The Empty Ark

Books by Philip K. Crowe

THE EMPTY ARK

SPORTING JOURNEYS IN AFRICA AND ASIA

DIVERSIONS OF A DIPLOMAT IN CEYLON

SPORT IS WHERE YOU FIND IT

The Empty Ark

PHILIP KINGSLAND CROWE

Charles Scribner's Sons

NEW YORK

PICTURE CREDITS

1–19, 27, 29–31, 33–38, 41–45—IRENE CROWE; 20—THE AUTHOR; 21–26, 28—IAN
STRANGE; 32, 51, 52—NEW YORK ZOOLOGICAL SOCIETY; 46—AMERICAN MUSEUM OF
NATURAL HISTORY; 47—MRS. OSWALD LORD; 48, 49—JOHN W. HANES JR.; 50—*The
New York Times.*

For my friends in The World Wildlife Fund

Preface

WITH THE CUTTING of the forests, the draining of the marshes, the plowing of the prairies, and the pollution of the rivers, the last refuges of wildlife are under steadily increasing pressure. In another fifty years the population of our world is destined to double. This means that by the second decade of the Twenty-first Century six and a half billion people will be struggling to survive and unless we act now the birds and animals which do not directly contribute to man's appetite will be only a memory.

Those who view this stark future with impunity have simply not bothered to consider the moral and ethical considerations involved. By any standards it is just as wrong to allow a species of life to be exterminated as it is to burn the Mona Lisa. Neither can ever be duplicated again. People enjoy looking at wildlife just as they enjoy looking at art and the wilful destruction of either is an aesthetic sin.

One often hears that wildlife must be exterminated to make room for the "march of civilization." This, of course, is sheer baloney. As the British naturalist, Peter Scott, points out, not one animal which has become extinct within historical times, such as the Dodo, Quagga, Great Auk, Passenger Pigeon, Blue Antelope, Labrador Duck, and Carolina Parakeet, to mention only a few, could have delayed the progress of the human race in the smallest degree had it survived.

On the contrary there are sound economic reasons for the protection of wildlife, especially in Africa. Tourism is a vital part of the economy of many of the new African nations and most of the tourists come to see the game. Game is also an important source of food and game will live in many areas where the land has no agricultural value. Regulated "farming" of game by cropping surplus animals is being successfully carried out in East Africa.

Since the time of Christ, man has been exterminating wildlife at an ever rising rate. Of the 250 species which have vanished since the beginning of the Christian era, two-thirds have become extinct during the past fifty years; and there are today another 250 rare species of birds and animals which are on the brink of joining the Dodo.

To meet this threat to wildlife the World Wildlife Fund was organized in 1962 under the chairmanship of His Royal Highness Prince Bernhard of the Netherlands with an international headquarters in Morges, Switzerland. Branches, known as National Appeals, were subsequently started in the United Kingdom, the United States, Switzerland, Austria and West Germany. The purpose of this non-profit organization is to raise funds which are then spent to save endangered wildlife.

These grants are used to succor rare species all over the world. World Wildlife funds support the Charles Darwin Foundation, which runs a research station on Isla Santa Cruz in the Galapagos Islands, where the Giant Tortoises, Land Iguanas and other unique species are now hard pressed to survive. These are the animals and birds which influenced Darwin in formulating his Theory of Evolution and their continuance is of historical as well as scientific value to humanity. Africa has profited from many grants, important among which is that of the African Wildlife Leadership Foundation which runs a school in Tanzania where Africans are trained to look after their own wildlife. The White Rhino Conservation campaign in Uganda, the Water for Animals Fund for the Royal National Parks of Kenya, and maintenance and equipment grant for the Albert National Park in the Republic of the Congo are other worthwhile projects which have been helped.

The Ne-ne or Hawaiian Goose, whose salvation was primarily due to the efforts of Peter Scott, multiplied to a point where thirty of these rare and beautiful birds (out of a world population of about 400) could be sent back to Hawaii from Scott's Wildfowl Trust at Slimbridge, England. The WWLF paid for the transfer. Half a world away the Fund financed a survey of the marine mammals of the

Falkland Islands in the extreme South Atlantic and at the same time helped to support a status survey of the endangered species on the Seychelles and Aldabra Islands in the Indian Ocean.

The purchase of the Coto Doñana estate in the Marismas or swampy delta of the Guadalquivir River in Spain was made possible partly by grants from the Fund. This famous 67,000 acre area, one of the most important wildlife refuges in Europe, is the last stronghold of the Spanish Lynx, and contains six eyries of the Spanish Imperial Eagle of which less than 150 are believed to remain in existence.

Projects aided in Asia have included the status survey made of the Indian Wild Ass in the Little Rann of Kutch by E. P. Gee, the well-known naturalist. I had the pleasure of visiting both the Kaziranga and Manas rhino sanctuaries with him. Mrs. Barbara Harrisson's two-year study of the decline of the Orang-utan in Sarawak was also paid for by the Fund.

In addition to aiding specific projects the Fund contributes to the International Union for the Conservation of Nature which maintains a constant check on endangered species. The Unions office is in the same building at Morges as the international headquarters of the World Wildlife Fund so that various national appeals are kept informed of crises in conservation. The IUCN may be said to provide a "war room" for the battle to save wildlife.

As a charter member of the Executive Committee of the board of directors of the American Appeal and subsequently as an International Trustee of the World Wildlife Fund, I became deeply interested in conservation and decided to spend a portion of each year working to help achieve the Fund's objectives. Having shot and fished around the world, I was familiar with many of the problems confronting conservationists and had come to the conclusion that the only way to promote the cause effectively would be to persuade men who ruled the various nations where rare wildlife is still found that it is their duty to help. Without the support of the top men, be they emperors, kings, presidents or dictators, little can be accomplished.

Accordingly I embarked on a series of missions for the Fund which began in 1963 with visits to five nations in Africa and four in the Levant Near East. In 1964 I journeyed to six countries in South America and the seldom-visited Falkland Islands. In 1965 I went to the Pacific Islands, Australia, New Zealand, Timor, Hong Kong, Taiwan, Japan, Siberia and Mongolia. My wife, Irene, accompanied me on all of these missions and my daughters, Phillippa and Irene, also came along at various times. The Hon. John Hanes, a director of the American Appeal, his wife Lucy, and Mr. and Mrs. Oswald Lord joined me for the trips to Siberia and Mongolia.

I am indebted to many people all over the world for their help and hospitality on these missions, but I want to express my particular thanks to H.R.H. The Duke of Edinburgh, president of the British Appeal, for his consistent interest in my endeavors and for his kindness in providing me with personal letters of introduction to a number of chiefs of state and governors. Commander Peter Scott, Chairman of the World Wildlife Fund, and Ian MacPhail, Director General of the British Appeal, were also most helpful.

I am also especially grateful to the Hon. Dean Rusk, Secretary of State, for his thoughtfulness in informing our various ambassadors and other diplomatic representatives about my missions. Without the consistent support of our embassies and consulates my work in many remote parts of the globe would have been infinitely more difficult.

For advice and help with the book itself I owe a great deal to Henry Volkening, my literary agent; to Stuart Rose, former editor of the *Saturday Evening Post,* for his careful editing of the text; to Colonel Jack Vincent and Noel Simon of the International Union for the Conservation of Nature for their review of the scientific terms used; and to Byron Dexter, former Managing Editor of *Foreign Affairs,* for his interest and encouragement.

Lastly I want to express my thanks to Dr. Harold Coolidge, the well-known international conservationist and fellow board member of the World Wildlife Fund. It was he who first interested me in doing something concrete about conservation.

PHILIP K. CROWE

Woodstock, Vermont
June, 1966

If anyone has the least doubt about the importance of conservation, one glance at this book should be sufficiently convincing.

The appalling disregard for the fate of wild animals and plants in almost every country in the world is a discouraging reflection on the selfishness and lack of consideration in mankind.

Howls of protest go up if one dog or one monkey goes into space, but not so much as a whisper is heard when a rare species becomes extinct owing to man's so-called progress.

This book has many sad stories of disappearing wildlife, but the ark is not quite empty yet. Philip Crowe's efforts to sound the alarm, to encourage a rational and intelligent approach to conservation, have met with considerable success in many parts of the world. I hope the book will do much to further his chosen work as well as the efforts of those who are interested in conservation all over the world.

1967.

Contents

xvi Contents

1963

East Africa and
the Middle East

ONE

Game of the Nile

"GAME," SAID THE PORTLY and effusive director of the Cairo Museum, "Mais oui, Monsieur L'ambassadeur, we have many books about les games in the library," and led me through the granite sarcophagi of the dynasties to high-ceilinged rooms where a small gnome-like lady presided over stacks of dusty volumes. I was given a seat while the curatoress rummaged among the shelves. Finally she returned with a book about "game," but it dealt with games of chance in the days of the Pharaohs, not the four-footed game about which I sought information. I explained at length that I meant animals, not gambling. She gave me a sweet smile and, after another period of research, returned with an ancient book in German dedicated to the wild life as depicted in the bas reliefs on the tombs. I thanked her and returned to the warm winter sunlight.

My next inspiration was the zoo. Certainly some one there would know about the Nubian ibex, rarest of the Egyptian fauna, which I had been assured was still carefully preserved in the reserve of Wadi El Rishrash, some fifty miles south of Cairo on the east bank of the Nile. After an hour's search among the byways of the fifty-acre zoo, I located Dr. Kam al Eddin Nagati, the veterinary surgeon of the Cairo Zoo. A small, energetic man of middle age, Dr. Nagati appeared genuinely glad to see me and said that word of my coming had been broadcast to his department from the Ministry who had the word from our embassy.

But when I mentioned the ibex his face fell. The reserve, he told me, had been completely wiped out during the war—he did not specify which war—and there is now no place in all Egypt where one can be sure of finding ibex. Perhaps in the wastes of the Red Sea Hills, perhaps in the Sahara, but for all practical purposes, except in the confines of the zoo where there are eight, the Nubian ibex is on the edge of extinction in Egypt. Furthermore, there are no laws protecting these lonesome survivors and no place in the length and breadth of the United Arab Republic where they can find sanctuary.

Then Dr. Nagati took me to the zoo's museum where he showed me the sad remnants of the fauna of Egypt: the gazelle, the ibex, the addax, the white oryx, all the delicate horned creatures that once adorned the deserts. The specimens were badly mounted and dated from at least fifty years ago when animals were "stuffed." Evidently no effort at conservation has taken place since the monarchy was overthrown and whether Farouk encouraged reserves for their own sake or as places to shoot is open to question. It may well be that in the not distant future the librarian of Cairo Museum may have the best information on the wild life of the Nile Valley and it may all be very ancient history.

There is little chance that the two-footed population of Egypt will fail to survive. It was a Friday and the thin grass plots of the zoo were overflowing with pregnant women, nursing mothers and those who looked as if they would soon be producing. "These children's children," said Dr. Nagati, "will never see a wild animal."

But in general my plea that a game reserve is as important to Egypt as the temples and that unless something is done soon to save her remaining fauna it will be gone forever, met with a good deal of interest. John Badeau, our ambassador, who, by the way impressed me very much—he was one of the few envoys we have had in Egypt who spoke fluent Arabic—showed considerable enthusiasm about my ideas and made an appointment for me with Mr. Desouki, the Governor of Cairo.

The concept of game reserves within reasonable distance of Cairo and other cities is practical. The total area of Egypt is a million square kilometers, but only about ten per cent of this is under cultivation. The rest consists of three barren deserts without any known use. The Libyan, or Western Desert stretches out from the Nile Valley for five hundred miles to the frontiers of Libya, and, with the exception of a few isolated oases like Siwa, is devoid of human habitation. The Eastern, or Nubian, Desert which lies between the Nile Valley and the Red Sea, consists of rocky wadis bisecting a low chain of mountains several thousand feet high. The Sinai Desert is an inverted triangle, bounded by the Mediterranean and the gulfs of Suez and Aqaba.

From the standpoint of harboring game, much of this vast area is useless. According to the old accounts—trust the British to document their sport—rain was then more frequent in the Western Desert and fair bags of oryx, addax and ostrich were taken in the northern areas. But with the gradual drying up of the desert and the advent of motor cars and high-powered rifles, the game had been so far reduced that by the start of the last war only a handful of Dorcas and Loder's gazelle, and a few Barbary sheep (Egyptian Arui) were left. Since then thousands of hungry tank crews have churned up the desert and it is unlikely that there is anything left at all but an occasional leopard or cheetah scratching a thin living from the desert hares.

The Sinai Desert, due to its seven-thousand-foot mountains, has been able to hold more game but the war gave guns to the local Arabs, all inveterate and pitiless hunters, who would just as soon shoot a pregnant ibex ewe as not. Pilots flying over these torrid wastes report almost no game now.

But in the remote vastnesses of the mountains lying some twenty-five miles in from the Red Sea in the Nubian Desert there may still be a few scattered herds of Nubian ibex, as well as Dorcas gazelle, and Barbary sheep. This is the only area which Dr. H. Saber, director of the Cairo Zoo and the man responsible for all wild life conservation in Egypt, told me he thought it would be worthwhile to conduct a survey in. "But," and he shrugged sadly and eloquently, "there is no money."

Egypt has game laws but Dr. Saber has not one piastre to enforce them. His budget allows for the running of the Cairo Zoo but nothing for the policing of Egypt's few remaining fauna. There is nothing to stop anyone at any time from killing as many head as he is able.

Wildfowl fare even harder. There is no law at all governing the shooting of the flocks of ducks and teal which migrate from the swamps of the Sudan to the steppes of Russia, and the market hunters trap and slaughter wildfowl by the thousands. Every restaurant in Cairo serves duck during both the spring and fall migrations. So far the flocks seem to be holding up—I saw three great skeins of what looked like teal flying down the Nile outside my hotel window—but a bad winter in the north or a dry one in the south might easily cut the numbers drastically, and the hunting pressure is constant. Dr. Saber said that mallard, teal, widgeon, pintails, pochards and shovellers are com-

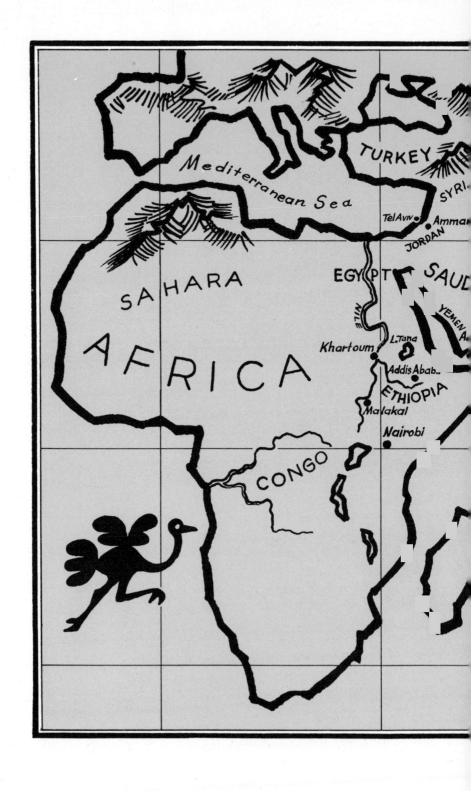

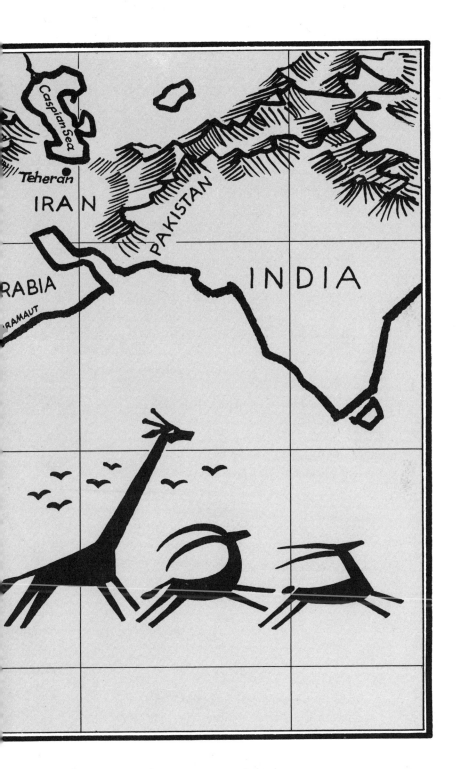

mon on the Nile flyway but the Egyptian goose has ceased to come to Egypt, and, like the sacred ibis, never flies north of the Sudan border.

I told Dr. Saber of the passenger pigeons of America. At the start of the nineteenth century the population of these birds was estimated at more than five billion. One flock was reported in Kentucky which was a mile wide and more than 200 miles long. Some ornithologists believed that more than a third of all the birds in America were passenger pigeons. It seemed impossible that shooting could make the slightest dent in these vast flocks and the market hunters shipped carloads of birds to city for a few cents each. But in less than a century the passenger pigeon was completely exterminated. The last one died in captivity in a Cincinnati Zoo.

Asked about the crocodiles, Dr. Saber said that the reason they have become so rare on the Egyptian Nile is not so much due to shooting as to cultivation. There are literally almost no wastes left where the old mugger can haul himself out for a sunbath. Crocodiles, like the wild fowl, have no protection by law.

The fellah, the poor masses of Egypt, do have some affection for birds and a particular affection for the white ibis, which they call the "friend of the fellah" because it follows their plows to grab grubs from the upturned earth. There were no white ibis in Egypt in 1914 but three small flocks were reintroduced and have flourished ever since. There is a thriving colony living half the year in a giant eucalyptus tree in the zoological gardens.

The only hope for Egyptian fauna in Dr. Saber's opinion is to make a game survey of the Red Sea Hills and possibly parts of the Sinai Desert. Second, establish a strict reserve in the area where game is found. Third, import animals—ibex, Barbary sheep, and gazelle—to the old Rishrash Park south of Cairo and make it a tourist attraction. He did not have estimates of the cost of such a program but I do not think it would be great.

A hundred miles above Malakal in the southern Sudan, the White Nile loses itself in a vast swamp known as the Sudd, and for a distance nearly half the length of Italy the great river is literally strained through an almost impenetrable forest of papyrus. This was the impasse which, since the beginning of recorded history, prevented the explorers from finding the sources of the Nile. The Pharaohs, the Romans, the Moslems all turned back when they came to the Sudd and it was not until the British tackled it in the late nineteenth century that the Sudd was conquered. Today there is a channel through it, kept open by frequent blastings, but only a tiny fraction of the morass has been explored, and a good deal of mystery still surrounds it. Not the least of the strange creatures who inhabit the Sudd is the shoebill, a bird that has a limited range in the marshes of eastern Africa and looks like no other bird in the world. With its strange shoe-like head which merges into a long and massive beak, the shoebill does look as if it is carved from granite and its habit of seldom moving even by the flicker of an eyelid helps the impression. When it does decide to advance it does so with deliberation, raising each spindly leg very slowly and then putting it down with the greatest of care.

From Mr. Medani, the director of the Khartoum Zoo, I learned that the shoebill is rigidly protected and that even the primitive tribes who inhabit the occasional islands of the Sudd leave it alone. But the shoebill is becoming rarer. Cultivation along the borders of the swamp may be restricting its breeding areas a little and the birds' eggs have always been a prey to the crocodile, the iguana and various hawks and buzzards, but there is no new factor resulting from civilization militating against the shoebill. Perhaps, like the great birds of the pre-ice age, the earthly span of the shoebill is drawing to a close.

In a completely different environment—the desert wastes of Darfur Province on the borders of Libya and the Republic of the Chad—two other creatures of the wilds are also growing rare and in this case something could be done about preserving them. The addax, whose stately twisted horns resemble those of a kudu, and the oryx el ghazal, a white oryx which differs from the common oryx in that its horns are scimitar-shaped, like those of the sable antelope, are seldom reported by the nomadic Bedouin who inhabit this remote part of the Sahara. That both still exist there is no doubt because recently one of the tribal chiefs sent an oryx calf to the President of the Sudan and there have also been more or less recent reports of small herds of addax in the area near the Libyan border, but no one really knows whether these desert dwellers are holding their own or declining and the chances favor the latter view.

I wanted to go to the area of the addax and the white oryx but it would have taken at least a month and entailed flying to El Fasher, driving from there along a sandy track to Kutum in the desert, and finally organizing a camel caravan to scout the area to the north and west. By way of compromise, my wife, and Sherman and Ann Haight of New York, who accompanied us on part of our mission while collecting artifacts for the American Museum of Natural History, flew to El Fasher and drove to the Jebel Marra, the great ten-thousand-foot mountain which rises from the desert in western Darfur. Their report on this excursion follows later.

Dr. Fraser Darling and George Merck of the Conservation Foundation made a trip to this general area in 1961 and recommended that the Sudanese Government establish a desert type of national park in the country north of Kutum or, failing that, a reserve elsewhere for the preservation of the white oryx and the addax. Both these ungulates breed well in captivity and there is no reason why a herd of both species cannot be established in an area near Khartoum where they can be watched. Mr. Medani has already done this with the Barbary sheep. In 1964 three rams and three ewes were settled at Sabaluka, a district ninety miles north of Khartoum. Now there are more than 200 of these attractive wild sheep in the reserve.

Mr. Medani thinks that before anything is done about deciding whether to establish a reserve in the desert where the sheep are or trying to capture some to build up a herd elsewhere, a survey should be made. He believes that the cost would not be great and the results would be of value in the preservation of these rare and beautiful animals.

During our long talk, the Minister of Animal Resources joined us and gave me a good over-all picture of the government's position on game conservation and its plans for the future. For an area of a million square miles there were exactly 225 officers, game scouts and game guides available. I am not a statistician but it seems to me that the ratio of guards to square miles is pretty low. Of course, not all of the Sudan has game but a surprisingly big percentage of the land carries some game and the anti-poaching force is certainly too small. The budget for fiscal 1962–63 was only 28,000 Sudanese pounds or about $84,000. Furthermore, the budget for the next ten years which had been recently approved, came to only $210,000.

Returns from wildlife are small. The sale of ivory comes to about 15,000 Sudanese pounds per year and another 4,000 to 5,000 accrues from game licenses, but tourism, potentially the best source of revenue, has not been scratched. The reason for this is obvious. Only one of the game parks in the Sudan has any facilities for tourists and this consists of a rest house in the Nimule reserve in Equatoria Province near Juba whose capacity is just twenty persons. Mr. Medani had plans to develop the Dinder River Reserve by opening up roads and building a central rest house but as of my visit there were no plans to develop the great game areas of Bahr El Ghazal in the south. Before the Sudan can attract the tourists in the droves which today swell the coffers of Kenya and Tanganyika, she must spend real money on roads, rest houses, and trained personnel. The game is there and simply has to be presented.

We also discussed licensed shooting and I pointed out the advantages to be had from the development of a reliable and profitable safari service. Today the government licenses a dozen safari firms but only two of them are functioning and neither one gives anything like the service provided by such firms as Kerr and Downey in Kenya. I learned later from Miralai Ahmed Bakr, Director of the Tourist Bureau of the Ministry of Information, that the Sudanese Government has already sounded out the possibility of making an arrangement with some of the reputable safari firms in Kenya but that negotiations have bogged down over the matter of the corporate set-up. Stripped of double talk, the government does not want it to look as if white men from another country were necessary to run their shooting. I said I saw no real reason why appearances could not be preserved and at the same time give the Sudan an efficient and profitable return from the organized hunting of expendable game.

Neither lions nor buffalo are protected and can be shot in any numbers by anyone. The Minister said lions are a menace in the south and that any form of protection for them would be unpopular. I agreed with this but said it still might be wise to put both animals on the game license for hunters. The villagers, whose cattle are taken and whose fields are trampled, are going to shoot anyway but that is no reason why the big game hunter should not pay for the privilege. Mr. Medani said he always felt that lions and buffalo should be on the license and hoped to bring the minister around to his view.

While few of the recommendations made in the Darling Report have so far been implemented, one of the most important has been. Dr. Darling's initial recommendation was that an ecologist of standing be attached jointly to the University of Khartoum and to the game department for five years with the purpose of initiating surveys and research, lecturing, and developing honor students for recruitment to the game department. Alan Brooks, the Canadian ecologist, went to the

Sudan on an eighteen-month job and funds for an additional three and a half years were made available under the United Nations Technical Assistance program. A start has also been made toward dovetailing the objectives of the game department with those of the tourist, agricultural and forest departments. Until quite recently each one of these agencies went ahead on its own without consulting the others.

Darfur means the land of the Fur, an ancient kingdom which lost its independence when it was annexed to the Egyptian Sudan in 1874. Irene and the Haights traveled to Darfur Province and the following is a report of their impressions.

El Fasher is a big military post and, since soldiers have guns and there is little to do besides drill, the game has suffered. According to old-timers in the district, there used to be quite a good herd of game with gazelle and kudu predominating. The country is park-like, with acacia trees and adequate grazing although the grass was straw-colored when they saw it. Large herds of cattle roam the plains. The surviving game, mostly greater kudu, had been driven high into the Marra ridge. In addition to the soldiers, local meat hunters shoot anything they see, including calves. No mention was made of a local warden.

Of oryx and addax there was not a word and I would bet that the surviving herds stay far out of the reach of the garrison. Certainly any attempts at a game park would have to be placed a long way out in the desert and be adequately patrolled by scouts.

Some five hundred miles southeast of Khartoum, where the borders of the Sudan march with those of Ethiopia, lies the Dinder National Park, an area of some 2,470 square miles lying roughly between the Dinder and the Rahad rivers. There are no villages in the park and since it is bisected only by a single dirt road there is little legitimate disturbing of the game. To protect the wild life from poachers a camel patrol is stationed there and it was as guests of the government of the Sudan that we made our way to the heart of Dinder Reserve and spent five intensely interesting days with the Chief Game Officer and his men.

The Dinder Reserve is not easy to reach. From Khartoum, where the Blue Nile joins the White, to Roseires, where the Blue Nile boils through its last cataract on its way down from the mountains of Ethiopia, is a dusty two-day trip by Land Rover. We chose to fly and in the little Cessna of Sudan Airways followed the river from above. The Blue Nile is a lonely river. None of the steamers which ply the White Nile can navigate the shallows of the Blue and even the sails of the fellucas are missing. Only the occasional skiff of a fisherman rides the river which, even from the air, in the dawn and sunset is definitely blue. As we stepped out of the plane at Roseires, the heat hit us between the eyes and our outdoor thermometer registered 120 degrees. But the Sudan is an arid country and a heat which would have floored us in the tropics or in New York City was not unbearable.

El Tahir Sid Mohomed, the Game Officer in charge of the Dinder Reserve, and A. G. Karkanis, Assistant Conservator of Forests for the Roseires District, met us with two Land Rovers and drove us— Sherman and Ann Haight and my wife Irene—and me—to the government rest house where we were served a good breakfast. Mohomed then accompanied me while I paid a call on Yousif Mohomed Saeed, the District Commissioner, a jolly gentleman with a strong British accent whom I found seated before a big desk.

The Commissioner's district runs to 18,000 square miles in which live 162,000 people, most of whom are members of Hamag, Berta, Berun, Oumiz or Ingessena tribes. Originally pagan and later Christian, most of the indigenous peoples of the Blue Nile Province are today Moslems and many have the finely carved features of their Arab ancestors.

Just outside Roseires a major engineering work was going up. An Italian firm had been working for three years on harnessing the Blue Nile and when the dam is finished, more than a million acres of cultivation will be possible. Cotton is the main crop of the Sudan and most of the newly irrigated land will probably be sown to the famous long staple.

Our safari was waiting for us on the road to the park. Under Mohomed's command was a staff of ten, including a junior game officer and four game scouts armed with rifles. We rode in a Land Rover and a large truck, and were a completely self-sustaining expedition, with beds, tables, chairs, food, water and even white napkins. The trip was a present to me from Dr. Santino Deng Teng, the Minister of Animal Resources, and was arranged through the efforts of Merghani Meeki Medani, Assistant Director of Animal Resources and the man in charge of the game parks. There are, in fact, no professional safari companies in the north of the Sudan and no extended trip into the bush is possible without the help of the government.

The road from Roseires to the border of the Dinder Reserve is not a bad one for a baked mud track, and we bowled along at a good thirty miles an hour. What the road would be like in the rainy season I hesitate to say. The first village we came to was Jebel Magano, a hamlet nestling beneath a vast stony outcrop where baboons were scampering in the twilight. Jebel Magano is inhabited by the Gumuz tribe, whose economy consists mainly in gathering gum arabic. Two of the old chiefs came to greet us with their long swords swinging from their belts. Mohomed told me that the villagers are not allowed rifles but can own shotguns, although few can afford this luxury. One of the chiefs said that the village water supply had dried up and that it was necessary to bring water from twenty-five miles away. Later we passed two tribesmen mounted on camels over whose rumps were thrown black goatskin water bags.

The farther one gets from civilization the more pleasant the simple comforts become. We camped the first night by a black pool on the Dinder and never has a bath seemed so good. It had been six months since the river flowed and since then every animal within miles had used the pool for drinking and bathing but even though nearing the consistency of light soup, it had a wonderfully refreshing property and in the deep parts was amazingly cool. Mohomed said there were a few small crocodiles but they would not bother us.

Early the next morning we mounted our vehicles and set out along the river to see the game. I kept a careful check of all animals and major birds sighted during the one-hour period from 8:00 to 9:00 a.m. The list is impressive. Hardly had we started along the river road when a herd of roan antelope, to my mind one of the handsomest grazing animals in Africa, thundered out of the reeds and dashed across the road a few feet ahead of us. There was one old bull with a magnificent set of horns and his harem of cows and calves. The roan carries his head like the sable and, at a distance, looks somewhat like his scimitar-headed cousin.

Behind the roan came a herd of hartebeest, the red antelope with rather an ungainly canter until speed is demanded. Little oribi, among the smallest of the antelope, dashed out of the bushes and, leaping like impala, made off across the plain. In many areas the grass had been burned and while this did not make for an attractive background, it did enable us to see the game more clearly. Unless burned or grazed off the "adar" grass grows five feet high and effectually hides everything. Reedbuck, a little larger than the oribi, scampered away before us and occasionally a family of wart hog, their tails as stiff as pokers, trotted by. Waterbuck were also numerous. We saw flock after flock of guinea fowl and occasional francolin. With the glasses I spotted one fish eagle and one greater bustard. Flying over the river were some large geese which looked like greylag. By the water holes were blue herons and flocks of dazzling white egrets.

The big animals were comparatively rare. We saw one herd of buffalo of about forty head and a small herd of giraffe. The buffalo are said to be far more numerous than is apparent and undoubtedly spend most of the long hot days in the denser parts of the bush. According to Sherman's trusty thermometer, the mercury climbed to over a hundred by 9:00 a.m., hovered at 120 from noon to 3:00 p.m., and then slowly declined to a comfortable 90 by suppertime. At night it grew so cool that we slept under blankets.

Among the rarer ungulates we saw was a small herd of oryx beisa, the common oryx; and several individual gazelle of both local varieties. In addition to several families of baboon, we saw both gray and red monkeys.

My tabulation for this limited period came to: roan antelope 75; hartebeest 45; waterbuck 43; oribi 60; giraffe 7; bushbuck 7; gazelle 4; wart hog 25; baboons 15; gray monkeys 10; red monkeys 3; buffalo 40; guinea fowl by the thousands, and a few francolin.

But the really big concentrations of game were found in the water meadows which were flooded during the rains and furnished succulent grazing afterward. We saw herds of thousands of roan and hartebeest, hundreds of waterbuck, oribi and bushbuck and a fair number of wart hog. When we approached in the Land Rover, the herds melted into a solid mass of moving animals and flowed away over the plain like a great brown snake. Near a diminishing pan of water we saw a flock of geese and around a kill a gathering of buzzards.

Strictly speaking, the Dinder National Park is not a park at all. Aside from the single dirt road, which runs along the Dinder and then winds across the Rahad, there is no means of getting about the country except by camel. Before the reserve can attract tourists in any volume, this road will have to be improved, subsidiary roads built and accommodations constructed. Even driving fast it takes about five hours to reach the boundary of the reserve from Roseires and if one cannot spend the night in the park there is little time for sightseeing before the sudden African night arrives.

Today there is no clearly defined border between the lands of Haile Selassie and General Aboud but there is a sharp delineation between the peoples. The Coptic Christians inhabiting the eight-thousand-foot mountains have never been able to sell their faith to the peoples of the Sudan and, likewise, the Moslem fanatics of the plain have been equally unsuccessful in making the hill people accept Islam. There is little trade between the two countries and Mohomed's patrols which pick their silent way along the ill-marked border do not deal gently with the Ethiopian poachers.

Waking in the dawn of our first day at the headquarters camp, we heard the guttural belchings of the camels and, lying on our cots, watched a patrol saddle up and prepare to move out. Perched high on the humps of their camels with their rifles slung from the saddles and their rations and water in leather bags draped on either side of the long withers, the game scouts looked like a patrol of the Foreign Legion leaving one of the outposts deep in the Sahara. Mohomed told me that his patrols are out for twenty days, riding every fifth day to the Dinder or the Rahad for water, but otherwise keeping to the borders of the game reserve. Each man has his own camel and, contrary to the usual opinion, a good deal of affection exists between the men and their mounts.

While we did not see lions, five of them serenaded us all one night and on another evening we heard the guards shoot to drive away a lioness which started to stalk one of their camels. Mohomed estimated the lion population of the park to be in excess of a thousand, a ratio of a lion to every two and a half square miles, and probably about the right number to keep the grazing animals in balance. The old and the infirm slow up and from these the lioness feeds her master and her cubs.

Water is a beautiful sight in this parched park land and the Lake of Rass Amer is particularly lovely. If the Sudanese Government ever decides to spend the money to open the Dinder Reserve for tourists, the rest house should be built on the shores of Rass Amer. About a mile wide and perhaps two miles long, the lake is in fact simply a bulge of the Dinder but it is deep and retains most of its water all year round. Mohomed said big fish—perch, catfish and others I did not recognize—swarm in its warm depths, but most important is the pleasure it gives the eyes. In a land of mirages a real body of water has a touch of paradise about it that only the thirsty understand.

We fared well in the camp. Mohomed Sala, the cook, labored over his pots and pans in the heat of the cook shack and laid before us four-course meals of soup, fish, meat and vegetables, and dessert. Clad in clean white tunics, he served us in great style, wearing a long gown in the evening and a short one for breakfast and lunch. The water was not exactly crystal clear but it was good and, laced with a bit of whiskey, a most acceptable drink.

By the last day in the bush we began to understand the heat. From eleven in the morning to four in the afternoon it became so intense that it induced a state of almost complete lethargy and one moved slowly, as if in a dream. The effort of doing anything was difficult and even one's mind became dulled. I found that I could not write except in the very early morning or the late afternoon. The typewriter was too hot to touch and the carbon paper stuck to the flimsies. Outside the grass shelter of our shack the heat waves shimmered over the baked compound and the trees in the distance danced strange dances. By mid-day even the crows ceased their chatter and a stillness descended on the land. Life seemed to be held in suspense and all one could do was to lie sweating on the cots, awaiting the time when the burning sun started to sink behind the palms by the river and the coolness came with the first evening breeze.

The southern Sudan begins at Malakal on the upper Nile. Instead of the beak-nosed people of the north with their much-prized Arab blood, one sees the Shilluk, blue-black Negroes with button-shaped cicatrices carved across their foreheads. Even the river is different. Islands of water hyacinth and masses of papyrus float past, a grim reminder that only a hundred miles or so to the south begins the Sudd. We were more than 2,000 miles from Alexandria and entering tropical Africa. Gone are the arid deserts of Darfur and Kordofan Provinces, to be replaced by the park lands and morasses of Bahr El Gazal, Equatoria and Upper Nile. There are also religious differences. The tribes of the south are ninety per cent pagan and ten per cent Christian as against the solid Moslem population of the north. A foreigner cannot travel to the south without a special permit issued by the Police Commissioner of the Sudan.

Malakal from the air is a pleasant little river town of conical native huts and the usual tin-roofed rest houses. Colonel Mohomed Nasr Osman, the military governor of Upper Nile Province, met us at the airport and assured us of his felicitations. Beshir El Hag Ali, the Inspector of Game Preservation for the province, and his assistant, Hamad Mohomed Abu Sin, also presented themselves and told me that the government paddle steamer was at our disposal. My friend, Medani, had arranged for us to live on the ship and travel up the Nile on her to the Boma Reserve, where Mrs. Gray's lechwe, one of the rarest antelopes in Africa, was now carefully preserved and was said to be thriving. A bit of talking, however, established the fact that there was no food aboard and it was necessary for us to go to the rest house and arrange for three days' supply. Another stumbling block proved to be the crew, who announced in loud Sudanese that they would not work the ship until they were paid. Mr. Ali, in the manner of all employers, shrugged his shoulders and said to me that labor was getting damn uppity these days.

The good ship *Wad El Nugomi,* named after one of the Mahdi's officers, is a wood-burning stern paddle wheeler of ancient vintage. Lashed to it were two barges, one with cabins for first class passengers and another with only deck space for less exalted riders as well as cattle and sheep.

While Mr. Ali was threatening the crew with life servitude and a long line of bearers were bringing aboard sufficient food for a month's voyage, I wandered down the bank where an active fish market was in progress. Tall and lean, the Nilotic tribes like the Shilluk often produce strikingly handsome and apparently happy people. Everyone enjoyed the fish market. After a particularly heated round of bargaining, the children and even some of the men would suddenly spring up and dash into the river for a cooling swim, where they joined the hump-backed cattle reposing peacefully in the mud.

There is a very small zoo on the banks of the Nile at Malakal and in the cool of the evening it was thronged with tribesmen staring fascinated at a modest exhibit of rabbits and ostriches. There is also a small and hungry lion, a hyena, and a very good lechwe buck. Black and white markings on the head and yellow under the belly, Mrs. Gray's lechwe is the only antelope without protective coloring. The horns of the buck are long and graceful and seem out of proportion to the slender legs. The lechwe has some religious significance to the Shilluk nation and the crowd around this yard was visibly respectful. Two armed guards accompanied me although no one could be more friendly than the natives of Malakal. Many raised their hands in the traditional salute and all smiled. The British evidently left a good reputation for the white man.

We had heard in Khartoum that the United States Navy maintained a medical research station on the upper Nile, but we did not know the station was at Malakal and were quite unprepared to be invited to a cocktail party by Captain Boyers, the commanding officer. His story is a fascinating one. It seems that shortly after the war the Sudanese government settled some emigrants from Wadi Halfa near Malakal and for some strange reason they immediately died. An appeal was made to the American Embassy and in the course of time a medical team was sent up-country. The British had already done a good deal of work on a strange disease named Kala-azar, which induced a high fever like malaria and was often fatal. Repeated experiments revealed that the carrier was a sand fly but it was still not known what the cycles of the sand fly's life are. If caught soon enough, the disease can be cured by certain drugs, but few of the poor Shilluk who suffer greatly from it apply for treatment.

Captain Boyers had a good team with him. There was Commander Rohers, an entomologist; and two civilian doctors, Hoogstaal and McConnell. Hoogstaal, a first class zoologist, had done a great deal of research on the mammals of Egypt and the Sudan. He told me that he saw no hope of saving the remaining ibex and Barbary sheep in Egypt but that there are more of these rare ungulates than most people think. Driven deep into the almost inaccessible crags of the Sinai and Red Sea Hills they survive in small herds. It was his opinion that the Egyptians would not make the effort to save them no matter what promise I was able to get in Cairo. He did, however, give my friend, Dr. Saber of the Cairo Zoo, full marks for interest and effort.

By four in the morning of the day after our arrival in Malakal, we were waked by a great commotion on board and with a wheezing of her paddles, the good ship *Wad El Nugomi* started chugging up the river. The Nile was narrow, barely wide enough for our steamer, and flowed between low, swampy banks which slope back to water meadows where lean cattle graze. Just behind the meadows were the conical thatch huts of the Shilluk, and we passed several rafts made of reeds and loaded with mats which young boys were ferrying down to town. The Shilluk are only one of the Nilotic tribes that inhabit the riverine reaches of the Nile above and below Malakal. There are also the Dinkas and Nuers who live on the river only part of the year and therefore lack a continuous fish diet which is high in protein. Deficiency diseases among the Dinkas and Nuers are more apparent than among the Shilluk.

There are many birds along this remote reach of the upper Nile. I saw a fish eagle just before it took off with the scream that is more typical of Africa than that of any other bird. I have seen and heard these beautiful birds on all the great rivers from the Zambezi north. Near the fish eagle sat a long-tailed cormorant with glossy black plumage, while in the shallows swam a small flock of knob-billed ducks. Cattle egrets perched on the backs of the long-horned cattle. Although this snow-white egret is said to eat ticks, it seldom does, nor does it warn game as does the true tick bird. My most exciting find was a crowned crane, a magnificent bird with a tuft of black feathers splashed with yellow on its head. The body is ebony black and shines in the strong African sun. Little blue and white malachite kingfishers hovered over the river competing for small fish with the purple herons.

Neither Mr. Ali nor his lieutenant knew the exact size of the Boma reserve for Mrs. Gray's lechwe but both more or less agreed that it is at least ten miles long. Part of the reserve is on an island near where the Bahr El Zeraf River joins the White Nile and part on the banks. The lechwe is one of the very few antelopes that can negotiate the floating islands so prevalent in this part of the Nile. Light and agile, it can maintain itself on packed vegetation which would let most animals sink into the water and the waiting jaws of the big Nile crocodiles. I saw a ten-footer slide into the water as we steamed past. There are also hippos on this reach but we did not see any.

At ten a.m., some six hours after we started steaming south, we reached Vanikan Island and almost immediately saw a large number of Nile lechwe grazing near the shore. There must have been at least a hundred in the herd and even though the steamer blew her whistle none of them ran off. Considered the property of the Shilluk king, they have learned not to fear man. Occasionally they are poached but if the culprit is caught he has to pay a heavy fine in cows. Later when we landed at a Shilluk village, I asked the chief for his opinion of the number of lechwe in the vicinity and he estimated them at at least a thousand. The Shilluk nation and the Sudan government both deserve credit for the preservation of this rare and delightful little antelope.

The divinity of kings has been out of fashion in most countries for quite a time but in the Shilluk nation, whose villages dot the west bank of the upper Nile, the king reigns today as a living symbol of the God Nykiang.

The village of Nyuya, across from Vanikan Island, is a typical settlement, consisting of about fifty conical huts, with thatched roofs and mud and wattle walls. Every hut we entered was spotlessly clean and that of Ayul Deux, the old chief, quite imposing. In the house of a teacher we saw paintings of birds and animals on the walls. This teacher, who spoke good English, said he had been educated by the Catholics but that only a dozen people in the three hundred or so who inhabited the village were Christians, the rest being pagans.

The Shilluk are tall, good-looking people with excellent manners. The men and women both wear a "lau," or type of toga, tied over their left shoulders. Unlike the town Shilluk who sometimes go in for bright colors, the tribes of the Nile villages wear dirty, rust-colored cloth and depend for color on ornaments. The young men wear a single feather in their hair and almost always carry either a spear or some sort of club or stick. The Shilluk have always resisted their Moslem conquerors and fought hard against the forces of the Mahdi. Because of this warlike bent, the warriors are not allowed to carry any sort of spear or side arm when they come to Malakal.

Excellent fishermen, they make heavy hauls from the Nile with their nets, by spearing and with hooks. Although they possess sizeable herds of cattle, they regard them as wealth and never kill them except for sacrificial purposes. The Shilluk are not true pastorals in the sense of the Dinka and Nuers, the other two important Nilotic tribes, and remain in their permanent Nile-bank villages all the time.

The village chief, whose title is "jal dwong pac," is chosen from the dominant lineage group of the settlement, and his elevation must be confirmed by the king. Plural marriage is the rule for chiefs, and while it would be unheard-of rudeness to ask him how many wives he has, we learned discreetly that he was not in need of female companionship. Unlike the Bantu of South Africa, whose women are often fat as butter tubs, the Shilluk women are lithe and graceful.

The Shilluk language is a complicated affair of gutturals and if it were not for one of the game guards, who is a Shilluk, neither Ali nor Sin could communicate with them. There are many different dialects in the Sudan which makes the problem of forging a single nation difficult.

As I noted earlier, the *Wad El Nugomi* merely furnished the motive power. We lived on a houseboat of four cabins, a bath and two toilets. There were also two screened porches and a dining room. We had a personal cook and two house boys. Meals were better than those of the Grand Hotel in Khartoum.

Kodok is the seat of the District Commissioner for the Shilluk nation. The village of Res Kur Popite, the King of the Shilluk, is some miles from Kodok, but His Majesty came there to see us. A man of about forty with a frank and pleasant face, the 33rd King of the Shilluk nation was simply dressed. Except for a coronet of leopard skin on his head, he wore buckskin shoes of the Bata variety, corduroy trousers, and a Hawaiian flowered shirt. His only jewelry consisted of two silver bracelets on his wrists and two similar ones on his ankles. He wore a pair of large dark glasses. I told the king that I was very pleased to see the number of Mrs. Gray's Lechwe in the reserve. He replied that the lechwe was royal game and he very seldom gave permission for one to be captured for zoos, much less shot. He was interested in the fact that I represented the World Wildlife Fund and said that animals and man should learn to live together.

When we left the king we drove to the royal village about five miles away where the king keeps his wives. It consists of about ten very large huts which literally swarmed with women and children. The royal guard, a group of about five elderly men with resigned expressions and rather dull-looking spears, told us that there was no estimate of the number of the king's wives but that there were "many, many." According to our Shilluk game ranger, the number is between 100 and 200, quite a spread.

At one end of the royal village was a raised hill of dirt on top of which rested three huts with bright woven rush roofs. The guards would not let us go into them for inside dwells Nyikang, the God of the Shilluk nation. Nyikang also lives in the person of the king and the Shilluk believe that if their king becomes ill or old or impotent, they will likewise suffer these maladies. There is no question even today about the fact that most of the Shilluk firmly believe that the spirit of Nyikang lives in the body of their lord. This implies a good deal of ritual for the king. He must follow the prescribed actions and do everything he can to promote a happy home for Nyikang. He is the common symbol of the Shilluk people and if he fails to do his job, his reign is not a long one. Nowadays, he is not walled into a hut or strangled as some of the kings were said to have ended their days, but he might well be helped to his end.

The Shilluk kings are chosen from one of three royal households in the royal tribe and, in theory at least, have the complete support of all their people. But times are changing and I was told that some of the better educated Shilluk of Malakal feel that Res Kur Popite (the word Res means king) is too much of a manikin of the government and no longer represents the best interests of the nation. There were even rumors that the king might be getting a cold.

From Malakal we flew southwest, skirting the vast papyrus swamps of the Sudd and stopping briefly at Wau, the capital of the province of Bahr El Ghazal. This is the land of the Dinkas, the cattle-loving Nilotic tribes who wander with their herds over the endless savannahs, counting wealth in their bulls and cows and oxen and finding in these sweet-breathed kine all the good things of life. The Dinka never kills his cattle except to make sacrifice and when a boy reaches manhood he takes the name of his favorite ox in addition to his own. The Dinkas have no divine king, like the Shilluk, but they do have men who possess powers of "wei," or life, who are known as the Masters of the Fishing Spears. I wish we had had time to study the Dinka but we had to fly on to Juba, the capital of Equatoria, our last stop in the Sudan.

As usual the Game and Forestry Departments had made good arrangements for us. Hassan Abdel Bagi, the Game Officer of Juba, and the representative of my friend Shawhi of the Forests, and Costis Yiaimanis, a Greek merchant who was to furnish the food, all met us at the airport and drove us to the rest house for lunch.

After lunch, we drove through a green countryside, the first we had seen since leaving England thirty-five days before. While waiting for the ferry to cross the Nile, it rained, the first rain we had felt since leaving the U.S.A.

The Nimule Game Reserve is 120 miles due south from Juba and its southern border runs to the border of Uganda. Although one of the smallest reserves in the Sudan, it has one of the best concentrations of big game and is the only park in the Sudan with rest house accommodations. There are two comfortable bungalows with baths, inside toilets (not always functioning) and adequate staffs.

We went out at dawn the next morning to see the game. Ferrying the Nile in a rowboat, we set out on foot. Four game scouts with loaded rifles under the supervision of Bagi constituted the escort, and also scouted ahead for the game. Of course, the major sight is elephant and we immediately spotted an old bull standing stock still in the open. There was something about his appearance that did not look right and under examination with the glasses he appeared ill and thin. The

Uganda poachers are active on the borders of the little park and this may have been one of the bulls which they had wounded and failed to bring down. Topping a little rise—the park country is rolling and lies between two sets of imposing mountains—we saw a pair of white rhinos, each with its white tick bird. Unlike the black rhino which can be dangerous to approach, the white has certain bovine characteristics and I got within ten yards to take pictures. As we crept up on the rhinos, one of the game scouts raised his hand and pointed to the left where a herd of about twenty Cape buffalo were quietly grazing. Luckily, the wind was from them to us, for we were much too close for comfort. These buffalo had not been shot at and, although they demonstrated, moved off quietly, after first allowing us some excellent pictures from a range of not more than twenty yards.

The park had a good stock of cob and waterbuck. There are also oribi, dik-dik and hartebeest, but we did not see them. Down by the Nile we saw the tracks of a hippo. The bird population was exciting. I saw a sacred ibis, the bird beloved by the Pharaohs. With white feathers and a black leathery neck and head it is to my mind one of the least attractive of the water birds. We saw both gray- and black-headed herons and a pair of hammerkops, the bird known for its enormous nest. Dancing across water lilies by the bank of the Nile was a pair of lily-trotters.

My main purpose was to find out about the game situation, and what I found out, especially in regard to the elephant, was disturbing. Simply put, the cost of the license is so low that a hunter, by selling the ivory and the meat, can make a handsome profit on the operation. Any native of the Sudan can purchase an elephant license for as little as 6 Sudanese pounds, or $18, and since ivory is worth about $2.00 a pound locally and the average bull carries 50 pounds on each side, the hunter nets $182 per bull on the ivory alone. He can also sell the meat for another $50. This is not all; a native can, by paying another 15 Sudanese pounds for each one, shoot two more elephants in a given year. Furthermore, the chiefs have much larger allotments of elephants and often employ professional hunters to bag their limit for them. Females as well as males are shot. I saw a good deal of ivory in the market in Khartoum which came from cows. Cow ivory is much finer grained than that of the bulls and therefore is much easier to carve. It is even possible for a foreigner, by picking a bull with heavy ivory, to cover his more expensive license and make a profit.

The elephant is to Africa what the buffalo was to America. Both are the largest and most valuable wildlife assets of their respective continents, but the buffalo was almost exterminated. In the days when the Indians had the great plains to themselves the herds were estimated to contain between 50 and 100 million buffalos. The massacre began soon after the War Between the States was over. The pressures were many. The United States army wanted the buffalo killed because without them the Indians would starve or be forced into the reservations; the market hunters wanted the tongues and hides; but the greatest pressure came from the cattlemen who wanted the grass for their livestock. First the southern herds and then the northern herds were decimated and by 1880 the buffalo for all practical purposes had been wiped out.

Elephant is not the only game that is being decimated in Bahr El Ghazal and Equatoria provinces. No license is required to shoot buffalo and the numbers killed for meat, according to a reliable source in Juba, is shocking. There is no interest in the horns, simply in the poundage of flesh, and it does not make the slightest difference what the sex of the animal is. My source has seen buffalo calf meat offered for sale in the market.

I have been talking above about the legitimate hunters, who at least bother to report their kills and whose rifles are licensed. By far the biggest drain comes from the poachers who slaughter the game with ancient guns and in ninety-nine cases out of a hundred get away with it. The Game Department of the Sudan has some very good and dedicated men but they are pitifully few and cannot begin to patrol the vast areas where game is found. The game scouts and their officers have little technical knowledge of how to handle game and game parks.

The game schedules for hunters are hopelessly out of date. I believe they have not been changed since the British made them up in 1905. For example, the giant eland is a very rare species, but it can still be shot on license.

This steady decrease in the game is reflected in the figures for professional safaris which are desirable from the standpoint of the Game Department. The two professional hunters I talked with were pessimistic about the future. These professionals, who are Europeans based outside the Sudan, told me that the weight of the ivory has been declining steadily and that few sportsmen worth their salt will shoot a bull with only fifty pounds on either side.

Another disturbing note in the game situation is the apparent willingness of the Sudanese government to allow distinguished visitors to shoot in the reserves. An Arab princeling turned the Nimule reserve into a minor abattoir, shooting from his car, and even Tito, reportedly a good sportsman at home, did not resist the offer to hunt in the reserve. This reflects little credit on the government. What would be said if Mr. Johnson invited Mr. Wilson, the British Prime Minister, to collect a few bear in Yellowstone?

In Juba, the Game Department maintains a tiny zoo with a sign "Animal Orphanage" over the gate. Inside there are a brace of buffalo calves who lumber about following the keeper, a baby zebra, a young hartebeest and a collection of small wild cats. The day may well come when zoos like this will hold the only examples of much of the game of Africa.

TWO

Crisis for Hunter's Antelope

I HAVE ALWAYS enjoyed Nairobi. There is something about the mile-high altitude and the clear blue skies that lends a special zest to living and on this particular visit I was even more pleased with Kenya's capital, for Major Ian Grimwood, Kenya's Chief Game Warden, had presented me with a project that seemed to fit into the objectives of my trip. It was not easy to find rare animals whose future may perhaps be secured by the expenditure of relatively small sums of money. The Egyptian ibex and the addax and white oryx of the Sudan all qualify as rare animals with uncertain future but there were no adequate local facilities through which I could work to help them. In all three cases it was necessary to make extended field trips simply to find out where the animals were located. Then would come the problems of getting the governments to establish reserves for them and the consequent need for adequate protection of these areas. Most of the funds would have to be raised by Egypt and the Sudan. Egypt has no budget for game and that of the Sudan does not include any extracurricular activities.

The Kenya project presented none of these difficulties. Of Hunter's antelope there may still be about a thousand left, and their habitat is well known. Ranging between the Tana River of Kenya and the Juba River of Somalia, they inhabit a narrow band of country between the forested hills which rise some twenty miles inland from the Indian Ocean and the semi-desert which lies behind them. Left alone, they would probably continue to exist in this restricted zone but two dangers have loomed on their horizon. The United Nations is considering starting a huge agricultural scheme along the Tana River which would mean new villages and new guns and ultimately perhaps no Hunter's antelope. Even more threatening is the political fact that most of their range lies in the territory which is now part of Kenya but which contains some 200,000 Somalis whose dearest wish is to join Somalia. The chances are that sooner or later the strip will be handed over to the latter country.

The project was to capture several brace of antelopes and take them back to a safe area in Kenya where they could be bred. The best man to do this job was Major Grimwood, who the year before had successfully captured specimens of the almost extinct Arabian oryx and brought them to Nairobi. He believed that a similar operation could be carried out for the Hunter's antelope and thought it could be done for a very modest outlay of funds, as he has adequate transport and equipment available in Kenya. The method of capture used in Arabia— lassoing the game from a car—would be equally feasible in eastern Kenya. Lastly, the cost of maintaining the Hunter's antelopes would be minimal.

Ian Grimwood at fifty is lean and rangy. After serving in the Indian Army, he spent fifteen years in the game department of Northern Rhodesia and moved on to the top job in Kenya several years ago. At his home, situated on the edge of the Masai Reserve about ten miles from Nairobi, he told me about Hunter's antelope while his pet otter played with my shoes. Almost nothing is known of the biology and ecology of this species. It is not even known if the species has declined within living memory. In any case, their numbers have never been great and the country they inhabit offers few other incentives for hunting. The latest information is that the range of the Hunter's antelope no longer extends far across the present Somali border and is more or less confined on the Kenya side to an area roughly contained by the line Maazinia-Ijara-Kolbio in the south and the Tana River in the west.

Grimwood had no picture of the Hunter's antelope but he had an ecologist working in the area where they are who was asked to take some photographs. The horns of Hunter's antelope resemble those of an impala but the body is larger, a male weighing over three hundred pounds.

Before leaving, we walked down to the Major's pond and watched the sacred ibis fly in to roost in the acacias. It was evening, with the beginning of a full moon just showing over the edge of the Ngong Hills. Out on the Masai reserve a lion roared and it was hard to remember that we were only eight miles from a big city.

Nairobi has 200,000 blacks and 15,000 whites, but for all practical purposes, only the whites and the Indians can afford cars and since one cannot enter the Royal Nairobi Game Park on foot, most of the city's citizens never see it. To remedy this, Colonel Merwyn Cowie, former director of the Kenya Parks, raised money to build a "Game Orphanage" at the entrance to the park, where the animals, mostly young ones, would be enclosed and could be seen by anyone with a shilling entrance fee. Thousands of Africans could then walk the four miles from the city to the park entrance and enjoy this display of their native wild life. Cowie told me that the scheme could be completed for $25,000, and he already had about $9,000. He said he had listed the project with the British Division of the World Wildlife Fund. I cannot imagine a better investment.

Another project of Cowie's that appeared to me to have decided merit was that of acquiring aircraft for the Kenya Game Parks. Tanganyika had light planes, and with them has been able to do a remarkable job in policing the parks, spotting fires and counting game. Cowie believed that he could get along with two light planes at a cost of about $30,000. Kenya has few parks in comparison to Uganda and Tanganyika but it is estimated that seventy per cent of the game of Kenya is located in the lands of the pastoral tribes such as the Masai, Samburu, Boran and Rendille who do not as a rule hunt it. Policing of these areas would be most helpful to the tribes who derive considerable revenue from safaris which hunt on their lands.

One of the most important factors in the salvation of the game in East Africa is an interest in its future on the part of the Africans themselves, and unless the duly elected representatives of Kenya's seven million people are moved to support conservation, the future is grim indeed. Cowie invited all the African ministers to spend the night at Treetops, the spectacular viewing station high in a great tree from which one can see elephant, buffalo, rhino and many other kinds of game as they come to drink at a water hole. The Mau Mau burned the old Treetops but Jomo Kenyatta, the convicted head of the Mau Mau and the first Prime Minister of Kenya, was among the first invited. The group reacted with the same fascination that all visitors do.

Seventy kilometers along a dirt track from the south Somalian seaport of Chisimaio lies the headquarters of Emilio Lucano, the lonely warden of Somalia's only proper game reserve. Aided by two police officers and a few game guards he is responsible for the wildlife in an area of more than 5,000 square miles. Known as the Riserva Assoluta Del Bubasci, the reserve is a rough rectangle bounded by the Indian Ocean, the Kenya border, the Buduna River and an artificial boundary. It was started by the Italians in 1926 and the government at Rome still pays Lucano's salary. He is not maintained in luxury. An old trailer, a few thatched huts and a truck which sometimes runs make up his camp. The only water comes from some brackish wells used by nomads for watering their camels. The dam, which used to store a large body of rain water, burst some years ago and the government has made no attempt to rebuild it. The result is that the nearest place the game can drink is the river thirty miles away where poachers wait by the banks.

Lucano speaks no English but we were able to get along in French. I was delighted to hear that the park contains at least 150 Hunter's antelope. While Lucano runs the Bubasci Park, all will be well, but the trend in Africa is to let the black man replace the white man and the chances are that a Somali will take over when Lucano leaves. This does not necessarily mean that the reserve will go to hell but judging from the state of conservation every place except in the reserve, I would not like to write an insurance policy for the game.

During the night we heard the laughter of the hyenas and in the morning Lucano told us that a lioness and two full-grown cubs had killed a brace of goats a few miles away. Lack of water had driven most of the game out of the area so that the lions are being forced to prey on the flocks of the nomads. Nor are the lions fussy about how many legs their supper walks on. Lucano told me that man-eaters are common in the bush of this part of Somalia and showed me pictures taken recently of a small boy who had been killed by a lioness. Having only their poisoned arrows and spears to protect themselves—the central government for various reasons does not allow the tribes to have firearms—they suffer a good deal from the big cats. There are, of course, no doctors, and the merest scratch from a lion's claws is certain blood poisoning.

Next to the tsetse, the big horse flies of Somalia are the most voracious in Africa. Only "6–12," the peerless insecticide, seems to have any visible effect, and even when it is used certain kamikaze-type flies still dive-bomb one's legs. There is much malaria in the district around Lucano's headquarters but weekly Aralin pills keep it under control. Disease, including leprosy, is rampant in the back land of Somalia.

The park contains many varieties of game, including about 5,000 elephant, 100 black rhino, 1,000 buffalo, 500 lion, 80 leopard and numerous giraffe, greater and lesser kudu, zebra, cob, oribi, oryx, Hunter's and common antelope, and a variety of smaller game. At Brava, a little port on the coast north of the mouth of the Juba, there are still dugong, that rare sea animal that looks like a mermaid if seen through the depths. The locals, unlike the Moslems of Ceylon who are avid dugong eaters, do not hunt it, and Lucano said there were fair numbers of them to be found grazing on the shallow weed beds just off the coast. In view of the rapidly declining numbers of these interesting sea mammals in other parts of the world, the Somalian abundance is fortunate.

Crocodiles swarm in the warm rivers of southern Somalia and sometimes, even without the urging of the crocodile men, they take humans. Lucano shot a fifteen footer in whose stomach he found a small boy. Another version of the story of crocodiles being used to eat people on command is as follows: One paid the "bar," the witch doctor, and gave him sand from the tracks of the intended victim. The witch doctor then summoned a crocodile who emerged from the water and laid its head in his lap while the witch doctor let it smell the sand from the tracks of the man he wished to do in. Later the crocodile waddled through the night, found the man, and ate him.

Although most of the game had gone to the river, we did see a small herd of oryx, numerous gazelle, a few wart hog, baboons and monkeys. Bird life was somewhat restricted but we spotted a flock of guinea fowl with beautiful purple and blue streaks in the usual spotted plumage of the common guineas. There were some francolin and a brace of lesser bustard. At high noon, one of Lucano's trackers came with news that a herd of elephant had been spotted nearby, and we all piled into the Land Rover to see it. The elephant, however, had moved into the bush and as the temperature was hovering over the 100 mark, I called off the chase after an hour's sweaty tracking. Lucano was almost in tears that he could not show us examples of his chief attractions.

As an officer of the country Lucano quite rightly did not comment on the state of game conservation, but I was able to find out a good deal about it from other knowledgeable sources. On the books there are a set of game laws. Drawn up by the Italians in 1950, the code had not been appreciably changed since, and it is quite out of date. Furthermore, there is a great deal of confusion as to whose baby the game department is. Administratively, it falls under the Ministry of Agriculture, but since that ministry has no enforcement agency, the police, a division of the Ministry of the Interior, enforce the game laws. A small squad under the command of Inspector Issa Mussa Uggiale is responsible for the protection of the Bubasci reserve and the inspector and three of his men were with us at Lucano's headquarters.

Poaching is rampant. With the skin of a full-grown Somali leopard, the finest in the world, now worth 700 Scelini, about $100 in the local market, every tribesman with a trap or a poisoned arrow is on the warpath to get them. Unlike the beaver in America which was saved because beaver hats went out of style in 1840, the leopard still commands a high price for women's coats and unless something can be done to make the wearing of these coats unfashionable the future of the world's most beautiful big cats is dark indeed.

The local price of ivory is 60 Scelini per kilo or about $4.20 per pound. There is no estimate of the number of elephant killed illegally but judging from the tusks coming on the market, it must be up in the hundreds. For some reason which I have not been able to fathom, the ivory and skin auctions are conducted by the government without much concern as to the source of the commodity.

There are other rare animals in Somalia in addition to the Hunter's antelope. The dibatag, a delicate little antelope, and the beira, a tiny deer about the size of dikdik, are only found in the mountains out on the Horn and are quite inaccessible for ordinary viewing without a safari into their arid and inhospitable country. Both of these little ungulates are native to Somalia only and are said to be declining. Unfortunately, there is no landing strip on the Horn or I would have taken a chance and flown up to see if I could find any.

General Mohomed Abscir, Commandant of the Somali police, through whose good offices I was able to fly down in a police plane and see the Bubasci Game Reserve, wrote me that all game law enforcement in his country was now being handled by a special force of thirty men. Barely able to cover the two southern regions of the country where most of the big game is concentrated, they have no extra men to try and cope with poaching in the other six regions. These northern regions include the areas of the dibatag, the beira and also the wild ass, known as the guduri.

An expedition to the Horn in the not distant future with objective of capturing and transplanting, perhaps to America, examples of these three dwindling species would certainly be a worthwhile project.

THREE

Rare Animals of Ethiopia

AUDIENCES WITH THE Emperor of Ethiopia are not easy to come by. There are ambassadors who have waited weeks to be summoned to the Presence in order to present their credentials. Lesser lights have an even harder time of it and I was extremely pleased when my request to see His Imperial Majesty was acted on in the record time of two days.

Ambassador Korry, immaculate in tail coat and gray waistcoat, called for me at the Ghion Hotel and we drove with flags flying to the Emperor's palace, only to be told at the gate that our appointment was to be at the Imperial Offices to which His Imperial Majesty would soon proceed.

On alighting from the car in the grounds of the Imperial Offices, the first thing I saw was a large black-maned lion who was seated placidly on the grass and took only a passing interest in the Emperor or his guests. I learned he was one of three tame lions, some of whom occasionally roared when they were not amused.

The Emperor received us in his private office, a large, pleasant room warmed by a big open fire. The furniture consisted of a carved desk where H.I.M. worked and a small throne flanked by ordinary chairs for his guests. We bowed as we entered the room, advanced to the throne, bowed again and then shook hands. Haile Selassie I, King of Kings, Lion of Judah, Emperor of Ethiopia, and the 255th monarch of the Solomonic dynasty, traditionally believed to have been started when King Solomon smiled on the Queen of Sheba, welcomed us with a kindly nod and asked us to be seated. He speaks some English but prefers French, and my conversation with him was conducted partly in French and partly by the Minister of the Palace who translated English into Amharic.

Although a small man, the Emperor, who was dressed in the full uniform of a field marshal of the Ethiopian Army, is an impressive figure. His eyes are clear, his expression intelligent and alert, and his general demeanor that of a man who commands and expects to be obeyed.

I told him of my mission and my particular interest in the mountain nyala, the Ethiopian ibex and the wild ass, the three rare animals of his country which are found no place else on earth. He replied that he was aware of their value and has issued firm orders that they be protected. He then smiled and said that any suggestions which I might have for their further well-being would certainly be welcomed by his government. I assumed this to mean that he knew that the game laws of Ethiopia are not taken too seriously. Indeed how could they be, for there are no game wardens? I told the Emperor that I intended to make inquiries about the status of these rare fauna and would see that he received a copy of my report.

When we took our leave the Emperor said to me in English, "I am glad to see you and hope you will come again." I found, as many foreigners have found, that with the Emperor's blessing anything is possible in Ethiopia and, without it, very little.

My next call was on His Excellency Ato Akale Worq, the Minister of Agriculture, whose department has responsibility for game. One of the ablest members of the government, Worq had served as ambassador to France and had more of an interest in international affairs than some of his colleagues. He had heard of the World Wildlife Fund and sympathized fully with its objectives. He was also well aware of the three rare species which are found nowhere else but Ethiopia, but here his knowledge stopped. He told me frankly that the Game Department consisted of little more than a set of laws which were seldom observed and a few scattered watchers in the areas where game is protected. He added that he would be delighted to have any suggestions which I might make toward improving this sad state of affairs.

Climbing lower down the official ladder, I talked with Hapte Sellasie (no relation of the emperor) who was the spark plug of the government Tourist Agency. Hapte, whose energy was somewhat unique among the aristocratic and work-hating Amharas, proclaimed himself solidly in favor of conservation but gave the subject rather a curious twist. Instead of working toward the formation of game parks, where tourists could see the animals, and legalized shooting which would attract sportsmen, he seemed primarily interested in issuing special licenses for the shooting of the very animals which should be protected from all hunting. The reason for this was apparent with the entrance of Ted Shatto, an American, who said he was Ethiopia's only white hunter, and who immediately wanted to know why I didn't think it was a good idea to pick off a few surplus ibex and mountain nyala. His reasoning was that only those hunters interested in rare species would come to Ethiopia and they should be allowed special permits.

My reaction was definitely negative. In the first place, the number of hunters who have the time and money to come to Ethiopia to hunt one or two species is very limited and would not produce any important revenue. Secondly, I believe it would be wrong further to reduce the numbers of these rare animals. As a matter of fact, the matter may be somewhat academic as the Minister of Agriculture had told me he was definitely going to put a total ban on the shooting of the three rare species.

Although it has been possible to get special licenses to shoot in Ethiopia, the most recent law has stated that no hunting is permitted. The result has been that foreigners, except in special circumstances, have not been able to shoot at all. This may not have been a bad move on the part of the government because previous to the prohibition there was some flagrant slaughtering of game. The U.S. Army and AID missions were among the guilty hunters.

Actually, only a minute percentage of the game killed in Ethiopia fell to foreigners. Poaching by the population is the great destroyer and until game laws with teeth are promulgated, the killing will go on. According to a reliable source, Ethiopia exports more than 10,000 leopard skins per year but the hunting of leopards is supposedly licensed. The leopards are trapped—not shot—so that the skins will not be scarred. A great many of the skins sold to Seventh Avenue in New York as Somali leopards come from Ethiopia. The skins of colobus monkeys, also supposedly protected by law, are so common that one can buy them in many stores in Addis Ababa.

Addis Ababa is the headquarters for a vast smuggling ring which imports leopard skins from all of East Africa. It is estimated that the traffic now exceeds the equivalent of $1.4 million per year. The native hunter probably gets only about $50 a skin, the smuggler gets about $150 and in a New York fur store a fine leopard coat consisting of eight skins can bring $10,000.

If a game policy were inaugurated and professional hunters were allowed to operate, an important source of revenue would accrue to the government. There is still plenty of game in Ethiopia. In addition to the three rare species mentioned, the list of common game is long and rewarding. In the savannahs and open woodland live many of the antelopes and gazelles. There are oryx, Soemmering gazelle and Grant's gazelle in the Danakil, Ogaden and Borana provinces. Roan and hartebeest are found in Wollaga, Illubador and in northwest Kaffa, while the eland thrives in Kaffa and Gamu-Gofa. Near the Kenya border are the common waterbuck. Both lesser and greater kudu are found in Ethiopia but the latter prefers the mountainous regions, and the lesser the lower hills, especially where sisal is growing. Kudu are plentiful in Danakil, Ogaden, Shoa, Arussi, Sidamo, Borana and Gamu-Gofa provinces.

Elephant roam the Sudan border in the area next to the Dinder Park. The Ethiopian elephant is said to carry very heavy ivory although the tusks are not long. Buffalo are also numerous along the Sudan border in Wollaga, Illubador and Kaffa. Lion inhabit the western parts of the country and those which live in the mountains have very dark manes. Leopards are found all over Ethiopia, although they are more plentiful where there are baboons and monkeys. Leopards have been shot at 12,000 feet above sea level where their only source of food is probably the gelada baboon.

Of the smaller animals there are also a great variety, including the wart hog, the forest hog, bush pig, Semian wild dog, aard wolf, otter, hare and porcupine. Game birds include bustard, guinea fowl, francolin, sand grouse, quail, duck, pigeon, snipe and dove.

The present game laws, proclaimed in 1944, sound well enough on paper, but do not provide for any enforcement. Like many other laws in Ethiopia, the government seems to think that its mere publication will insure its observation. The law gives maximum protection to the ibex (walia), the mountain nyala (dega agazen) and the wild ass (ahia). It also protects the female dibatag, gerenuk and kudu. Among the protected birds are the heron, hammerkop, marabout, stork, ibis, spoonbill, flamingo, and hornbill. There is a closed season for all shooting from July 1 to October 31. Sad experience also prompted the government to issue a prohibition against tracer bullets, hand grenades, bombs or shooting from aircraft.

Such enforcement as exists is left up to the local police who have many other duties besides roaming around in the bush.

The year before my visit a technical team of the International Union for the Conservation of Nature spent a few days in Ethiopia and recommended that a countrywide survey be made of all game and that special research projects be set up for the ibex, nyala and ass. The team also recommended that wildlife conservation be coordinated with the other natural resources. This report makes good sense but would entail considerable money which the government seems loath to spend.

Fortunately, the animals in which I am primarily interested are protected by nature. The Ethiopian ibex and the mountain nyala are found only in the wildest and highest reaches of the mountains and the haunts of the wild ass are in a desert area almost completely devoid of water or roads. To get exact information on the locale of these three I appealed first to Youra Lappine, a White Russian who, before he became the General Motors representative in Ethiopia, conducted extensive safaris all over the country for twenty years. He told me that previous to the shooting ban of 1958, while hunting in the Chelalo Mountains southeast of Addis at the 12,000-foot level, he saw a herd of twenty-seven nyala, among which were some very big heads. He did not try to shoot any. He was told by his boy that some of the native tribes in the area shoot female nyala in the belief that the urine is a sure cure for syphilis. He also saw nyala in the Chercher Mountains of Arussi Province and was told that the natives there occasionally shot them for meat which they ate raw.

Lappine said the Ethiopian ibex is now restricted to the Simien Mountains northwest of Lake Tana. Hunting there six years before he saw a pair of ibex and was told that small herds existed farther up in the mountains.

I was interested to hear that there are still some hippos in the lake regions of Ethiopia and that an attempt was made to preserve those in Lake Hora Abyato without much success. The tribes still value hippo hides for their shields. Crocodiles are being shot out, as is happening all over Africa. A Swiss has a concession to eliminate them in one of the few lakes where they are still plentiful.

My next source was Ronald Peel, counselor of the British Embassy. Peel, who had been in Ethiopia for seven years, was keen about wildlife and had made a trip to the Simiens where he saw tracks of ibex although he did not see any animals. He told me that the British Consul stationed at a small town on the border of Kenya had a good deal of information on poaching and the smuggling of skins. In the event that it is decided to make a survey of the ibex or the nyala, this man, who was expected to retire from the consular service, would be a very good one to retain.

The next day Shatto and I talked again and he gave me a map of the places where he said he personally knew there were ibex, nyala and ass. Questioned on specific views of these species he said that in November of 1962 he saw 220 nyala in the mountains of Bali Province and later in the same year saw 40 nyala in the Chercher Mountains.

He estimated that there are 400 to 500 ibex in the north escarpment of the Simien Mountains. There are only one or two passes into the area where they are and one of these passes is guarded after a fashion by the local police. When Shatto went into the area, he was guiding a gentleman from Washington state. He said the hunter collects for some small museum in a town near Tacoma. I always wonder about these "small" museums.

Shatto had not seen wild ass but had talked recently to an American group who drove across part of the Ogaden and reported seeing several herds. Seen from a distance the wild ass look a great deal like Grevy's zebra and it is possible that the Americans saw zebra. On the other hand, there is no question but that the wild ass does exist in the Ogaden and, even though occasionally poached by the nomadic Somalis who graze their herds there, is still said to be holding its own in the more desolate areas. Wild ass are also said to be in the Danakil, although the hostility of the tribes—they are apt to collect a certain part of one's anatomy—makes surveys risky.

From these relatively slim pickings, my opinion was that the best chance we had to contribute toward conservation in Ethiopia would be to make a survey of the ibex.* Unlike the mountain nyala which are spread over quite a big area, the ibex are concentrated in the Simien Mountains and have not been reported outside this restricted range.

---

* Mr. Leslie Brown made a preliminary study of the Walia ibex and the mountain nyala for the World Wildlife Fund in 1963 and plans another expedition in the future.

Shatto said that a team could cover this area in a two or three month trek and come up with a very fair idea of the numbers of ibex left. Helicopters would of course make the job easier as the mountains rise to Ras Dashan which towers 15,158 feet above sea level and is the highest peak in North Africa.

I could not climb around the Simien peaks myself but I could go to the foot of the mountains and, I hoped, find people there with first hand and recent knowledge of the ibex.

At Gondar, the ancient capital of Ethiopia and the main city of the Amhara people who run the country, we were met by an inspector of police and driven to the administration building where Kanazmach Bekele, the deputy governor of the province, assured us that everything possible would be done to make our stay pleasant and interesting. A Land Rover with driver as well as the services of police lieutenant Getare Yohanes Asfan were placed at our disposal. The Iteghie Menen Hotel, named after the Empress, is one of the best little hotels in Africa, with clean rooms, garden vistas through the windows, and good food.

My purpose in going to Gondar was to find out all I could about the ibex, the rare Ethiopian walia. Accordingly, on a fine, bright morning—it had been raining almost all the time since our arrival in Gondar—we departed in the Governor's Land Rover with a good chauffeur at the wheel and Lt. Asfan to translate. The road from Gondar to Debarek, the village at the foot of the Simiens, is one of the best in Africa. Constructed by the Italians during their five-year occupation of Ethiopia, it has been well maintained since and makes the 550-kilometer run from Gondar to Asmara one of the most dramatic I have ever seen. Initially we climbed from the 6,000-foot elevation of Gondar to a plateau country of more than 10,000 feet, where the rolling green pastures stretched away to the blue line of the Simiens, far in the distance.

We saw several monkeys and in a particularly rough stretch of country a pair of large doglike animals which I thought at first were jackals—there are two types in Ethiopia, the side-striped and the black-backed—but after putting the glasses on the retreating pair, I saw that they were gray and too large for jackals. The chauffeur said they were "kay kabaro," wild dog, and that they were killers of sheep. According to Harper's *Extinct and Vanishing Mammals of the World* very little is known about the "Abyssinian wolf," also known as the kay kabaro.

I learned that Mikirel Tarekeque, our highly efficient and careful chauffeur, had a wife who hails from Debarek and had spent a good deal of time in the Simiens. He said that while staying in the Lemalino Valley, the year before, deep in the mountains, he had seen three small herds of walia, numbering about a dozen each. He added that these wild goats are extremely wary and always walk on the ridges of the mountains so that they can see on either side.

At Debarek we picked up Turekque Gebrehisvet, a constable of the local police who had trekked all through the mountains. He told us the fine for shooting a walia is 100 Ethiopian dollars and not worth the meat. He had seen several hundred walia during the past year and was of the opinion that the species is increasing. He said that when he was a small boy—and I would judge him to be about thirty—many people shot walia and sold the horns for drinking cups. Horns were still sold in some of the back country stores but he did not go into detail as to how the storekeepers came by them. He remarked that there is snow on Ras Dashan most of the year and that the walia wander close to the snow line on the north face of the mountain.

An old resident of Debarek told me that walia frequent the district near the village of Ambaras which is known for its ancient church of Kidusyared. He estimated there are hundreds of walia in the high mountains and that they are so hard to shoot that few bother to hunt them. He said there are twenty police in the area and the risk of being caught is too great.

We had several reasons for going to Lake Tana, the great island-dotted body of water in northwestern Ethiopia which forms the source of the Blue Nile. The first was curiosity. We had seen the river at Khartoum where it joins the White Nile and at Roseires where it thunders over its last cataract and in both cases the waters were blue-gray. Was it also clear at its birth? The second was in the line of my work. I had been asked by Mrs. P. B. Hall of the British Museum to find out what I could about *Francolinus harwoodi,* a rare francolin which was reported to inhabit the gorges of the Blue Nile or its tributaries northeast of the lake. Lastly, we wanted to visit the ancient Coptic monasteries which still exist on some of the islands.

We set out early in the Land Rover to drive the forty miles of the winding dirt road from Gondar to Gorgora, the village on the edge of Lake Tana. It is sometimes difficult for me to tell colors from far away but the impression that Lake Tana was muddy, which I'd gained while flying over it, was more than justified by a closer look. The great basin of the Blue Nile was the color of Old Miss in the spring.

In addition to the Emperor's speed boat, an ex-smuggler from Aden, Gorgora boasts a slow but dependable launch which I promptly hired. The captain, a Yemeni from Taiz, knew the lake well and was a good source of information on everything, from the birds to the habits of the monks.

I kept my binoculars trained on the mainland and the islands and was soon rewarded by the sight of a Goliath heron, a big striped-neck heron which is fairly common along the shores of Lake Tana. There are also said to be gray heron and black-headed heron but I did not see any. A little while later I spotted a crowned crane. An old friend from the Nile, this handsome long-legged bird, with its red and white face and crown of stiff yellow feathers, is one of the adornments of African waters. Sitting in a tree on one of the rocky cactus-covered islands I saw a fish eagle, a bird whose strange distinctive cry is heard from one end of the continent to the other. Swimming near us were darters and wading along the shallows I saw both the sacred and the glossy ibis.

Asked about francolins, the Yemeni captain said there is only one kind found near the lake, the common yellow-leg variety. The male *Francolinus harwoodi* has a distinctive U-shaped pattern on the black and white feathers of the breast which differs from the plainer feathers of the East African *hildebrandti*. It is not known if the female *harwoodi* resemble the male or have orange breasts like the female *hildebrandti*. Unfortunately, the Ethiopian name for francolin is "kok" and it applies to all varieties of the pheasant family. By dint of much explaining—I talked in English to Lt. Asfan who translated into Amharic for the captain—I was able to find out that there were other kinds of francolin along the river ravines and that he would be glad to have the different types brought to me. Alas, we had to return to Addis Ababa the following day, and there was no time to try and collect a skin of *harwoodi*.

The first monastery we came to was that of Teklehaimant, a collection of thatch huts around a large round hut surmounted by an ornate Coptic cross. It is forbidden for women to land on any of the islands and, as I did not fancy the stiff climb to the cliff face, we settled for the binoculars and the captain's knowledge. The best ecclesiastical painting, however, is not found in the island monasteries but in the mainland church of Debra Sena.

Back in Addis Ababa I reviewed my notes on the game situation in Ethiopia and put them in the form of a letter to the Emperor with a copy to the Minister of Agriculture. I believed that a sincere effort was being made to preserve the ibex in the Simien Mountains but felt that the mountain nyala and the wild ass needed additional protection, particularly against the so-called "collectors" who are always trying to get permits to shoot rare animals in order to mount them in their own "museums," which are often no more public than their bedrooms.

I also urged that a game department be established with clear-cut duties in regard to conservation and enforcement of the laws governing the protected species.

FOUR

Aden and the Oryx

MANY YEARS AGO when I was sailing to Bombay in the old Peninsula and Oriental liner, *Viceroy of India,* we stopped at Aden and I had a memorable evening ashore with some young subalterns of the Indian cavalry. Those were the days of Empire, and Aden was a vital link in the line of naval bases that ran from Gibraltar to Singapore. The Royal Navy ruled the Red Sea and the approaches to the Indian Ocean were securely in the hands of Engand. The Union Jack still flew over Aden and it was greatly to the advantage of the West that it did for the West must have oil and Britain's Middle East Command of some 40,000 troops guaranteed the flow from the Persian Gulf. Since then it has been decided to move the troops out of Aden and rely on the Royal Air Force, based in Africa and Cyprus, to keep Nasser's ambitions in check.

In 1963, however, the British were firm in their desire to stay in Aden and despite the continual screaming of the Cairo radio and the heady wind of Arab unity the man in charge at Aden was keeping a stiff upper lip.

Sir Charles Hepburn Johnston, K.C.M.G., former High Commissioner for the Federation of South Arabia, is a career Foreign Office man with definite ideas as to his mission. After an excellent lunch on the wide patio of Government House, overlooking the blue waters of Aden harbor, he puffed his cigarette and told me something of his parish and his problems.

Strategically located where the Red Sea joins the Indian Ocean,

42

Aden itself consists of only some seventy square miles of black volcanic hills on the southwestern tip of Arabia. But the hills surround the best harbor between Suez and Bombay and on the long air strips rests the most powerful air force in the Middle East. The city of Aden, a free port almost since the days when Britain took it over in 1839, is one of the busiest in the world and, by and large, its 300,000 inhabitants have prospered under a beneficent if tight imperial rule. Lately they have been given a considerable amount of self government and Britain plans to give them more. This, however, does not satisfy the masses, many of whom are from neighboring Yemen. Claiming that the Imams of Yemen once held Aden and its hinterlands, the Aden mobs recently rioted, shouting "One Yemen, One People, One God." Why anyone would want to join the Yemen is one of the mysteries of the mysterious East, but nationalism is potent, especially when imperialism, however good it may be, is fast disappearing elsewhere.

Sir Charles's job did not stop at the sandy borders of Aden proper. It included the Aden Protectorate, a matter of 112,000 square miles, mostly sand, but populated by some 650,000 Arabs, some of whom are nomadic Bedouins and some of whom live sedentary life in towns. But unlike Aden, where British rule is more obvious, control of the Protectorate is exercised through twenty-four local rulers ranging from His Highness Sultan Fadhl bin 'Ali of Lahej (11-gun salute) to a bevy of Sheiks and a few Amirs. Eleven of these petty princes, mostly in the western end of the Protectorate, have been merged with the city of Aden into a Federation, a title with a much more democratic connotation than that of Colony or Protectorate. Federations, in fact, develop eventually into self-governing dominions. The eastern end of the Protectorate has not been federated and the sultans of the states in the fabled Hadhraumaut are still tied to Britain by their original treaties.

Most of these little sultanates, sheikdoms and amirates have their own internal security forces in the shape of tribal guards, and two of the larger ones, Lahej in the west and Mukulla in the east, have their own small armies. In all cases these units are British trained and in some cases are still commanded by the Queen's officers. Among these picturesque units is the Hadhrami Bedouin Legion whose scout cars and camels patrol the lonely sand deserts on the borders of Saudi Arabia. To see what life is like in these remote monarchies, I made two trips out from Aden, one to the neighboring sultanate of Lahej, a matter of an hour's drive, and another to the Hadhraumaut, the fabled valley of the Eastern Protectorate. The latter trip involved a vast amount of planning, permissions, and luck, and included flights of nearly a thousand miles.

My reason for going to Aden was not to study the people or to see the country. The south coast of Arabia is no summer resort, especially in late April, when the thermometer passes a hundred at noon and there is no real relief until the evening breezes blow. My mission was to find out all I could about any remaining Arabian oryx, that rare antelope whose future is now so dubious. A year before, an expedition headed by Major Ian Grimwood, Chief Game Warden of Kenya, succeeded in capturing four oryx in the Eastern Protectorate, but since then no new sightings had been reported and it was feared that the oryx might be near extinction in this part of South Arabia. I did not have the time or the facilities to explore the borders of the Rub al Khali, the sand desert where the oryx lives, but by going to the Hadhraumaut and talking with the officers of the Hadhrami Bedouin Legion who patrol that border and with the various rulers whose caravans traverse the area, I hoped to get some news.

The Arabian oil princes are still keen about gunning down oryx from cars. Careening over the desert with guns blazing, they have blotted out virtually every herd in the Protectorate. There were said to be still a few herds in the neighboring kingdom of Muscat and Oman, but all Arabs have guns these days and the single Bedouin on his camel is just as apt to take a pot shot at a free dinner as his oil-rich cousin in a Land Rover.

Luckily, the Political Adviser to the Sultan of Lahej, a young Britisher named M. A. Crouch, was the very man who, in a letter to Colonel Boyle of the Fauna Preservation Society in London, in January of 1961, suggested that a few of the remaining Arabian oryx be captured and transplanted before it was too late. Ian Grimwood's successful expedition was the result. Crouch sent his Land Rover for us and we drove out to Lahej in the late afternoon. Only thirty years before trees lined the twenty-mile road from Aden to Lahej, but refugees have cut them down and today there is only a strip of macadam running across the shifting sands of the desert. We passed Sheikh Othman, a hodgepodge of camels, goats, rickety trucks, and fly-specked coffee houses, and soon afterward entered the Sultanate. At the Residency, an imposing but curiously truncated edifice, the sentry snapped to attention and Mr. Crouch and his wife welcomed us to Lahej. Before settling down to talk, he showed us the Residency and explained that it was formerly the palace of the Sultans. The reason for the truncated effect was due to the fact that the top two stories had been lopped off so that the British Advisers could not look down into the harem gardens of the Sultan's new palace across the road. Two peacocks screamed in the ghost-haunted ground. Not so long ago, one of the Sultans had tied his two cousins to a tree and shot them neatly through the heart. Both seemed to have had ambitions.

Crouch is a student of the oryx and from his voluminous files of correspondence and clippings I was able to glean a few facts which may be of interest to my readers. Although the Arabian oryx (first described by Gray in 1857, who named it oryx Beatrice, after Princess Beatrice) was once common over much of Arabia and Mesopotamia, where it was known as the Baqr al Wash (the wild cow); it is now nearly extinct except for a few survivors in the southern part of the Arabian Peninsula. But even in this last toe-hold its survival is tenuous. In 1961 Qatari raiders killed forty-eight oryx near the edge of the Rub al Khali at longitude 52 degrees east.

The Arabian oryx is the smallest of the four species of oryx and the only one found outside Africa. The others are the gemsbok, which I have shot in Southwest Africa and which is in no danger of extinction; the oryx beisa of Kenya and Tanganyika which is also plentiful; and the scimitar oryx of the Sudan which is fairly rare. This is the white oryx which I have written about previously. The horns of the Arabian species which are only about 35 inches long as against 48 for the African varieties, have always attracted hunters. Some people say that the oryx seen in profile, when its long pointed horns appear to be one, furnished the origin of the legends of the unicorn. In medieval times these horns were thought to possess magical qualities, and for centuries the kings of France drank out of cups made from oryx horns on the theory that poison could not be introduced into them. Other legends concern the aphrodisiac properties said to lie in the ground-up horns, and some Arabs are said to believe that the mere killing of an oryx somehow strengthens one's virility. The net of it is that the oryx's crowning glory has proved his undoing and only the education of several million Arabs can hope to save him from extinction. In the meantime, the breeding of a small herd in a safe place such as Phoenix, Arizona, where it is planned to move the Kenya specimens, offers the best hope of keeping the oryx from joining the dodo bird.

Among the most ancient lands in the world are those forming the southern coast of Arabia. Along the inhospitable littoral which runs from Aden to the borders of Muscat and Oman, a matter of nearly 700 miles, there is little means of transportation except by sailing dhows or caravans. There are few roads to speak of and only two air fields. Like the cities of Tibet and Yemen, those of the Hadhraumaut, the hidden land of the Eastern Aden Protectorate, have no tourist trade and seek none.

Sir Charles Johnston introduced me to Arthur Watts, Resident Adviser to His Highness, the Sultan of Mukalla. Watts in turn invited me and my party to stay at his residency in Mukalla and also arranged for our further journey to the inland cities of the Hadhraumaut. So far so good, but we seemed doomed to a bitter disappointment. Aden Airways' weekly cargo and passenger plane was booked solid for some trips to come. There were no planes to charter and no ships to hire. Then my daughter came to the rescue. As a result of a conversation in Mogadiscio with the wife of the French Ambassador there, she had a letter of introduction to Anthony Besse, a name that stirred a host of memories in my mind. There are certain great trading families in the East and Besse is one of them. Grabbing a taxi, Renie and I drove from the Crescent Hotel and drew up in front of the block-long house of Besse. About thirty-five and by all odds the richest man in Aden, Tony Besse controls a trading empire which includes almost every kind of enterprise from oil to insurance. He was leaving for Paris the next day but listened patiently to our troubles and called the manager of Aden Airways himself, saying he would consider it a personal favor if we were given the space. The next day the space was confirmed, and on the 20th of April we took off in an ancient DC3 for Mukalla and a journey into the past.

Arthur Watts was also taking the same plane back to his job, and, as we droned along the coast, he pointed out places of interest and told me something of his parish. As Resident Adviser and British Agent Watts is the supreme authority in the Eastern Aden Protectorate, an area of some 80,000 square miles, which includes three sultanates and some other smaller units. By means of astute diplomacy and with the backing of the Hadhrami Bedouin Legion, an irregular force of some 1,200 men, he maintains the Queen's Peace.

The Eastern Protectorate includes the sultanate of Mahra, whose sultan rules from the islands of Socotra. But the term Hadhraumaut,

1. The Nile at Aswan

2. Egyptian ibex

3. Shoebill

4. Hartebeest

5. Waterbuck

6. Shilluk warrior,
Upper Nile

7. Black rhino

8. Zebra

9. Giraffes

10. Kudu

11. Ethiopian shepherd boy, Simien Mountains

13. Ibex with tame goats, Hadhramaut

12. The village of Shibam,
Hadhramaut

15. Arab Legionaires, Jordan

14. Yemeni tribesman

16. Nile lechwe

17. Gazelle

18. Red deer fawn

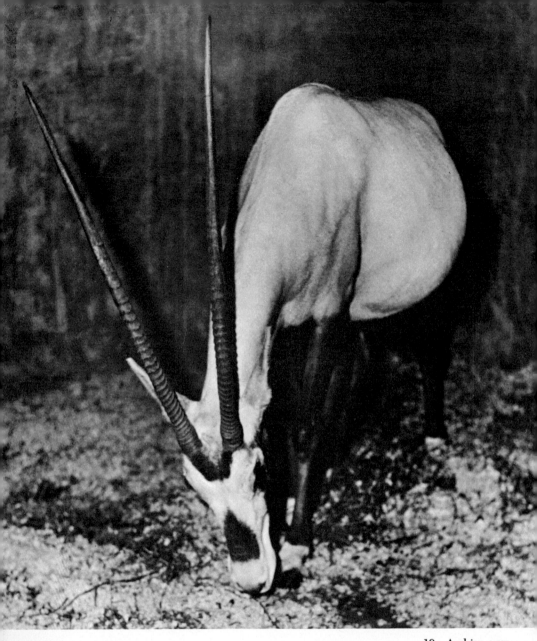

19. Arabian oryx

which means "death is present" applies only to the Qu'aiti and Kathirit sultanates, and the three fabled cities—Saium in Kathiri and Tarim and Shibbam in Qu'aiti. All located near each other in the Wadi or Hadhraumaut Valley about a hundred miles inland from the sea, they were the real object of the trip.

We landed at Mukalla, the seaport capital of the Qu'aiti Sultanate of His Highness Awaah bin Salih al Mukalla Qu'aiti and the city where Watts has his Residency, and, driven by Watts himself, we headed toward town.

In the courtyard of the Residency, also a former palace, we found a guard of honor drawn up. After reviewing it, Watts stepped forward and shook hands with every man in the squad. This is the custom but his relationship to the soldiers of the Legion goes deeper. Watts personally chooses those permitted to enlist from a great number of applicants.

Modeled on the famous Arab Legion of Trans-Jordania, the Hadhrami Bedouin Legion was started in 1938 by officers lent by Glubb Pasha to Harold Ingrams, then the Resident in Mukalla. There are only two British officers, Pat Gray, the Qaid, or commanding colonel, and his deputy.

Gray's forces dot the borders of Oman and Saudi Arabia, the areas where the Arabian oryx are still said to roam, and I found him greatly interested in the possibility that Ian Grimwood might consider another trip to the Eastern Protectorate to capture additional oryx if a sizable number could be located. He promised to send us full information on any sightings and to ask his men to question the Bedouin in the area.

The economy of the Eastern Protectorate is based almost entirely on the export of people. There being few other fields of endeavor in the Protectorate thousands of Hadhrami emigrate. In the old days they went to the Dutch East Indies and Malaya and today most of them find work in Saudi Arabia and in the oil sheikhdoms. These adventurers send their money home and it is due primarily to these remittances that the Hadhraumaut citizens are able to get along. Some families get along very well indeed. The owner of Raffles Hotel in Singapore is said to be an Hadhrami. Mukalla is the port of entry for the inland cities and import taxes go quite a way toward defraying the costs of the Sultan's government. However, the Aden Protectorate as a whole costs the British taxpayer 6½ million pounds sterling per year with the Hadhrami Bedouin Legion accounting for about 340,000 of it.

The British are making strenuous efforts to build up local industries.

The trip from Mukalla to the Hadhraumaut takes a strenuous twelve hours by Land Rover but in the DC3 of Aden Airways the trip can be done in forty-five minutes, providing the landing field is not a sea of mud. Even the flying is tricky. Drafts from the ovenlike desert suck up and down above the walled-in plateau; the floor of the valley is 2,000 feet above sea level but the cliffs of the plateau rise to 7,000. Nevertheless, our pilot made a serene landing and drew up before the little white building of the Ghuraf airport with the flag of the Sultan of Kathiri hanging in the still, dry air.

Yacob Al Kaff, a scion of the famous Al Kaff family whose founder Sheikh Al Kaff made his fortune a hundred years ago in Singapore, welcomed us and drove us to one of his father's mansions in the city of Tarim. En route we were stopped at two customs posts. The Sultan of Qu'aiti charges a 25 per cent levy on all goods crossing his territory and the Sultan of Kathiri reciprocates by an equally stiff tariff. But my good friend Arthur Watts had sent word ahead of our coming, and we were not subjected to the usual red tape.

Gasir Alnaeem, the Al Kaff house where we stayed in Tarim, has great charm. Situated in a flowering oasis of date palms and roses, the big white building has large, airy rooms, a swimming pool, an indoor bath into which one walks and stands up in four feet of water; it also has a flush toilet, the only one in Tarim.

Although all the houses in the Hadhraumaut are made of mud brick, some of the fronts are glazed with a kind of plaster made of lime and sugar which gives them a high gloss. Only the houses of the rich are so glazed and tinted pastel colors; most of the dwellings are simply sun-dried brick. All of the houses of Tarim, however, consist of at least four stories.

Tarim is completely surrounded by a wall and has five gates which are closed at night. The days when the Bedouin waylaid anyone caught outside have passed but relations with the neighboring state of Qu'aiti are always uncertain and the blood feud is still a factor in the Valley. At each gate a soldier of the Sultan of Kathiri drowsed in the late afternoon sun.

There are public wells in Tarim and believe it or not several public toilets, the only ones I have ever seen in an Arab town. The water, coming from deep wells, is good and has a mild taste of rain water. On the ramparts of one house I saw three sets of ibex horns and was told that the owner had participated in last year's great hunt. Several hundred citizens of Tarim take part in these hunts and when a herd of ibex is located they surround it and drive the antelopes slowly toward a ravine where other hunters lie in wait. Every single animal is killed, even the kids, and for the rest of the year tiny pieces of the dried carcasses are handed out as favors to friends, while the horns, some pathetically small, are mounted over the door. I asked about oryx but was told that there are none in the Hadhraumaut. There are some gazelle, foxes, cheetah, and hyenas, but wildlife in the bare and sun-baked jebels of southern Arabia is rare.

In the evening we visited the home of our friend Yacob and his brother. A vast new building of fifty-plus rooms, it had everything that passes for luxury in Tarim. From our standpoint there is virtually no furniture, most of the rooms simply having rugs on the floor and faded photographs on the walls.

If Tarim with its mosques is the Rome of the Hadhraumaut, then Shibbam is the New York. As one approaches the old city across the plain, it looms like the skyline of lower New York. Actually, the buildings are only ten or twelve stories high but rising from the floor of the valley they appear gigantic. With steel and concrete this would be no feat but the skyscrapers of Shibbam are built of sun-dried brick with wooden beams. I learned some are 350 years old, and there is a mosque in the city which goes back 1,000 years.

The capital of the Kathiri Sultanate is Saium. It is here that His Highness Hassan bin Ali al Kathiri (13 guns) has his palace and where Arthur Watts' assistant has his residency. Next to the Sultan the most important man in Saium is Sir Abu Bakr Al Kaff, the son of the original Sheikh Al Kaff and the man who persuaded the sultans of Kathiri and Mukalla to accept British protection.

We called on the old gentleman, who is Yacob's grand uncle, in his white-walled palace in Saium and were most courteously received. Leading us to a reception room where we took off our shoes, we sat on the handsome rugs and drank spiced tea. If it had not been for Sir Abu, the Hadhraumaut today might be either an impoverished province of the Yemen or, worse still, one of Nasser's socialist republics. In 1940, by dint of some fast and delicate diplomacy, he got both sultans to sign the Treaty of Protection. This meant that Kathiri and Mukalla were given security, a sound administration, and a great deal of help.

All visitors to the Valley visit the three cities but few take the rocky road east where the Wadi narrows and the walls of the great jols press in on the valley bed.

Flying out of the Valley the pilot kindly swooped low over Shibbam and I was able to get the kind of picture that Lowell Thomas made when he flew over the Hadhraumaut some years ago. But I believe that was before the days when it was possible to land in the Valley, and his movie did not include a travelogue of the old cities. The time will of course come when tourists will hear about and insist on visiting the Hadhraumaut. I am glad we beat them to it.

FIVE

The Yemen and the Oryx

F̲ew̲ ̲w̲o̲r̲l̲d̲ ̲t̲r̲a̲v̲e̲l̲e̲r̲s̲ sailing down the Red Sea on their way to the East know anything about the southern half of the Arabian coast. They see a barren sandy shore and conclude, if they think about it at all, that this part of the Peninsula is just as much of a trackless waste as the Sinai Desert they saw when passing through the Suez Canal. They can be corrected. The coastal plains merge into a great mountain range averaging 8,000 feet whose peaks, some of which rise to more than 12,000 feet, catch the rain-laden clouds of the monsoon and give this part of Arabia such a generous fall that it was known to the ancients as Arabia Felix in contrast to Arabia Deserta, the name for all the rest of the arid Peninsula.

Most of the tableland lies in The Yemen, which once played an important part in the history of the Middle East, but which for centuries has been virtually inaccessible to foreigners. Not only was the terrain extraordinarily difficult but the Imams, the priest kings, feared innovations as only absolute rulers of closed kingdoms can fear new ideas. In many respects the average Yemeni lives in the same huts, eats the same food and wears almost the same clothes as he did in the days when the Queen of Sheba ruled a part of the country. But in September of 1962 the last Imam was overthrown and since then, despite the fact that the country has been wracked by civil war, a trickle of correspondents have been able to get in, and the world is beginning to hear a little about the Yemen.

There are still no tourists and it is extremely difficult to get permission to visit. The royalist ambassador who represented the exiled Imam refused to hand over his seals to the new man appointed by President Sallal so that it was not until we arrived in Cairo that we were able to get the visas.

The legal barrier was overcome but there was still the matter of actually getting into the country. We learned in Aden that Yemeni Air Lines, a private concern with two antiquated DC3's, flies into Taiz and Sana when the weather allows. We decided to fly and after a good deal of phoning finally located a gentleman named Salim who said the flights were all booked for the immediate future. Appealing to the manager of the Crescent Hotel, I learned that one of his assistants was related to Mr. Salim and as a result of this personal approach we were informed at midnight (the assistant manager himself simply burst into the room with the good news) that we were leaving at dawn the next morning.

At eleven we were still in the Aden airport but progress was being made. The Yemeni plane had arrived from Taiz and the pilot, a capable-looking Norwegian named Linder, was engaged in persuading the Aden authorities that his passengers were really who they said they were. Saudis often try to enter the Aden Protectorate by claiming they are Yemenis with relations and jobs waiting for them. Finally the matter was settled and, seating ourselves in the plane along with a load of cargo and some Yemenis, all of whom hugged ancient rifles, we roared down the Aden field, soared out over the water and turned inland toward the distant line of jagged mountains. Unlike the flattened tops of the jols which guard the approaches to the Hadhraumaut, the bastions which ring the Yemen are a series of saw-toothed peaks. Far down the sides we saw terracing and in deep valleys, where the sun shines only at noon, ran muddy rivers. It was the season of the southwest monsoon and storm clouds were always hanging low over The Yemen.

The Taiz landing field is short and there is always a ten to twenty mile cross wind. Linder slipped in sidewise and we came to a bumpy halt. I had wired James Cortada, our chargé d'affaires, that we were coming, but knowing the state of communication in The Yemen, I had scant hope of having anyone meet us. We were pleased when Jim Murray, the administrative officer of the Embassy, was on the tarmac. He said Cortada had had to jeep to Sana, but would be back in a few days. In the meantime the embassy residence was at our disposal and his deputy, Dick Blalock, and Jim Megellas, the AID Director, would show us around.

Taiz is 4,500 feet above sea level and a welcome change after the wet heat of Aden. The embassy is a comfortable modern building with bathrooms, a fine view and a capable staff. Soon after our arrival, Blalock arrived and took us for a tour of the city. Said to be the most beautiful town in The Yemen, Taiz is an old walled city built on the side of the Jebel Sabir, whose rugged heights protect the side not enclosed by the ramparts. The city has two gates, the Bab Al Kabir and the Bab Sheikh Musa, which are always guarded and sometimes closed.

The people all appeared to be chewing gum and I learned that they are addicted to Qat (pronounced Gat), a drug that is said to produce excitement both mentally and physically. Everyone was chewing it: the policeman who waved us on, the guards at the gates, and the old women who hawked their wares in the streets. Taken to excess, and Yemenis chew it for several hours a day, the drug has a debilitating effect which in the end causes impotence as well as other unpleasant results. So popular is the habit that Sallal has not banned it although the sultans of the Eastern Aden Protectorate made its importation illegal many years ago. Qat consists of the fresh leaves of the *Catha edulis*, a small tree with white flowers which flourishes in the highlands of Ethiopia and Arabia under about the same conditions as those favorable for coffee. A man with a grove of Qat trees is a rich man and much of the soil which could grow foods or coffee is devoted to it.

The U.S. presence in Taiz is considerable. The AID mission is building a road from the ancient port of Mocha on the Red Sea to Sana and there are 120 Americans engaged in the job. A few men have their wives and children with them and to house these families we have built a modern cantonment complete with prefabricated houses and a community hall. There is also an AID project to give Taiz a better water supply. Bilharzia, dysentery and various other forms of digestive tract diseases are endemic.

Russia and Red China have embassies at Taiz but their major aid efforts are being made elsewhere. The Red Chinese have built a good hard-top road—ours is gravel and therefore somewhat easier to maintain—from Hodeida to Sana, and the Russians have built the port of Hodeida. We have some contact with the Russians but none with the Red Chinese who keep very much to themselves. They imported all the coolies necessary to build the Hodeida-Sana Road and seem to have little intercourse with the Yemeni. There are West German, Ethiopian and Italian ministers, and we were handling matters for the British whose minister had been withdrawn.

The old Imam, known as Ahmed the Devil, who died in his bed of pneumonia a year before our visit, was quite a ruler by any standards. He was immensely fat, weighing over 300 pounds when he died, but he never was soft in his handling of his people. He feared Sana because his father had been assassinated there and preferred to live in Taiz. His palace is now a rest house for the Egyptians.

While his people feared him, most foreigners liked him. He was fond of children and had as many as he could. His son, Badr, had all the vices but none of the stamina of the old man and the revolution broke out when he had ruled The Yemen for little more than a week. Sallal, the man who overthrew him, had been one of Badr's friends.

From seven centuries before Christ to five after, Mocha was one of the great ports of the ancient world. From her harbor sailed galleys and dhows laden with fragrant coffee beans grown in the valleys of the high Yemen and in her stately palaces dwelt generations of merchant princes. So famous did the city become that the very word for coffee was "mocha." But with the triumph of Islam, contact with the West was cut off and in 1533 a fleet belonging to Suleiman the Magnificent captured Aden and reduced the Red Sea to a Turkish lake. Mocha still carried on some trade, however, and in 1709 there was even a Dutch "factory" there engaged in exporting coffee and spices. In 1904 the Germans presented the Turks with a lighthouse for Mocha, but in 1917 the beacon went out for the last time and Mocha sank into a ghost city where a few hundred fishermen eked out a bare living with their nets.

In 1961 Mocha took on a new lease of life. The powers that be in Washington decided that America should do something for The Imam of Yemen's government and the best thing they could think of was to build a road. True, the port of Hodeida, farther up the Red Sea coast, had a harbor where freighters could tie up while at Mocha they had to lie several miles off the coast, but a road linking Hodeida and the capital of Sana had already been begun by the Red Chinese. There was, however, no decent road between Taiz, the second city of Yemen, and Sana, and we decided to construct this link. The only way that we could bring in the materials necessary to do this job was to use Mocha and incidentally build a road from Mocha to Taiz in order to get these supplies up country. The road at the time we were there had progressed past Taiz to the old city of Ibb in the high Yemen and is about half way to Sana.

To see this engineering feat and visit the old port, we set out with Dick Blalock, the Embassy Second Secretary, to drive the road to Mocha. Taiz is 4,500 feet high and as we left the highlands it became steadily hotter.

There are gazelle in the hills along the road and Blalock said it was easy to hunt them but few of the Yemenis bothered to do so. There are no game laws in The Yemen but certain animals have protection under the law. Despite the fact that baboons are highly destructive to crops, anyone killing one of the big apes is fined 25 silver dollars.

Mocha from across the coastal plain is a scene of glistening minarets and some white-walled palaces but as one draws nearer the illusion fades. The minarets project from mosques half choked with sand and the palaces are empty shells with gaping windows. There are people still living in Mocha, about 700—an increase of 400 since we started using the port—but they live in shacks along the derelict main street and even the sub-prefect, who governs the town, flies his flag from a shabby building.

Our American installation, a set of oil tanks, an LCM to lighter supplies in from the ships, and a few warehouses are the only modern construction in the town. There are three Americans stationed in Mocha, two port directors and a captain for the LCM. It is not an easy life. In summer the thermometer rises to 120° and in winter the wind blows the sand for months at a time.

We had heard in Aden that Yemeni Air Lines was a risky business but how risky we found out when we took off from the Taiz airport. Irene's and Renie's seat belts were non-existent and mine broke when I tried to tighten it. The stuffing was coming out of most of the seats and the brown, scruffy interior was dirty and scarred. But the important factor was the engines and early in the flight I sensed trouble. We climbed slowly off the short Taiz strip and barely rose above the peaks surrounding the valley. Then the purr of the motors faltered and we swung suddenly around and headed back to Taiz, losing altitude all the time. We landed on the very end of the strip. A brace of Egyptian "newspapermen" who had the seats in front of us said shakily, "We must have left the oil behind."

The truth was somewhat grimmer. Antoun Kiamy, the pilot who had once flown for an American company, told me that he lost power in his port engine soon after take-off and by the time he turned around he had to feather it completely. He added bitterly that the plane had gone 900 hours without a check. Maintenance, such as it is, is done in Cairo but owners are loath to waste time on such details.

Two hours later, in another plane, with the careful Kiamy still at the controls, we took off again. It was nine o'clock and the last moment we could begin the trip and hope to arrive in Sana before the clouds hid the 10,000-foot peaks and made flying too unsafe, a relative term in The Yemen. Then the rugged peaks suddenly fell behind us and we flew into a great valley, the 7,500-foot high plateau in which lies the city of Sana. I noted three airfields with a good many military planes parked on two of them. These were the Egyptian bombers and fighters. The commercial field is cup-shaped and when it rains, as it does every day during this season of the year, the water collects at the bottom of the saucer and makes take-offs and landings impossible.

The telegram from Taiz announcing our arrival had not arrived —one never expects any such miracle in The Yemen—but Harry Sizer, the third secretary in charge, and Thomas Tindale, an American adviser to the Yemeni government, arrived just as we were about to risk our necks in a local taxi and took us to the "office" where James Cortada, the chargé d'affaires, made us welcome. I have seen some primitive missions in the Far East but our office in Sana is the smallest so far. The actual working space consisted of a room no larger than a bathroom in which were the code machines, a desk, a chair and a filing case. Cortada and Sizer had no assistance and coded their own cables.

Living accommodations were in very short supply in Sana and if it had not been for the good Cortada we might have ended up in the Government Guest House, an almost sure chance to acquire most of the known diseases. Instead we were given one of the best rooms in the Liberty Hotel, the new name of the last Imam's palace. It was this palace that Sallal shelled during the revolution and it was from this palace that the Imam Badr escaped over the garden wall. The top floor was still pockmarked by shells but Shakir Haqq, the young English-speaking Yemeni who ran it, was making progress with repairs.

In the late afternoon Cortada's chauffeur, Bahari, drove us around the old city and as we passed through the walls by the gate called the Bab Al Yemen, we might well have been in the fifteenth century. The unpaved lanes are a maze of sharp turns and blind alleys which only a citizen of Sana can negotiate. The houses of Sana have beautifully traceried windows made of carved alabaster, and huge iron-studded doors with shovel-shaped iron knockers. The houses rise to four or five stories and have little observation platforms from which one can see down into the street. Motley crowds jam the streets. Unlike the Egyptians who seldom carry rifles in the streets, the Yemenis of all ages and all walks of life lug around various varieties of shooting irons and festoon their bosoms with fancy cartridge belts. Most Yemenis ride rather large and handsome mules and some have Arab horses fitted out with elaborate saddles and red leather bridles.

The Gates of Yemen all have a fascinating significance. There is the Bab ar Rum or Gate of Tome. This was the portal through which the travelers of ancient times set out by caravan for Constantinople. The trip up through the spice road of the Arabian Peninsula took three years.

There has never been a census in The Yemen but there are estimated to be about four million persons living in this wild, rocky land. Sana is said to have 60,000 and Taiz, Hodeida and the smaller towns much smaller urban populations. The great majority of the people, however, are the tribesmen who live in lonely walled fortresses and cultivate with infinite care their terraced fields. To see something of the countryside we drove out of Sana by the Bab as Stran gate, where the road built by the Red Chinese winds down to Hodeida on the Red Sea coast.

Sana is built in a great bowl of the mountains which sweep down in ravines to the plain, and it is in these ravines that we saw the most interesting terracing. Never except in the Yunnan mountains of China have I seen so much effort go toward protecting so little soil. Walls as much as fifteen feet high support a ledge of earth barely ten feet long and five feet wide. All of the villages are fortified and the blood feud still rages between these grim outposts.

We were impressed with Cortada and his staff, all of whom spoke fluent Arabic and took a real interest in their jobs and in the country. No desk envoy, Cortada was always on the go, risking his neck in the crates of the Yemeni airlines, or jeeping in his "black maria"—he had the only black jeep in the country—over the hopeless roads. His relations with Sallal and his government were excellent.

I asked frequent questions about game and found that there is a considerable amount of wildlife in The Yemen: gazelle and some leopards which are said to live on the baboons and a good many hyena and foxes. Up in the northern sections there are still gray wolves. Game birds include quail, francolin and partridge. Although there are no game laws, there is certainly no indiscriminate slaughter. The Yemeni occasionally kill the gazelle but only when they are really hungry. Asked if they would like a game reserve where the animals could be seen, the men I asked replied that the gazelle live in such rough country that no one would climb up merely to see animals.

But it was not until we went to a dinner party at the embassy and I had a long talk with Mohammed Abdel Wasea Nu'man, Deputy Minister of the Interior, that I really struck pay dirt. I asked Nu'man if he had ever seen oryx in his many travels around The Yemen and to my great surprise he said he had seen five in the region of Jauf, the area in the northeast corner of the country where The Yemen borders Saudi Arabia. Part of this border includes the Rub al Khal, the sand desert, where the oryx spend part of every year. I thought he might have seen ibex and asked him to draw the head. Sure enough, the picture he made showed the long unicorn-like horns of the oryx. He also said that he had seen oryx on the massif which rises from the coastal plains of the Red Sea coast. The mountains there do climb to over 5,000 feet but the terrain is so broken that I would doubt if oryx, essentially a plains animal, would live there. However, the minister, one of the few able members of Sallal's government, stuck to his story and said he would ask the nomads to capture an oryx and bring it back to Sana where Harry Sizer, the vice consul in charge, would be able to photograph it. If Nu'man is right and oryx do exist in The Yemen, an entirely new dimension will be added to their previously reported haunts. Furthermore, the disinclination of the Yemeni to shoot game may well mean that the herds are not being decimated as they are in Saudi Arabia, and in Oman and Muscat. Almost alone among the Arab people, the Yemeni seem willing to let game share life with them.

Just why this is I don't exactly know but the Minister explained it as a result of the extremely strict Moslem code under which most Yemenis live. There are prohibitions in the Koran against useless killing and the Yemenis evidently take them more literally than the Saudis and other Arabs. Nu'man also said that he liked my idea of establishing a reserve for the oryx and would be glad to cooperate, if sufficient numbers are found to make such a scheme feasible.

In order to interest other members of the government in the oryx I called on Mustafa Yacoub, the Foreign Minister. A nice-looking young man in his thirties, Yacoub has been in the diplomatic service of his country for a good many years and has a much wider viewpoint than most of his colleagues. He told me a little about his problems and they are certainly great. The Imam did not run a government, he simply ruled, with the result that the new government began without a single functioning ministry. Despite these headaches Yacoub, whom I called on while he was in bed recovering from a dinner given at the notorious Government Guest House for a visiting U.N. delegation, showed a real understanding of my wildlife objectives and promised to help in any way he could. He quite understood the point that if oryx are found in the Yemen and some can be captured for transfer to America, the resulting publicity would be excellent for his country.

It is just as hard to get out of Sana as it is to get into it. We were at the airport at six-thirty and were assured by Ali Al Arashy, the director, that the plane for Taiz would be in at seven-thirty. The only other passenger was a genial Russian engineer, named Anatole Khaleev, who said he was based in Cairo and had been inspecting the port of Hodeida which his country had built. Seven-thirty came and went and at eleven-thirty we were informed that our plane had gone to Hodeida and would have to return to Taiz before coming to Sana. Arashy then invited us into the VIP room, furnished with several thrones, probably looted from the palaces, and served us spiced tea and small green apples. Questioned on when the plane might be expected, he said he did not know but I could ask the radio man upstairs. Duly climbing the tower, I insisted that the operator contact Taiz and find out the facts. He did and told me that Linder, the wise Norwegian pilot, had refused to fly to Sana on account of the condition of his plane and had gone without passengers to Aden for a check out. The good sense of Linder as well as that of the Egyptian pilot, Kiamy, may well have saved our lives. In any other country, Yemeni Air Lines, a private corporation, would have been grounded and found guilty of criminal negligence.

My daughter, Renie, who had gone to the Yemeni Air Lines office in order to find out the next plane to Taiz, reported that the manager had told her that President Sallal called and asked him why he would not transport some government officials. The manager replied frankly that the Yemeni government owed his airline 9,000 riyals and since the Treasury was empty, there was no hope of being paid. Sallal laughed, said he understood, and would not ask the line for any more free seats. The manager, a bright young Yemeni who had gone to school in Aden and whose dearest wish was to go to a university in England, also told Renie that he had in his safe an order from the government banning Ethiopian Air Lines from running into The Yemen. Renie asked him not to implement this order until we got out and he promised to hold it up a while longer. The only way to leave The Yemen, besides risking one's neck on Yemeni Air Lines, is by Ethiopian Air Lines, a stepchild of our own TWA, which runs twice a week from Taiz to Asmara. Ethiopian Air Lines had already been banned once on account of tardy recognition of Sallal's government.

As the plane which never arrived was the only one which could get us to Taiz in time to make our reserved connections with the Ethiopian plane to Asmara, we decided to drive with Jim Cortada, down to Hodeida on the Chinese road. Two days later we left Sana at ten, waving to the Egyptian sentries who guard the gates of the city under the "unified Araba command" a fiction which gives Nasser effective control of all the key points in The Yemen.

The Chinese road, an asphalt strip that runs 226 kilometers from Sana to Hodeida, follows the old Turkish road and is one of the wonders of The Yemen. After crossing 10,000-foot Manakha pass it winds through some of the most spectacular country I have ever seen. Only the gorges of China match its rugged grandeur. Running along the sides of the mountains with a sheer drop of hundreds of feet, the road has few guard rails and I counted seven trucks lying far below in the terraced valleys. The Egyptian drivers, used to tearing across the flat land of the Nile, simply could not cope with the hairpin turns.

Hodeida itself, which we reached after a sweltering two hours' ride across the sandblown flatlands, is much more of a city than Mocha. It is the main port of The Yemen and almost all the upcountry trade flows through it. Thanks to the Russians, there is a modern port at which half a dozen freighters can tie up to the quay at one time. The only American living in Hodeida was Michael Harris, the representative of Mecom Oil Company. Headed up in Houston by John W. Mecom, the company had so far drilled four dry wells in The Yemen and was presently inactive.

The weekly plane of the Ethiopian Air Lines flew from Addis Ababa to Sana, and by dint of a good deal of persuading we managed to get seats on it. Ethiopian Air Lines pilots were trained by our own Trans World Air Lines, and the old but efficient DC3's which they flew on this little-used route were also maintained by American-directed ground crews. To say we were glad to be flying under those pleasant circumstances was an understatement.

SIX

Game Trails of Jordan

HIGH ON THE escarpments and deep in the desert wadis of the Hashemite Kingdom of Jordan there still roam small bands of gazelle and ibex but every year their number diminishes and unless drastic action is taken they may soon become as extinct as the dodo. Rich city Arabs in Cadillacs and poor Bedouin on camels shoot them whenever the opportunity offers. There are game laws but there is no game department to administer them and no game wardens to enforce them.

His Majesty King Hussein told me that he is well aware of the problem and is seriously considering formation of three game parks: one for ibex, one for desert gazelle and one for birds and wild fowl. The establishment of such sanctuaries would be extremely important in this last-ditch effort to save the remnants of Jordan's wildlife but it should be supplemented by a nation-wide campaign to prevent poaching. Steps toward such an effort had already been taken: a law was about to be published prohibiting all hunting for the twelve months starting June 1. Enforcement, however, still remains a problem. The police are charged with implementing the game laws but poaching is one of the least of their problems. The law states that a poacher can be fined ten Jordanian dinars ($28.20) or imprisoned for fifteen days or both, but convictions are few, especially where the culprit is a man of means.

I learned that responsibility for wildlife is a function of the Department of Agriculture and was about to make an appointment with Saleh Majgali, the Minister of the Interior and Agriculture, when I learned that 99 per cent of His Excellency's time is taken up with his Interior duties. Subsequently, I arranged to see Sami Ayoub, the Permanent Undersecretary of Agriculture, and had a very pleasant talk with that functionary who then referred me to a Mr. Doudi, the Assistant Undersecretary. Official calls in Jordan, and for that matter in all Arab countries, include the drinking of coffee, tea or fruit drinks, so that by the time one works down or up in a given department, one is apt to be afloat with various liquids. And it was while I was finishing my fourth coffee that I learned from the courteous Dr. Doudi that his bailiwick included the Veterinary Department, and that Dr. Kamal Izzat El Taher, the Director General of the Veterinary Service, is the only man in the Jordanian government directly charged with the responsibility for wildlife conservation.

On the wall of his small office was a chart of the Dogs of the World and in his library about everything that has been written, all of it in Arabic, unfortunately for me, about the fauna of Jordan. He told me sadly that there is very little left. A few small herds of desert gazelle (Gazelle Sahara Arabic) could still be found along the borders of Saudi Arabia and Syria. He estimated the numbers at less than 500, when ten years earlier he had counted these graceful desert dwellers in the thousands. The increase in Land Rovers and jeeps capable of negotiating the sands has sealed the fate of hundreds of gazelle. The hunters simply chase the herds till they are exhausted and then shoot them down wholesale, sparing neither the pregnant females nor the fawns.

The ibex which inhabit the steep cliffs of the Madala Mountains were also nearing extinction. Although extremely wary and requiring infinite patience to hunt, the new scope rifles, which the richer Bedouin can now afford, are steadily thinning their numbers. Dr. Taher estimated there were less than 200 left. The mountain gazelle (Gazelle Jebel) also had some protection from the nature of their habitat but were vulnerable to the persistent gunner. Dr. Taher thought their numbers were not more numerous than the ibex.

Cheetah have virtually vanished from the Jordanian scene but the previous year a female was shot and her cub presented to the King, who sent it to a zoo in England. Wild boar are still hunted along the Jordan River. The law states that there shall be no hunting between October 1 and July 1 but this prohibition is seldom observed. The law also states that the limit on gazelle is six per day per licensed gun. The law makes no mention of sex or size.

The wild cattle (Arabian oryx—Baqr al Wash) which used to roam the southern desert are now extinct, according to Dr. Taher, who remembers seeing herds of them twenty years ago.

A sad commentary on the methods sometimes used to exterminate the game of Jordan is found in a clause in the game laws which states that "No one shall shoot from an aircraft."

But shooting was not the only reason for the lack of wildlife in Jordan. The ancient land had been ravaged by man and goats for centuries and probably not since the days of Romans had the land been a fit habitat for animals and birds. As George Perkins Marsh, the Vermont-born naturalist whose *Man and Nature* is one of the great conservation books of all time, succinctly put it: "The ravages committed by man subvert the relations and destroy the balance which nature established—when the forest is gone the great reservoir of moisture stored up in its vegetable mould is evaporated; the well-wooded and humid hills are turned to ridges of dry rock; and the earth becomes an assemblage of bald mountains, barren turfless hills and of swampy and malarious plains."

The King told me that a game reserve was under consideration at Azraq a swampy oasis some 200 kilometers from Amman in the western desert. The oasis holds a large winter population of wildfowl and wild boar could be introduced along the reedy borders. There is a camp of the Arab Legion at Azraq and stiff conservation measures would not be hard to enforce if the orders were issued by His Majesty.

The second site being considered was an area in the Wadi Rum, near Aqaba. This wild hill terrain still holds a few ibex and gazelle and since there is very little vegetation, the Bedouin seldom go there with their flocks. Scenes for the movie, *Lawrence of Arabia,* involving the attack on Aqaba were shot at Wadi Rum.

Lack of time prohibited discussion of the third prospective game park but I gathered from Dr. Taher that it would be a refuge for the desert gazelle. Immediate establishment of these refuges plus adequate protection would go a long way toward saving the few remaining herds of the country's last three species of game.

As Jordan is an ancient land and at times has been a hungry one, trapping of game birds, and possibly all birds, has gone on to a point where there are few left. Bill Macomber took us for several long and interesting drives in the country near Amman and the only birds I saw were lone crows and a small kind of sparrow. Dr. Taher told me that almost every country market has game bird eggs for sale during the mating season even though this is strictly prohibited.

On a sunny Sunday we drove to Jarash, among the best preserved ancient ruins in the Middle East. First one of the Greek Decapolis cities, Jarash was later a Roman town and was one of those visited by the Emperor Hadrian. To commemorate this honor the town fathers erected an arch, which still stands. In Roman days the country around Jarash was heavily wooded but today only olive groves and the odd cedar or eucalyptus dot the stony hillsides. The goat is mainly responsible, although it is popular to say that the Turks cut down all the trees to make ties for the Hejaz Railway.

As we drove through the countryside—still green because the rains had been late—we saw many small encampments of the Bedouin. The tents, woven from the wool of the black goats, were sometimes pitched in the middle of newly plowed fields but the camels, sheep and goats of the desert dwellers are not allowed to graze on the growing crops. Now reduced to some 50,000 the nomadic Bedouin are steadily declining in numbers. This does not mean they are dying out; it simply means they are becoming settled. The Arab Legion has been largely recruited from the nomadic tribes and after a hitch in the army the returning soldiers become dissatisfied with a life which gives their children no chance to attend school and their wives few of the comforts of village life. Furthermore, the camel, the wealth and pride of the desert Bedouin, has ceased to have the same economic value. A truck now hauls in a few hours the load which a fleet of camels took weeks to move.

The Arab still cherishes his horses, however, and we passed some very good-looking stallions and mares ridden by men who did not look wealthy. There seem to be few geldings in the country. Glubb Pasha was said to have urged King Abdullah to geld the horses of the Arab Legion, but the king refused flatly on the grounds it was not fair to the horses. Bill Macomber had a very good-looking white stallion named Mah Bout which he greatly enjoyed. I always kept horses during my own tours in the service and found that a long ride is the best change of pace one can find.

No wonder the paradise of the Arabs is green. After crossing the desert the sight of the palms of an oasis is balm to the eyes and refreshment to the soul. Yet from afar it is often hard to recognize the real thing. So persistent are the mirages that one can almost swear one sees a shimmering lake just a few hundred yards away across the sands. Many times during 132-kilometer drives from Amman to Azraq we thought we had arrived at the swamps which surround that little Arab village only to have the illusion fade into the baked plains.

It was not until we saw far in the distance the stark outline of an Arab Legion fort that we knew we were near our journey's end. Azraq is at the head of the Wadi Sirhan, a long, shallow valley that leads down to the undemarcated border of Saudi Arabia, and a more desolate land to cover would be hard to imagine. It is the edge of the lava country where the sharp flints knife through the sands and play hell with the feet of the camels and the tires of the trucks.

Near the fort we saw the black tents of the Bedouin and learned that these were members of the Beni Sakhr, the largest camel-breeding tribe in Jordan. It is said to number 6,500 tents and to own upward of 15,000 camels, as well as some very good horses. The Paramount Sheikh of the Beni Sakhr is a rich man who could have a Cadillac and move to town but he still follows the ways of the nomad. The tribe has an ancient feud with the Huwaytat but both are fiercely loyal to the Hashemite dynasty and members of both tribes in the Arab Legion rallied to Hussein's defense in the crisis of 1957. Nasser holds virtually no appeal for these stern traditionalists.

The remains of a black basalt castle rise above the plains and it was in the one sound room of this old pile that Lawrence planned his advance on Damascus. Today there is no plaque to tell of these brave days and the old Arab who followed us into the ruins had never heard of the man who wrote *Revolt in the Desert.*

The colonel commanding the Azraq garrison happened along as we were viewing the ruins and volunteered some news about the duck situation, one of my objectives in going to the oasis. His English was picturesque but I got the point. "Only a few pieces left," said the colonel, and he shrugged sadly. Later I questioned several of the officers working on the United Nations Ground Water Project and learned that the migrations have been decreasing steadily and in the last year were less than half of what they had been ten years before. Abdullah Bazian, one of the chief engineers and an alert and intelligent officer, told me that he had been at Azraq since 1957 and had noted a progressive decline in the wildfowl population. The year before, the migration was so small that the government had stopped all shooting and it would remain closed. Of course, Azraq is only one of the places which these ducks and geese visit. Unlicensed and unlimited slaughter in the Lebanon is probably largely responsible for the decline but a safe refuge at Azraq could certainly help a great deal.

Just a month before we arrived in Jordan a British expedition, led by Guy Mountfort of the Nature Conservancy in London, had spent several months in the country and prepared an excellent plan to make Azraq a desert national park. He discussed the broad outline of this and other conservation plans with the King, and when I talked with His Majesty he gave me the definite impression that he was going to proceed along the lines suggested by the Mountfort memoranda.

I was particularly pleased to learn that the proposed park would not be confined to the swamps of the oasis but would include about a million acres. There are still gazelle in the basalt plateau within a twenty-mile radius of Azraq and a park of this size would afford them some protection. Bazian told me that during his six years at Azraq he had only seen ten gazelle and he saw seven of those about a month prior to our visit while driving ten miles north of the oasis. Ahmen Shawki, a farmer who owns land in the oasis, told me that in his opinion there are still at least a hundred gazelle within a fifty-mile radius of Azraq. Shawki used to be a great hunter and spent a good deal of time exploring the surrounding country. He said that parties from Amman used to come out and shoot twenty to thirty head from cars and then give the meat to any Bedouin they happened to see on the way back.

The ban on shooting has also been extended to fishing, although why the government should object to the taking of catfish is hard to understand. Tilapia might be profitably introduced. They grow much faster than any other food fish and taste a great deal better than catfish or perch.

The local population of about 2,000 like to hunt rabbits and ducks and it is up to the Arab Legion to see that the closed season is enforced. This is not a very satisfactory arrangement. The primary duty of soldiers is to keep the peace, not to lurk about in the marshes to pounce on a boy with a bent pin or an old man with a duck trap. Jordan should have a pukka game department with its own enforcement branch, and until such a department is set up, poaching will never be controlled.

SEVEN

Tigers and Caviar in Iran . . .

WE WERE CAMPED in a little valley high in the Kopak Dagh range of northeastern Persia. The horses were grazing in a meadow sprinkled with poppies, blue cornflowers and purple delphinium, and our Turkoman cook was making a savory stew of rice and chicken. From Teheran to the camp was quite a jaunt. Specifically, it took us sixteen hours by train and Land Rover before we mounted the horses for another three-hour climb into the mountains, but like all touring in Persia there was never a dull moment. The night train to Gorgan chugs up to the rim of the snow-capped Elburz Mountains which surround the capital and then strikes north to the Caspian, which is three times bigger than our Lake Superior, the second largest inland body of water in the world. Khosrow Sariri, Assistant Chief Inspector of the Game Council of Iran, or the number two wildlife officer, accompanied us on the train and made all subsequent arrangements for our transport and comfort.

At Gorgan, the railhead, we were met by one of Sariri's men in a Land Rover and driven through the town. Once famous for perfumes and polo, it is now a dusty little provincial burg. The Persians invented polo and according to the record some pretty grim versions of it were played in Gorgan, the heads of raiding Turkomans from Russia being used as balls. There are still Turkoman heads in Khorassan but they are firmly attached to bodies. There are also Kurds because centuries ago these fine warriors were sent to Khorassan to check the raids of the Turkoman. Needless to say a fine time was had by all concerned.

The Kurds are some of the toughest boys in this part of the world and see no reason why they should not have their own nation. This is going to be hard because they are scattered in Iraq, Iran, Syria, Turkey and the Soviet Union. Iran's Kurds are mainly concentrated in the western sections of the country and are a cause of concern to the central government.

Because it was a religious holiday, we passed trucks full of black-shirted men and boys en route to the local mosques to scourge themselves in sympathy with Hassan, who was foully murdered 1500 years ago on his way to Mecca. The scourge, known as a "zangir," consists of a bunch of chains tied to a wooden handle and makes Captain Bligh's cat-o'-nine-tails look like a means of administering love pats. Foreigners are not welcome in the holy cities at this period of "moharan" and we were on the road to Meshed even though not going there. From Gorgan we drove on a bumpy dirt road to Gonbad Ghabus, which is dominated by the 1,000-year-old funeral tower of Quabus-iben-Washmgir, a curious brick pile whose fascination I missed. Another 100 kilometers of equally poor road but increasingly superb scenery—we were getting into the mountains—brought us to the police post of Dasht, where the horses were waiting.

Both the Turkoman and the Kurds are proud of their horses, and some of them are very good steeds indeed. In the old days they fed their favorites on "nahari," a diet of flour and fat, which so stimulated the chargers that they were able to gallop for twenty hours "with a Persian captive bound on their back." Today the local horses of Khorassan are a mixed bag, some showing Arab blood and others looking a good deal like our thoroughbreds. Most of them are on the small side with good deep chests and powerful quarters.

Our shikar party consisted of the two best game scouts in Iran: Mir Mohomed and his brother, Nur, who had taken out the Shah and other royal hunters who came here to hunt, and seven other retainers. Mir and Nur are Kurds while the others are Turkomans. All of them wear curious homemade shoes and woolen hats, and have fantastically keen sight. Scarcely had we climbed out of the first valley before Mir pointed toward a granite cliff and whispered "Kal," Parsee for ibex. I could see nothing with the naked eye and even with my binoculars it took minutes before I could detect a tiny brown speck on the cliff face. It moved and I spotted another behind it. They were a pair and Mir said that the male had fine horns.

The mountain Kurd's idea of distance is wonderful to read about but hell to follow. According to the legends a "farsakh" is four miles, or the distance one can hear a drum or distinguish between a white and black horse. Another norm is the distance a laden mule can traverse in an hour. Again and again I was told that a spring or a valley was just over the hill but hours seemed to go by before we reached them. We did not really mind. The horses were sure footed and the mountains enchanting. Every vista held new perspectives and every meadow wild flowers and birds. We heard many more birds than we saw and those we did see were mostly strangers. I only recognized an eagle soaring above the peaks and some small hawks.

The particular part of the Kopak Dagh Mountains where we were looking for game is known as the Chakar Lou and is the best range for wild sheep in all of Iran. We had started into the mountains at three in the afternoon and saw our first herd of sheep at four. There were two males and four females. The leader had a big spread of horns and would have made an imposing trophy. Both Riahi and Firouz had urged me to take a rifle and collect a good head but I declined.

Near a spring we found the remains of a urial ram (urial are the type of sheep found in this part of Iran) which had been killed by a leopard a few days previously. The pad marks of the big cat were plain to see in the mud around the spring. I was told the mountains are full of leopard who dine well off the numerous wild pig and sheep. Such a diet is also good for tiger and, according to both Mohomed brothers, the rare Persian "babr" can still be found in the area. Asked exactly when they had seen a tiger last, Mir said that the last one he personally saw was in September of 1957 when he was guiding a hunting party a few miles south of where we were. A stag was roaring and approaching a water hole where the hunting party was waiting for a shot. Suddenly, Mir said, a big tiger burst from the underbrush only thirty meters away and made off. The hunter fired and wounded it, at least they found blood, but the wound must have been superficial for the blood spoor soon vanished. The next news of tiger was reported in December of 1960 when a villager found a tiger feeding on the carcass of one of his cows. The coats of these tigers are reported to be long, as indeed they should be, for the winters are cold in northern Iran and the snows lie for many months on the mountains.

Leopard and tiger are not the only predators that roam the Kopak

Dagh. There are also gray wolves, wild cats and bear. The brown bear of Iran is usually content with honey, ants and other small sources of food but occasionally one will attack the villagers' flocks. Sariri once saw a bear eating a lamb and shot it.

Before we arrived at camp, called "Al Meh" or small spring, we had seen five herds of wild sheep, none close enough to photograph. The stag at this time of year stay in the forest and are difficult to find. The Maral stag is the great red deer of Europe and Asia with a magnificent spread of antlers. The Persian record, shot in these same mountains, is a twenty pointer. In Scotland a royal stag has only twelve points. Some of the Kurdish hunters are very proficient at calling stag and use the horns of an ibex. The Persian stag does not bellow like the Kashmir or Scottish stag but roars like an ox.

Another virtue of the ibex is the "bezoar stone," a kind of gall stone that is secreted in the stomachs of certain rams and is believed to have magic properties. It is said to be a sure antidote for poisons and can also turn away bullets. How one shoots an ibex possessed of this excellent stone is not explained. If the bezoar is genuine it will stick to the palate and will make water boil.

While we did not, at first, see any game birds we twice heard partridge and Nur put on a spectacular show of calling them. Placing a leaf in his hands and blowing on it, he produced a sound so like the birds that he was answered immediately and the partridges later appeared on a rock. There are also pheasant, quail and pigeon.

Irene saw a viper, one of the few poisonous snakes in Iran. According to Mir, these snakes occasionally bite humans but the wounds are not always fatal, as they often are when domestic sheep are the victims.

After a good dinner of rice, eggplant, cherries, Persian bread and coffee, we sat around the fire and talked. A guard had been sent to watch the horses in case a marauding leopard happened by and the rest of the men were mumbling in the shadows. The cook, who was a Persian, not a Turkoman as I had thought, announced that he could sing and gave us a rendering of the love songs of the poet Hafiz. We were reminded of old Omar and his book of verse and loaf of bread.

The last day of our stay in the mountains dawned foggy and cold. It was so cold every night that we slept in sleeping bags with our heads inside, but by seven the hot sun thawed us out. That morning there was no sun and the mist, driving over the peaks, lent a weird quality to the landscape. Mir and Nur were not optimistic about finding game but said if we did see any we would be able to get close to it.

Muffled in sweaters and letting the horses pick a dripping path across the bracken, we had covered about four miles when the fog suddenly lifted, revealing a deep valley on the opposite side of which we saw a herd of seven urial lying down in a meadow of short blue grass. The wind was right and the fog would kill the sound but the stalk involved a hard climb and I declined the honor. Sariri and Mir vanished in the mist with Irene, and were gone about forty-five minutes. The stalk was a complete success. Mir took Irene and her telephoto Nikon camera to within thirty yards of the herd, where she got some excellent pictures.

The grand finale of our trip came just as we had completed the descent to the forest which borders the main road. A huge boar dashed out of a thicket and almost ran into us. I have stuck pig in India and shot them in many other countries but I don't believe I have ever seen a bigger or nastier looking customer than this Persian version of the porcine species.

On the train going home, Sariri took my map and inked in the game reserves of Iran. There are nine of them, ranging from Al Meh in the northeast, where we had camped, to Khark, an island in the Persian Gulf. In the extreme northwest a reserve has been made of an island in Lake Rezaieh, on the border of Turkey, and down near the Saudi border is Duz, the refuge of the fallow deer. Except for Duz, all of these refuges hold both sheep and goats. Unfortunately, there is no refuge for either the wild ass or the gazelle.

Enforcement of the laws promulgated by the Game Council is quite tough. The guns are confiscated, the convicted poachers fined 400 to 4,000 rials and a jail sentence may be added. But a much greater dissuader than any of these is the really severe beating administered on the spot by the game guards. Almost alone among the enforcement officers of Iran, the Game Council's men have a reputation for honesty and a lust for doing their duty. This is good because a rich poacher may be able to persuade the judge to let him off but bribing won't prevent his initial licking.

No villagers are allowed to pasture their flocks on the Game Council's reserves, so that the value of these rich grasslands is very high. It would be relatively simple for one of the wardens to allow a friend, for a fee, to run some sheep in at night, but so far there has never been such a case brought to Sariri's attention.

Iran is twice the size of Texas and the hundred plus wardens in the pay of the Game Council are pitifully inadequate to cope with a conservation job of this size. All they can possibly do is watch the reserves, but most of the nation's game is not in reserves and is being slaughtered whenever the hunters feel like fresh meat. Sariri told me that hunting parties in jeeps make regular sweeps of the deserts and gun down every wild ass or gazelle they see.

From my brief sojourn I would say that the Game Council needs a lot more money for the following projects:

1. A survey of the remaining tiger, wild ass, fallow deer and gazelle.
2. A game park in the desert to serve as a refuge for the wild ass and gazelle.
3. At least double the present number of wardens and higher pay scales for these dedicated men.

The gates of four of Teheran's royal palaces face each other at the corners of a small intersection, and so similar are the great wrought iron structures that it must be hard for the princes to know which one is home on a dark night. After attempting to enter several of the wrong ones, we finally arrived at Prince Reza's, a handsome stone pile about the size of the Grand Central Station. Before the door was parked the red bicycle of one of his sons. Shown in immediately, we, John Friar and I, found the Prince waiting for us in his library. About thirty-five and in good shape, the Prince obviously keeps fit in a land where many in his position would be showing the effects of easy living. He has a frank, pleasant expression, and appeared genuinely glad to see us. His major interest is hunting and he has collected rare animals from all over the world. He told me of his work for the Game Council and repeated the opinion of his colleagues, Riahi and Firouz, that the most effective way I could help the cause of conservation in Iran would be to put the case to his brother, the Shah. Later the Prince led us downstairs to his private museum where he showed us a really remarkable collection of heads. The African room included the head of an elephant and the American that of a bison, while the Asian group included a good Indian bison shot in the forests of Mysore where I shot my own bull of that mighty species. In the Iranian collection I saw the wild ass and the Mesopotamian fallow deer, two of the rare species which the Prince and the Game Council have succeeded in putting on the protected list.

The Prince has never shot an Iranian tiger but he has seen the pug marks in the Al Meh reserve, the 220,000-acre tract in northeastern Iran that used to be part of the Crown Lands and has now been taken over by the Game Council. Firouz had told me previously that he also saw pug marks in the mountains behind Chalus on the Caspian Sea. There are a few skins around Teheran but the last man to describe killing an Iranian tiger in print was Major R. L. Kennion in his book *By Mountain Lake and Plain,* published by William Blackwood in London in 1911. Referring to the tiger as a Hyrcan tiger, the Major describes shooting two in the Eastern Elburz. He was only able to recover one of these which, when pegged out, measured eleven feet, six inches. Rowland Ward, the British taxidermist, told him that the only difference he could see between it and the Indian tiger was the somewhat thicker coat of the Persian specimen and the fact that the skull was a little broader.

The area where he shot the tiger, the forest of Mazandaran, was full of both wild pig and deer so that there was no question of the scarcity of the breed being due to lack of diet. But even half a century ago the Iranian tiger was very scarce. Just why this should be no one seems to be sure but Professor Haltenorth of the Bavarian State Game Commission has advanced the theory that abundance has been bad for the species, which has grown lazy and impotent by the very ease of its existence. A similar case might be made for the Gir Lions in India which are also decreasing even though rigidly protected.

The Mesopotamian fallow deer, a gentle little creature, lives between the rivers Dez and Karcheh, in a narrow strip of territory only five or six miles long. The Prince told me that the Game Council now keeps sufficient guards there to insure its immediate future. He estimates there are between 50 and 60 deer in the reserve. The park, however, is in the midst of the oil-producing region of Iran where the population is increasing.

Unlike the tiger or the fallow deer, the Iranian wild ass is found over a great area bordering the great Kavis Salt Desert. The Prince estimated that there are about 300 to 400 left and the job of policing them is very difficult.

I told the Prince that in my opinion one of the first things to be done from a conservation standpoint would be to make a survey of these three rare species. Available information about the tiger and wild ass is much too sketchy and even the estimates of the fallow deer are conjectures.

Broadening the base of our game discussions, the Prince said that there is no reason why the commoner game animals of Iran should not be cropped in the same manner that game is cropped in Kenya and Tanganyika. Gazelle can live almost everywhere on the arid plateau of his country and with protection could multiply to a point where they could constitute an important source of meat. Only fifty percent of the land area of the country is under cultivation even some of the time, so there is no danger of the game interfering with agriculture. In addition to the desert areas for gazelle, ibex and mouflon could be raised in the mountains, and wild pig in the forested sections.

We talked of wildfowl and the Prince said that some limits must be placed on the duck and geese bags. There is now no legal restraint and market hunters slaughter the flocks during both the fall and spring migrations. He also said that the black cock and native pheasant are becoming scarce.

Game is not the only national resource of Iran that is not being conserved. Both Firouz and Riahi told me that the fishing industry in the Caspian, which produced 30,000 tons of fish in 1900, today markets only 2,800 tons, and the hauls from the rivers have decreased just as alarmingly. Dynamiting, the use of nets with meshing so small that few breeders are allowed to live, and a complete disregard of the ecology of the waters is responsible.

Sport fishing for trout has, however, been protected on certain rivers and one of our Military Aid Group, Colonel Lloyd Marr, told me that he has caught some very good "golden" trout on the Lar River, only forty miles northwest of Teheran. These trout live at altitudes of about 10,000 feet and swim in the icy snow rivers of these rare heights. The colonel said that he was able to use both wet and dry flies and that the trout averaged about a foot long. The fish sounded to me very much like the golden trout caught in the high Sierra of California.

To show us something of Iran's forests and streams our host, Jack Friar, took us to the Caspian Sea, stopping off on the way for a half day's trout fishing at the Charistanak River which rises in the snow-covered peaks of the Elburz Mountains, some fifty miles north of Teheran. The water was dirty, due to heavy rains in the high passes, and flies proved useless. Later, with spinners and even less aristocratic forms of lures, we did take a few small trout. They were "brookies" very similar to those of the eastern United States.

But whatever the river lacked in fish was more than made up by the grandeur of the scenery. Only in the Simien Mountains of Ethiopia, the Wadi Rum of Jordan and on the Chinese road from Sana to Hodeida in The Yemen have we seen such spectacular mountains. High on the slopes live the ibex and mouflon which add so much to the interest of this far western branch of the mighty Himalayas. Only a few miles from where we were fishing lies the Valley of the Assassins, where the Old Man of the Mountain and his descendants held their dread sway for several hundred years.

We saw few ruins in the mountains but were charmed by a small castle erected for a favorite horse by a long-forgotten Persian king. Stabled in this handsome house and having the entire little valley reserved for his grazing, this lucky mount lived out his days in peace and plenty.

From a pass of 11,000 feet in the Elburz Mountains, the road to Chalus on the shore of the Caspian drops dramatically in a series of hairpin turns and dark, cavernous tunnels to 85 feet below sea level, and the landscape changes with the descent. The naked snow-capped peaks give way to pines and later to poplars; the high pastures of the fat-tailed sheep to terraced paddy fields, reminiscent of South China; and the rugged peasants of the mountains to softer visaged peoples of the Caspian littoral. And at Chalus, a little provincial town with Russian architectural overtones—the houses reminded me of Odessa—we saw the Caspian, an oval sheet of silver in the afternoon sun. The second largest inland body of water in the world, the shores of this inland sea encompass some 169,381 square miles of water.

To get an idea of what the average Iranian thinks of the game laws, I asked a banker from Teheran who appeared to be in the middle income bracket. He felt that the $20 yearly fee for shooting was much too steep for 95 per cent of the population. He also objected to the 100 per cent duty on shotgun shells and fishing equipment. Rifle ammunition is heavily taxed and hunters are allowed only about 100 rounds per year. He believed that the only way to broaden the interest in game and fish is to make sport much cheaper and I think he has a good point.

From Ramsar we drove along the Caspian, where flooded fields of paddy alternated with plantations of tea, and arrived for lunch at Bandar Pahlavi, the biggest port on that inland sea, where Mr. Nabavi, the co-director of the government caviar and fish freezing plant, showed us around. He said that, ten years before, the Russians produced 700 tons of caviar and this year only 350 tons, while the Iranian share a decade ago was 97 tons and is now 205 tons. He added that most Iranian caviar, which is the best in the world, is shipped to America. At the canning plant we saw sixty-pound casks of the precious stuff and were invited to eat all we wanted. This is not easy with the Iranians watching.

We inspected the freezer, a cavernous complex of icy caves, where the sturgeon, mullet, herring and whitefish were stacked like cordwood. Sturgeon grow to great size, some reaching 300 pounds, and live as long as fifteen years. There used to be a fine run of salmon trout in the Caspian but netting had reduced the catch drastically. Salmon have been officially closed by the government for the next five years but it is still possible to buy the big silver fish in the black market in Teheran at $2.50 per pound.

Nabavi told us that the Caspian is drying up and recedes an average of two meters per year. He attributes this to the gradual rise of the temperature in the Middle East. In the last half century it has risen a full degree with a consequent increase in the evaporation rate. Others say that the vast Russian irrigation works have siphoned off an important volume of water which formerly flowed into the Caspian. When we swam later at the broad beaches outside Bandar Pahlavi, I noted that the water was slightly saline. The drop in the water level of the sea also affects the marshy lakes around it and Lake Mordat, one of the most important habitats of wildfowl in the Middle East, is also slowly drying out.

1964
South America

EIGHT

Mission to South America

NORTH AMERICANS GENERALLY know little about South America and even less about the wildlife that lives in that vast continent. To many, a jaguar is simply an expensive British car and a tapir is a big candle in a church. Anaconda stands for a copper company and condor for a passenger plane. The vicuña only became known for a short period because of the propensity of those in high places to accept presents of its handsome fur, and the giant sloth is thought to refer to a Senator.

The reason is mainly because South America has relatively few animals and only a handful of these are large. The 300-pound tapir can hardly compare with its two-ton relative, the rhino, and the guanaco, the wild version of the domesticated llama and alpaca, is puny next to its cousin, the camel. True, the jaguar is bigger than the Asiatic or African leopard but it is smaller than both the lion and the tiger. The spectacled bear, the only member of the bear family living in South America, compares in size with our small eastern black bear. All of the South American deer are little and range from the Ecuadorian pudu, which stands at a bare 14 inches, to the marsh deer of Brazil which is somewhat smaller than our white-tails. None of the monkeys compare with African gorilla or the orang-utans of the East.

But there are other forms of life in South America which attain great and sometimes terrifying sizes. The tucandera ants grow nearly the size of mice and are highly carnivorous. Tarantulas of the rain forests measure 10½ inches across and attack rabbits and snakes. The beautiful atlas moth has a wing span of 13 inches, larger than many birds. There are huge rodents like the paca, agouti and capybara, a sort of riverine guinea pig which is 3 feet long, has webbed feet, and can weight 150 pounds. The pygmy anteater is barely as big as a squirrel but the giant anteater is nearly 8 feet long. Armadillos, living tanks, range from 3 inches to the giant variety whose carapace was 12 feet long. Whether this huge animal still lives is debatable. The last signs of one was a huge carapace found near Mercedes, Argentina, in 1870.

How big are the anacondas and boa constrictors? Tales, often as suspicious as those of the trout fisherman, put these inhabitants of the Amazon Valley at incredible lengths. Major Percy Fawcett, the famous explorer who vanished in the Central Brazilian Plateau in the summer of 1925, claimed to have killed an anaconda of 62 feet, and the great German animal collector Hagenbeck, director of the Hamburg Zoo, had a photograph of a "sucuriju gigante" killed by the machine guns of the Brazilian Boundary Commission in 1935 which was said to be 115 feet long. Four men could not lift the head.

The purpose of my mission, however, was not to measure the anacondas or test the pincers of the tucandera ants. It was primarily to persuade the various governments to take more interest in the conservation of wildlife. Time for many of the rare forms of South America's wildlife seems to be running out rapidly. The manatee, a harmless water mammal that nurses its young and appeared to some nostalgic Europeans to compare favorably with a mermaid, is now rare in the Amazon Basin. Like its equally charming colleague, the otter, it is being hunted toward extermination. Game laws have little validity in the vast rain forests but there is just the outside chance that an approach to the powers that be in the capitals might someday be translated into action before it is too late.

This was my second mission for the World Wildlife Fund. Next to appealing to the men at the top I spent a good deal of time in the field, visiting the national parks, collecting recent data on the rare animals, birds and reptiles, and looking for possible projects to recommend to the Fund for action. In addition to these major objectives I was asked to be on the lookout in Argentina for a small weasel skin for Dr. Van Gelder of the American Museum of Natural History, and in Peru for a whole pearl gray opossum for Dr. Davis of the Bronx Zoo. Dr. Dowling

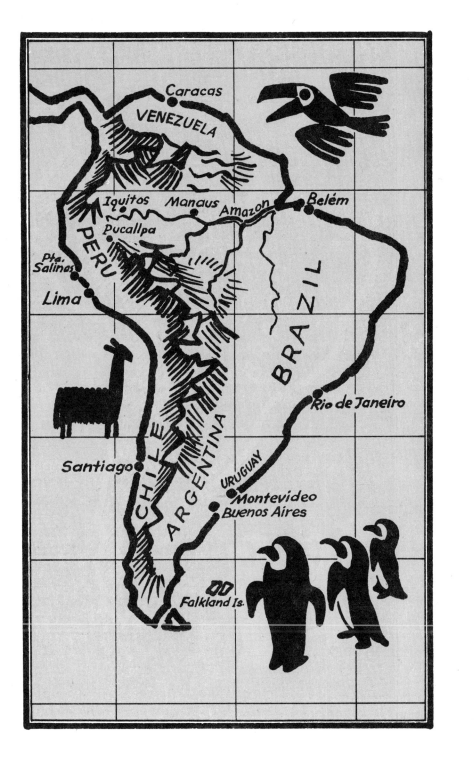

of the same institution wanted any factual data I could gather on the length of anacondas and boa constrictors.

I also promised my good friend Harold Coolidge to see about getting the various governments, which have not done so, to ratify the 1940 Convention on Nature Protection and Wildlife Preservation in the Western Hemisphere, and to assemble a list of persons in South America who would be useful to the Fund as correspondents on rare and endangered species.

Before sketching the outline of my trip, a few words about the geography of South America. With an area of 6,800,000 square miles, the continent is nearly twice the size of Europe. Yet, of the total area, it is estimated that only 20 per cent is arable. Swamps and the vast mountain chain of the Andes which stretches 4,400 miles from Venezuela on the sun-bathed Caribbean to freezing Tierra del Fuego on the South Pacific, make agriculture virtually impossible on four fifths of the land. It is further estimated that a fourth of the cultivatable land has been ruined by erosion due to bad farming methods. The irrational clearing of forests has left the watersheds unprotected so that surface water has nothing to hold it.

Few people, even among the educated minority, understand the inter-relation between man's desires and the necessity of preserving the land. Indiscriminate killing of predatory birds and other carnivori has led to a multiplication of crop-destroying insects and rodents. As Fairfield Osborn so eloquently put it: "The tide of the earth's population is rising and the reservoir of the earth's living is falling. There is only one solution: man must recognize the necessity of cooperating with nature. The time for defiance is at an end."

Despite its size, South America today is underpopulated. In England there are 350 persons to the square mile and in America there are 50, but in South America only 11. Even with this relatively small population the life of the average man is a hard one. Plagued by poverty, illiteracy, hunger and ill health, his life expectancy is only 45 years, as against 70 in the U.S.A. What will be the condition of these 150 million people when they have more than tripled forty years from now?

Who are these people? They can be divided by race into Indians, Europeans, Negroes and Mestizos, or half-castes. The Indians are more or less concentrated in Ecuador, Peru, and Bolivia, and comprise about one person in ten in South America. A very few live almost as they did before the Spanish Conquest in the sixteenth century. Europeans make up the bulk of the population of Argentina, Uruguay, and Chile, and while the first great migrations were Spanish and Portuguese, substantial members of Italians have migrated to Argentina and Uruguay, and Germans have become important factors in Argentina and Chile. The Negroes were imported to the country as slaves and make up parts of the populations of all South American countries. In Brazil they comprise 40 per cent of it.

NINE

Venezuela

IN HIS SUNLIT patio, the hummingbirds sipped bottled nectar while William Phelps, Jr., told me something of the animals and birds of Venezuela. A well-known ornithologist as well as a fellow director of the World Wildlife Fund, Billy Phelps did a great deal to make my stay in his country interesting and productive. He told me that aside from one bird—a red siskin which has the footloose habit of mating with canaries when kept in captivity—there are no Venezuelan birds in danger of extermination. The mammals are also in pretty good shape as far as vanishing species go, but additional protection is needed. The red siskin enjoys full protection now, as do the deer, but there are other birds and animals against which the hunting pressure is great and relief is necessary.

To get a more detailed view of the conservative picture as applied to game, I called on Dr. Edgardo Mondolfi, executive director of the Consejo de Bienestar Rural, a civilian organization that makes special studies for the government and private industry on all phases of land use and conservation. Dr. Mondolfi and his able assistant, Fernando Rondon, told me that deer shooting has just been closed for two years and that the capybara, a rodent about the size of a big pig, and the arrau, the river turtle, are also being given complete protection; but the hunting and trapping of some other animals is unrestricted. The jaguar, the jungle cat bigger than the African leopard, is hunted all year round and is growing rarer. The cattle interests fight any attempts to protect it. The puma, a smaller member of the cat family, is also hunted hard and becoming more difficult to find. The spectacled bear, due to the wild nature of the mountain terrain it inhabits and its extremely shy nature, is still extant but seldom seen. The lapa, a rodent smaller than the capybara but many times bigger than our largest rat, is licensed but is still under pressure from hunters. Tapir, anteater, and armadillo are also on the diet of the country folk. Nor are the aquatic mammals safe. The manatee is fast disappearing from the Orinoco and its tributaries, and eggs of the arrau, despite the law against taking them, are poached regularly.

With Dr. Juhani Ojasti, a Finn who is professor of biology at the Central University of Caracas, we visited that volatile and handsome institution. Dr. Ojasti's specialties are turtles and bats, and in the laboratory of the Biology Department he showed me a collection of vampire bats that would have delighted Dracula. Common in Venezuela, the vampires take an evil toll of cattle and sometimes attack man. They are occasionally rabid and, if one finds the telltale marks of the teeth and great difficulty in stopping bleeding from the puncture, it is well to get the anti-rabies injections. When the vampire bites it injects a substance into the wound that prevents coagulation. So quiet are the attacks that, if asleep, man or beast may not be aware of being bitten. There are 120 species of bats in Venezuela or about the same number as there are rodents.

Dr. Carlos Rivero, the curator of reptiles, showed us a variety of snakes, including the deadly bushmaster, assorted rattlers, and a young boa constrictor. The boas are somewhat smaller than their water-inhabiting cousin, the anaconda, but still grow to upward of 20 feet. Asked about the reports of giant anacondas, Dr. Rivero said that accurate information is extremely difficult to get as the anacondas live deep in the swamps and the Indians leave them strictly alone. The longest skin he had ever seen was 28 feet but it might have been stretched. A handsome olive-green snake with black spots, this great constrictor has been known to attack human beings in the Orinoco valley but is usually contented with animals. I was also shown a tank of tiny "pipa" frogs who live all their lives under water, the only species in the world which seems to have resisted the impulse to sit on the bank and croak.

As we planned to spend almost a month on the Amazon and its tributaries, I was particularly interested in the piranhas, the small but voracious fish which relishes flesh—human and otherwise. The curator of marine biology told us that there are many varieties of piranha and showed us several specimens. Short and plump in the manner of our sunfish, the piranha is endowed with a set of razor-sharp teeth that can slash the flesh off the toughest cow with lightning speed. Asked if they invariably attack, the curator said he believed that small schools seldom do but larger numbers are more apt to. Blood in the water would naturally tempt them more than a smooth pair of legs. Stagnant and slow-moving water is more apt to be populated by piranha than fast currents. The piranha, despite its unsavory diet, is itself quite good to eat.

Crocodiles have no protection in the rivers of Venezuela and are being hunted hard for their skins. Unless some relief is granted them under the laws they will become as rare in the Orinoco as they now are in the rivers of Africa and Asia. Friends of the crocodiles, and I number myself among this small group, have a hard time selling their ideas.

There are no game wardens per se but the National Guard, a quasi-military organization stationed in the hinterlands, has responsibility for enforcement. Game watching, however, is only one of the many duties of the guardsmen and therefore does not necessarily get priority with all of the 10,000-man force, but there is a special 900-man division whose duties are entirely concerned with conservation and which operates under the control of the Ministry of Agriculture.

Colonel Francis Jenkins, our army attaché, took me to call on Brigadier Parades Maldonado, commander of the National Guard. Also present were Colonel Nieto Bastos, the chief of staff, and Captain Diez-Cardenas, the officer commanding the special conservation force. I found all three officers interested and cooperative. According to General Maldonado there are three kinds of poachers in Venezuela: the small group of rich "sportsmen" who kill illegally for fun; the poachers who kill to sell the game, and the poor who kill to eat. The second group of poachers give him the most trouble. We also discussed the danger to habitants from the constant firing of the bush, and the Brigadier said his men did their best to stop the fires and punish the offenders. He did not think that insecticide spraying of the crops has had an important effect on wildlife to date.

There is no magistrate system in Venezuela and those arrested by the national guardsmen are turned over to functionaries of the Department of Agriculture who have power to fine or imprison. I gathered the penalties are moderate and the officers felt that the game laws, which are twenty years old, should be overhauled.

Conservation is a division of the Ministry of Agriculture and I was pleased to find that the Minister, His Excellency Dr. Miguel Rodrigez Visa, is keen about wildlife and conservation in general. An energetic young man of about thirty, the Minister took a degree in veterinary science at Cornell and owned a cattle ranch before going into politics. He had been in office only a few months but had already made history in the Department by setting up a new department devoted entirely to fauna and issuing an edict against the shooting of deer for two years. He assured me that he was delighted to have me come to Venezuela and was pleased to make arrangements for me to visit several of the game parks. Also present at our conference was Dr. Altuve Gonzalez, head of the division of Renewable Natural Resources, under which the new Game Department was organized, and Dr. Gonzalo Medina, the chief of this department.

I was astonished to hear that a game license cost only about 15 cents and permitted one to shoot a wide variety of game. For instance, the daily bag allows for five kinds of pheasants, of which one can take a total of 24 birds. In addition, the pampered Venezuelan hunter can kill 6 ducks, 12 quail, 12 doves, 3 rabbits, 2 tinamou, 1 tapir, 2 pigs and 2 lapas. I urged the Minister to include jaguar on this license and asked why the licenses were so cheap. He replied that it was difficult to get the National Congress to vote for anything as unpopular as licenses. The poor peasants would, in fact, have a hard time paying for them. I learned later that a good deal of the poaching is done by recent immigrants, most of whom are Italians. Knowing the fate of the song birds in Italy it is not strange that the fauna of Venezuela is also suffering. My net impression was that these three men are dedicated to wildlife and will do their level best to improve conservation.

I had a long and interesting talk with Allan Stewart, our ambassador. A former AP newspaper reporter from San Francisco, Stewart came into the Foreign Service through the United States Information Service, and has a good reputation as a tough and able representative. He was a close friend of Betancourt, the outgoing President, and was equally friendly with Leoni, the new chief of state. Stewart is a keen fisherman and feels that the tourist possibilities of Venezuela as a game fisherman's paradise have hardly been scratched. There are trout in the mountain streams, bass-like fish in the tropical rivers, and big game fish in the warm seas.

Caracas, with a population of about three quarters of a million, is a modern city set in an almost perfect climate, for, though it is only a bit more than ten degrees north of the equator, the city is situated 3,000 feet up in the coastal range and the temperature averages 70. "Heaven," said a travel brochure, "has the same climate as Caracas."

Caracas lies in a valley of the coastal range, and the wise policy of proclaiming an area of the mountains which dominate the town a national park makes it possible to escape quickly and completely to the country. In the cable car or in a jeep one can climb a mile high and find a cloud forest replete with birds, stately trees and grand vistas. Our first trip to the campo, or country, was not to the Avila National Park which lies north between the city and the sea, but to the range of mountains to the south of the city where our good friend William Phelps, Jr., had his cottage. As guests of Billy and his wife Cathy, we spent a delightful and informative weekend.

Not only has Billy classified more than 200 birds of his country but he and his father have made a famous collection of 66,000 birds which includes all of the 2,300 birds of Venezuela, as well as migrants from other areas. He told us that there are more different kinds of birds in his country than there are in all the nations north of the Rio Grande. Sitting on the green lawn watching the hummingbirds drink from flasks of nectar and the tanagers and thrushes partake of fruits, was a pleasing way to enjoy nature.

Another day we visited the Avila National Park as guests of the Ministry of Agriculture. Joe Pojan, a bright young forestry engineer who had just returned from a year in America where he studied with our parks and wildlife people, called for us in a Land Rover and, after taking us as high as that capable vehicle could climb, we mounted mules and plodded still higher into the cloud forest. Giant majagua trees gripped the steep cliffs with iron-hard roots, while the smaller eucalyptus and cypress strained for the sunlight under their canopy. The guacharaca, a mountain pheasant, made its harsh clucking call and the blue flash of a mountain tanager showed bright against the green of the forest. Here and there we saw groves of carricillo, the mountain bamboo, and stunted coffee bushes. Long ago there was a coffee finca there and some of the bushes still bear fruit and are harvested by the park people. Joe pointed out the great waxy leaves of the ocumo plant whose roots are highly favored by the peasants as food. Only about 400 of the trees and bushes of the mountains have been classified since the park was proclaimed in 1958.

Venezuela has done well by her parks. Since 1958, when the National Park Board was set up to assist the Ministry of Agriculture, eight parks, three water reserve areas, and three national monuments have been proclaimed. She has also ratified the 1948 Convention on Nature Protection and Wildlife Preservation in the Western Hemisphere and has sent delegates to all the important international conferences since then.

The parks are carved from a vast, thinly settled country. With 352,143 square miles, Venezuela is twice the size of Germany and larger than Great Britain, but its population of eight million is about that of the city of London. It has the smallest population per square mile of any country in Latin America. There are four well-defined natural divisions: the Maracaibo lowlands, under whose swamps and waters lie 11 per cent of the world's proved oil reserves; the Andean ranges; the Llanos, or great plains of the Orinoco Basin; and the Guiana highlands, which cover about half the country.

The Orinoco is the third largest river in South America and extends 1,700 miles from its source on the Brazilian border to the Atlantic. In 1800 the great German explorer Baron Alexander Von Humboldt ascended the river and established the existence of a water link between the headwaters of the Orinoco and the Amazon.

On a sunny morning we started from Caracas with Dr. Gonzalo Medina, the director of the Game Department of Venezuela, to visit Rancho Grande, the nation's largest national park, and the Llanos, the great plains. Oil revenues have produced some fine roads but accidents are frequent and we passed numerous wayside crosses, often decorated with flowers, to commemorate traffic deaths.

The dry season had just begun and the hills were starting to turn brown. Until June there would be no more rains and the sugar cane and rice in the valleys would depend entirely on irrigation. At Maracay, the capital of the State of Aragua, we stopped at the University. I inspected the experimental station where talapia from Trinidad were being studied with a view of stocking the Venezuelan rivers and lakes. Amazingly fast breeders, the talapia have a high protein content and can be raised in almost any body of water no matter how stagnant. In the laboratory I saw an electric eel and was told that it could deliver a shock of some 400 volts, enough to give one a nasty jar.

Headquarters of the Rancho Grande National Park is a fascinating old pile started as a hotel by Gomez, but the Dictator died in 1935 and that day work stopped on the partially completed building. Since then the park service has finished a few rooms and made a small natural history museum out of some of them, but the great bulk of the building has been left open to the weather. Bats roost in the empty halls, and the jungle tide was starting to push in sections of the walls.

A cloud forest is not as wet as a rain forest but it is still damp, and when the mist swirls through the branches of the giant trees and the howler monkeys roar their deep challenge, the jungle becomes an eerie world. The caudelo, a huge tree whose trunk is supported by flying buttresses of roots, rises more than a hundred feet in the air and sustains a hanging garden of orchids and Spanish moss. We saw yellow orioles and vividly colored butterflies flit through the long allées of the forest. According to Medina snakes are common, but we never saw the brightly banded coral snake or the duller but just as deadly fer de lance.

There are no jaguars in the park but pumas are plentiful, and we saw the pug marks of one in the soft earth near a mountain spring. These big cats live on the smaller mammals of which there are some strange varieties. There is a water opossum, the only aquatic marsupial in the world; the cuchi cuchi, a strange little creature looking like a minute compromise between a monkey and a bear; and the picure, a ratlike animal with the hindquarters of a deer. The park teems with game birds which range from the giant pauji, a bird the size of our wild turkey, to minute quail. There are also tinamou which look like guinea hens. They are more apt to run than fly and are easy to kill. Before the park was formed in 1947, a man from Caracas built a hunting camp near Rancho Grande for the express purpose of hunting tinamous.

The tiny red siskin, the rarest bird in Venezuela and the only one which is in danger of extermination, can still be found in the park. Dr. Medina knows, but wisely will not tell, the location of a small flock of siskins. As I noted earlier, the red siskin mates in captivity with the canary and the resulting offspring is an operatic singer avidly desired by the world's canary fanciers. There are said to be some two million of these and they will pay up to $60 for the siskin-canary cross. With such an incentive the illegal trapping pressure on the few remaining birds is heavy, and recently a Caracas gang, which purchased the birds from the Indians, was caught red-siskin-handed.

From Rancho Grande we drove down to the Llanos, the great plains which occupy more than half of the area of Venezuela and are only a few hundred feet above sea level. It grew much hotter but the atmosphere was dry and we did not mind the change.

We arrived in the forenoon at the ranch of Tomas Blohm, a young Caracas businessman who runs cattle on a 22,000-acre estate as an avocation. A graduate of Cornell with a fluent command of English and a deep interest in wildlife, Tommy Blohm laid himself out to show us the fauna and flora of the Llanos. A flat country, watered by the few rivers but inundated for half the year during the rains, the Llanos looks a good deal like the bush country of Florida, with tall oil palms rising from grassy savannahs and dense islands of thorn trees dotted here and there. Luckily there are small hillocks where the cattle can go during the rains, for a calf born on the flat land is drowned.

After the siesta we drove in a jeep across the plain and found, just as Tommy had said we would, a family of howler monkeys. Middle-sized primates with handsome red coats and curious oval-shaped mouths, the howlers have an ivory bone in their throats which enables them to emit a series of roars which can sound like a pride of hunting lions or the wind screaming down a canyon. They were not afraid of us and remained in their trees quite willing to be photographed.

On a pond in the savannah we found a great flock of tree ducks which rose and wheeled continually over our heads. About the size of teal, the tree duck flies much slower and is all too easy to shoot. Tommy allowed no hunting on his ranch and the ducks seemed to know it. There were also a few brace of blue-winged teal migrants from Canada, and half a dozen garçon-soldat, the largest stork in the world, with a truly amazing wingspread. The muscovy, the biggest duck in South America, was represented by a pair who refused to fly and remained on the placid waters while I took their picture. Near the pond we heard the call of the troupial, the national bird of Venezuela.

Rooting in the long grass was a sounder of pigs, the European species, which had gone wild and provided Tommy with a yearly crop of hams. They were rounded up by his gauchos on horseback, lassoed, and those not wanted for slaughter were castrated and released. The big boars are formidable-looking customers whom I would hate to tackle on foot. We also saw a family of peccaries, the small native South American wild hog. These handsome little pigs have no closed season and are hunted all year round. We saw one deer, a doe. Very much smaller than our whitetails, the Venezuelan deer are supposed to have a closed season of six months but in fact they are hunted all twelve months and usually highjacked with lights during the nights. The poachers are hard to catch and even harder to convict. The ranchers are loath to report the local peasants who do most of the illegal hunting. In a small community no one wants to make enemies.

We spent the night at Tommy Blohm's ranch house, a comfortable cement building which he constructed himself. We slept in hammocks, a mode of rest popular in the British Navy during Captain Bligh's time. One can see why bunks were later substituted but a hammock in the Llanos is a wise precaution against the numerous creeping things that would have little trouble scaling an iron bedstead.

In the morning we again toured the ranch and found a tree blooming with lilac flowers. The ranch was named Flores Morades after these jacaranda-like blossoms. By the edge of a water hole we saw a five-foot alligator and Tommy said that he had shot one in the river fifteen feet long. These 'gators sometimes grab a calf but do not attack humans. Sitting on a dead tree was a king vulture, a bird fairly rare in Venezuela, and trotting across the lilies was a family of jacanas, water pheasants similar to those I saw so often on the tanks of Ceylon. A sick-looking horse came to drink and I learned that there is a local form of horse anemia that makes it necessary to buy new mounts every other year. So far nothing can be done for the animals infected. By the banks of the Guarico River, which forms a border of the ranch, we saw the tracks of ocelots, those handsome cats that harry the howler monkeys, and capybara, the huge rodent. We did not see the giant anteater but found a dead lesser one. The claws of these burrowing animals are long and sharp but their skulls are so delicate that the merest tap will kill them.

Summing up my impressions of conservation in Venezuela, I would say that the park system is excellent and is well staffed by dedicated and intelligent officers. I was particularly impressed by Dr. Medina, with whom we spent three long and interesting days in the field. He told me that the only major section of the country which now lacks a park is the Llanos, and that one should be proclaimed soon in order to preserve the many types of fauna found only on the great plains.

I felt that the fish and game laws should have a thorough revision. A much shorter season for deer would help. Six months, in view of the shooting pressure, is too long an open season. Many other animals, such as the jaguar and the puma, should be put on the license and the legal number restricted. The cost of a hunting license, now virtually given away, should be raised to a reasonable level, and the proceeds from these sales used exclusively for conservation. Fishing inland waters should be licensed and more effort made to stop illegal catches.

Enforcement of the game and fishing laws should be a function of the Ministry of Agriculture and should be organized and run by Dr. Medina's department. Under the present cumbersome arrangement, the poacher has an easy time of it.

TEN

Amazon Journal

FEW TOURISTS GO to Belem and fewer still use the old city as a jumping-off place for the vast hinterland of the Amazon Basin. Today Belem is a curious mixture of the old colonial and a degree of modernity. The opera house, relic of the rubber boom of the turn of the century, still stands but it is a long time since the divas have made its ornate theater echo. Near it rose two huge skyscrapers, one of which had been under construction for two years and was still far from finished. Our hotel, Belem's one and only and of course named the Grande, had much in common with the old Raffles in Singapore. Nothing really worked well; the water sometimes ran and sometimes stopped; the lights flickered; and the servants shuffled through the dingy halls bound on long, aimless missions. Even time in Belem was a matter of opinion. His Excellency, Aurelio do Carmo, the Governor of the State of Para of which Belem is the capital, and the American Consul, Hyman Blum, both adhered to daylight saving time while all the rest of the 450,000 inhabitants of the city persisted in keeping their watches at the old time.

Eighty miles from the Atlantic, the city is the main port, too, for an area of more than two million square miles, nearly the size of the continental United States, and in the zoological park one can see a good collection of the birds, animals, fish, and reptiles of this vast area. Dr. Fernand Novaes, an ornithologist and deputy director of the Goeldi Museum which is part of the park, told me that game laws have little meaning in Amazonia and that the crocodiles, deer, and river turtles are being exterminated just as fast as the hunters can manage it. The price of a twenty-pound turtle had risen to around $8.00 or just about half of the monthly wage of a lower-class inhabitant of Belem. Only the very rich could enjoy tartaruga. I believe this is either the same turtle or one closely related to the arrau of Venezuela which was also under extreme pressure from the hunters there.

According to Dr. Novaes, there were game laws on the books and there was some effort to enforce them in the populous states of the south, but few people had even heard of them in the remote reaches of the Amazon and there was not even a pretense of conservation in the state of Para. He said there were a good many rare birds in their collection but he knew of none which were facing extinction due to hunting. The cost of a game license, if anyone bothered to get one, was about 30 U.S. cents.

Asked about the length of the largest anaconda he had ever seen, Dr. Novaes smiled and said five meters. If one of Brazil's leading naturalists puts these river snakes at only 15 feet, the explorers who claimed to have killed monsters of 60 feet may well be regarded with mild skepticism. There was, however, in the ponds of the zoo a mammoth freshwater fish which weighed several hundred pounds and was said to be the largest freshwater fish in the world. The Nile perch and the huge catfish of the other African rivers would dispute this. Unfortunately the ponds of the zoo were so murky with algae that neither this fish nor the shy manatee, which was also on exhibit, could be seen. The only evidence of the manatee was the occasional downward movement of a piece of grass, apparently pulled under by these strange mermaid-like creatures. Dr. Novaes said the manatee were also getting rarer on the lower river but few people eat them, and he did not think they needed special protection in most parts of the Basin.

In the zoo's great aviary where a wide variety of birds live a socialistic existence, I saw an "arapapa," a cormorant, lay a solitary white egg on the sandy ground and proceed to sit on it. A similar bird, presumably her mate, stood beside her looking disconsolate. Indeed, the housekeeping facilities were limited. The only nesting places provided were several wire platforms high in the eaves, and two snowy egrets were in residence there.

Although Belem is relatively prosperous for northern Brazil, most of the people are very poor and the galloping inflation—the cruzeiro was 1,400 to the U.S. dollar as against a par of 350—made living even harder. A missionary told me that the peasants almost never taste meat and seldom have more than two meals a day of farinha, a food derived from manioc root, beans and rice. The police were three months behind in their salaries and had to appeal to the businessmen for help.

In the early 1900's the rubber tree, indigenous to Brazil, was smuggled out of the country and planted in the East where cheap labor soon drove the Brazilian product off the market. Black pepper, indigenous to the East Indies, was today being produced by Japanese near Belem and the new industry was doing very well indeed. But neither rubber nor pepper makes any real difference to Brazil. She has a one-crop economy and there is too much coffee in the world. In 1961, the world's exportable crop was estimated at 40 percent above what people would drink and Brazil produces nearly 40 percent of this exportable surplus. Coffee prices have been falling since 1957 and there are no signs of a reversal in trend.

Belem has a well-earned reputation as a smuggler's city and a good percentage of the waterfront population was said to be engaged in the illegal importation and exportation of luxury products. British whisky was available at prices so far below the controlled price that little was sold in conventional stores, or, if it was, at the government price. It may be an exaggeration to say that grand pianos were available on the black market but objects nearly as big certainly were.

Back at the turn of the century the city fathers of Belem wisely decided to enclose some twenty-five acres of the surrounding jungle and, aside from a few paths, leave the magnificent forest exactly as it was. Today the city has grown around the enclosure, or Bosque as it is called, but the primeval playground is still intact. Tapirs wander along the paths and stop to have their ears scratched by equally tame quatis, a coon-like animal with a ringed tail and a long nose almost like the tapir's. Little pacas, looking like a cross between a rabbit and a deer—they are the same animal as the lapas of Venezuela—scurry through the dim forest aisles, and a variety of monkeys chatter in the upper terrace of the giant trees. In a cave flit hundreds of bats, some of the vampire variety, and in a jungle pool bask alligators who must be thanking the jungle gods that they are in the Bosque and not part of a suitcase. The shy and dangerous animals are confined to cages. There are neat little peccaries, looking like silver fox furs moving about on tiny feet. The puma snarls in his cage but he looks well fed and no wild cat really likes a zoo. The brilliant macaws are free but other varieties are caged.

The jungle itself is as fascinating as the animals and birds which inhabit it. Slim assai palms grow in groves, their smooth stems culminating in feathery foliage thirty feet in the air. Banana trees, with velvety green leaves ten feet long, are also handsome but the real attractions of the forest are the giant hardwood trees, whose column-like trunks rise a hundred feet from the jungle floor before a single branch reaches out. At the base these trees are buttressed by roots so large that the space between them forms a stall for a good-sized horse. One of the most useful of these great trees is the Massaranduba, or cow tree, whose fruit is delicious and whose bark yields a milky substance which tastes a good deal like cow's milk. Red dye is made from the bark. We saw no orchids or other flowers. Unlike the cloud forest of Venezuela, the equatorial jungles of Brazil are on the whole unadorned by any color but the deepest green. The trees blanket the noise of the city and it is easy to imagine what it must be like to explore the real jungles which run for thousands of miles just outside the city limits. Occasionally a fruit or a dead branch falls, less often a bird calls, but generally the jungle is silent.

Glancing down at one of the sandy paths on which we walked I was delighted to see an army of sauba ants gathering leaves. The ones I had seen in the streets of Belem were the fertile females and males winging their way abroad to breed new tribes, but the ants in the Bosque were workers engaged in their endless missions. Each tiny sterile worker—they are one-fourth the size of the fertile females—had hefted a circular leaf about the size of a penny and was moving steadily forward with it toward a hole in the sand just large enough to permit the worker and his burden to enter. Out from the hole came a stream of empty-handed slaves rushing to get another leaf. The "inspectors," the large-headed ants, were ambling along the lines of workers and stopping occasionally to salute one with their feelers. They may have been conferring merit badges similar to those handed out by the Russians to heroes of Soviet labor.

Hyman Blum took us for a long drive into the country where I could see what strides, if any, were being made in soil conservation, not strictly an objective of my mission, but important as it affects wildlife habitats. Burning of the forest, a really tragic policy when the trees destroyed are hundred-footers, goes on uninterruptedly. We rode for some miles beside the blackened stumps of forest giants between which a scanty crop was growing. Actually, the soils of the Amazon Delta are poor and sandy and nothing much can be produced without fertilizer which the peasants cannot afford. I was impressed with the government experimental farm where effective farming and soil conservation methods are being taught. I learned, moreover, that Brazil's forest legislation is excellent, with specific penalties for infractions of the laws but that these laws are either not enforced or enforced so mildly that the disastrous cycle of "burn, sow, move and burn" is steadily consuming the remaining accessible forests not already ravaged for fuel and charcoal. Of course it will be a long time before a major dent is made in the vast Amazon jungles but the forests near the growing cities are being relentlessly destroyed.

New species of mammals are rare but in the myriad world of smaller creatures they pop up quite often. Dr. Robert Shope of the Rockefeller Institute, who was working on viruses, told us that in a three-month period, prospecting in a small area in the nearby jungles, he had come upon three new species of bat, and in an even smaller area his field team had found 80 different species of mosquito, some of which are new.

To show us how he gathered data on the viruses, Shope, a good-looking young man of thirty-four, took us on a tour of the jungle where his men were working. First asking us if we had up-to-date yellow fever inoculations and had taken our weekly malaria pills—both diseases are endemic on the outskirts of Belem—he led us down a narrow path deep into the forest. Great trees, many of them figs which had choked other trees in order to reach the sun, overhung the trail, while tree ferns and creepers made so dense a canopy over us there was perpetual twilight. The ground was wet and swarmed with ants, some of which bit me painfully. Shope uses a number of devices to catch the mosquitoes which he later examines for viruses. Most startling of these was the sudden appearance of a ragged Indian who held in his lap a number of small glass tubes. Whenever a mosquito lit on his legs or arms and began to bite him he would clap the tube over it and seal it in with a stopper. Here certainly was a hero of science. A less willing attraction to the mosquitoes was a monkey in a small cage which was hoisted high into a tree. Certain mosquitoes, including one kind of yellow fever carrier, live only in the high branches. This monkey, a sentinel which had been imported from an island off the coast where the winds always blew from the island to the mainland, was a valuable control source as he had never been exposed to the mosquitoes, and therefore viruses, of this area.

Many small denizens of the jungle such as rats and marsupials were trapped, and as it is important for Shope to know exactly when the animals were caught, he used an old alarm clock which stopped when a wire which closed the trap door was tripped.

Dr. Dalcy Albuquerque, the director who was away during my first visit to the Goeldi Museum, said that a new French process for curing alligator and crocodile skins has widened the demand and that a factory now runs in Belem solely to process these unfortunate reptiles. He added that the manatees are sold for food, oil, and their skins, and that they are now found only in the more remote tributaries of the big rivers. He knew no way of controlling the traffic at the source but thought that something might be done in the way of limiting sales of the processed skins.

The best road to Manaus, 850 miles up the Amazon, is the water route, and we embarked on a little ship, the freighter *Veloz* of the Booth Line of Liverpool, for the first leg of a journey that took us all the way to the foot of the Andes in Peru. Only the Nile, with an overall length of 4,037 miles, exceeds the Amazon, but the Nile is studded with cataracts and is navigable by shallow draft vessels, while the Amazon can carry sea-going steamers for 2,300 of its course of 3,900 curving miles. The area drained is more than two million square miles, nearly as big as the continental United States, and the Amazon sends twelve times more water to the sea than the Mississippi, the so-called "father of waters." And, to top the superlatives, there is the incomprehensible statistic that the Amazon consists of one fifth of all the river water on earth.

We got underway at 8:00 A.M. on January 29 and sailed up the Para River, passing innumerable little islands and fishing boats whose sails varied from dirty brown to the purest azure. We had to take on a cargo at Macapa, a river port on the other side of Marajo, the island in the mouth of the Amazon that is bigger than Switzerland and where the Brazilians hunt Indian water buffalo which have gone wild. We passed the mouth of the Tocantins, the river on whose tributaries—the

Araguaia and above that the Rio das Mortes—Peter Fleming made his gallant effort to find out what happened to Colonel Fawcett, perhaps South America's best-known modern explorer.

In the summer of 1925 Colonel Percy Fawcett, a retired British officer, vanished with his son Jack on the banks of the Kuluene River, a tributary of the Xingu. He was looking for an ancient city which, according to a Portuguese map of 1743, was located in a range of mountains somewhere in the vast tract of jungle lying between the headwaters of the Kuluene and the Rio das Mortes. There are tens of thousands of square miles in this remote section of the Matto Grosso and the Indians range from indifferent to extremely hostile.

Peter Fleming went to find Fawcett in 1932 and wrote an entertaining book, *Brazilian Adventure,* about his exploits. It was Fleming's considered opinion that Fawcett and his son were killed by the Suya or the Ananquas Indians. He also inferred that if they had not been killed, they might well have starved to death in the almost gameless jungles. Rumors that Fawcett is alive can still be heard on the Amazon, and a rubber buyer in Belem told me that his Indian agents are always reporting a strange white man who has lost his memory and lives like a vegetable in a remote village.

In the afternoon we entered a series of channels between islands where we were close enough to the shore to see the dense green wall of the jungle, relieved here and there by the long sheds of plantations and crude wooden huts of the workers. Pale children came out to meet us in narrow canoes, using heart-shaped paddles to propel themselves over the brown flood. A few yellow-billed Amazon terns were following the ship and the ubiquitous urubus were sailing above the jungle clearings, hoping for death on which to feed. With the glasses I made out rubber trees, oil palms and behind them the towering masses of the hardwoods, and once, when we ran close to the shore, I saw a number of birds: white egrets, a brilliant blue little fellow that may have been a kingfisher, and the green flash of parrots.

Macapa is on the Equator but the temperature compares favorably with New York in July. We stopped to deliver an earth-mover to the Brazilian company which mines manganese for the Bethlehem Steel Corporation. As this huge hunk of machinery was removed from the hold of *Veloz* we wandered along the port and watched the small boys catch tiny translucent catfish on nylon lines of about the same shade. In a ramshackle store I saw the belly of a little alligator, the hide of a baby ocelot, and the skin of a large brown animal with a long tail that proved, on closer examination, to be a lontra, or otter. The storekeeper said the latter was rare and he wanted the equivalent of $20.00 for the dusty remnant.

Just before we left Macapa in the late evening Irene saw a dolphin rising and diving on the silver surface of the river. The two species of dolphins which inhabit the waters of the Amazon are, with the exception of an Indian species found in the Ganges, the only freshwater dolphins on earth. I inquired from the pilots and found that no one tries to catch them as bad luck would certainly result. There are so many superstitions that destroy animals—the Chinese belief that rhino horn makes old men young, and the Arabian faith in oryx horns—that it is good to find folklore operating to save them.

Above Macapa for hundreds of miles the river appears utterly uninhabited and it had for us the same ominously empty appearance it must have had for the Spaniard, Orellana, who in 1541 was the first white man to go down it.

A century later the Portuguese mounted a big expedition of 45 canoes and 900 men which made its way without any great misadventures to Quito by way of the Napo, and returned to Para, the journey taking two years. It is interesting to note that the Portuguese spoke of the gentle dispositions of the aborigines.

Santarem, 538 miles up river, lay off our port bow and we saw the red tiles of the roofs. Among the Portuguese families who live in this little river town are the descendants of 200 Americans, who, with their slaves, left the South immediately after the Civil War and migrated to Brazil. Now the Jennings and Bretts and Rikers speak only Portuguese and the old color lines have blurred.

The great river Tapajos, itself more than 1,000 miles long, joins the Amazon at Santarem but its black water makes scarcely a dent in the muddy flow of the main stream. There is said to be a good deal of malaria and yellow fever on the upper reaches of the Tapajos.

Seventy miles above Santarem lies Obidos where Bates, the naturalist, spent more than a month collecting animals and insects. He reported four species of monkeys. The coaita, a large black monkey with coarse hair, which we call the spider monkey, is the largest of the Amazonian species in stature but is exceeded in bulk by the barrigudo of the Upper Amazon. The Indians tame them and at the same time prize them as food. They catch them by shooting them with poison arrows out of blowpipes and then restore the monkey to health by putting salt, an antidote for the poison, on their mouths. I saw several spider monkeys in the Belem zoo and noted their long prehensile tails which serve as a fifth limb.

The river near Obidos is rich in butterflies and as we ran close to shore some brilliant specimens landed on the ship. I did not see any of the genus Morpho, the great blue butterfly with ten-inch wing span, but there were a number with rich velvety black and gold wings and others of an almost translucent pink and green.

The *Veloz* left the tawny flood of the main Amazon and sailed five miles up the black waters of the Rio Negro to her anchorage at the floating docks of Manaus. We were a thousand miles from the Atlantic but the altitude was only 105 feet above sea level. Capital of the State of Amazonas, the biggest in Brazil, Manaus is the trading center for more than a million and a half square miles of jungles and rivers, and from the standpoint of the naturalist the best place to gather information about the wildlife of this vast and still largely unknown area.

Through the kindness of Noel Bowmer, the Booth Line agent, and also the Consular Agent of the United States, we were introduced to H. W. Schwartz, a German who has spent twenty years collecting animals, fish and birds in the hinterlands of Amazonas. A burly man of about fifty who presides over a welter of tanks and cages in a big dark house on a side street, Herr Schwartz was in the midst of filling an order of tropical fish for the Smithsonian of Washington but turned the job over to one of his dark-skinned employees, chucked a cat out of an ancient rocking chair, and invited us to be seated and state our business.

He was immediately interested when I told him something of the aims of the World Wildlife Fund and while he thought little or nothing could be done to stop the killing in Amazonas, he was most anxious that I should know all the facts and present them to the powers that be in Rio de Janeiro later on. He started with the peixe-boi, reporting that this curious and inoffensive manatee was slaughtered by the thousands in 1963 when the river fell to its lowest level in recent history. The price, which had been steady at about $20.00 per adult weighing 250 pounds, suddenly slumped to 50 cents. This price was for the fat, which is boiled down and canned in 40-pound drums. The skin brings only about $1.00. Easy to find when the river is low and quite unable to take evasive action, the manatee was speared in such numbers in 1963 that Schwartz thinks their numbers may be permanently reduced. Asked if the Indians were responsible, he said definitely no, explaining that it was the hunters, mostly half-breeds and whites, who kill off the great percentage of the game. The Indians, having no way to preserve the meat, only kill what they can eat, while the skin and flesh hunters wipe out everything they can find. He cited the case of a German hunter who maintained a pack of forty dogs with which he exterminated every wild animal with a worthwhile pelt along river after river.

He did not think, however, that the manatee faced extinction but he definitely believed the giant otter was on the way out unless something drastic was done to help it. Six feet long and not shy of man, these big brown otters have become so rare that a skin now brings $70.00 and few come down from the upper rivers. They are mostly killed by the Indians for meat.

According to Schwartz, the denizens of Amazonas whose chances of survival are the poorest are the black alligators, for the skin of these big caymans makes the best leather. Ten years ago two million skins came into the Manaus market and today fewer than 200,000 are sold. Prices have skyrocketed. A belly skin six feet long sells for $8.00; one of nine feet for $11.00, and one of ten feet for $12.50. In Manaus, two tanneries are still processing alligator and other skins of wild creatures but more and more the volume is shifting away from the saurians to the skins of pacas, capybaras, deer, etc. There are, of course, many different species, and the smaller brown alligator, also killed for his hide, is not in short supply. According to Bates, the jacareuassu, or big cayman which we call the black alligator, may grow to 20 feet. The natives fear the great cayman and there are a good many well-authenticated stories of people being eaten by them. Like the turtles, the alligator has its annual migration for it retreats to the interior pools in the wet season and returns to the rivers in the dry season.

Turtles are also on the wane and Schwartz thinks that they will soon be in as bad shape as the black alligators. This freshwater species grows to a very large size, a full grown one measuring three feet by two. Today they are beyond the price of any but the rich. Not only are the adult turtles taken whenever the opportunity offers, but the eggs are dug up as well. The eggs are eaten and mashed up for oil, a wasteful process by which some 6,000 eggs are required to make one three-gallon jar of oil.

Jaguar skins brought $65.00 in the local market, and fewer were coming in. Black jaguar skins were even rarer, although in some districts they seemed to be as common as the yellow ones.

In a dank tank in the rear of his menagerie, Schwartz showed us a 20-foot anaconda and said that he had never seen one of more than 26 feet and did not believe larger ones existed. He also showed us a handsome harpie eagle, a gigantic bird with a crest and a far from tamed expression. When we opened the door it gave a piercing scream and raised its taloned feet. Schwartz said the rarest animal which he is now trying to find is a pacarana, a paca with a tail. He then took us out to a set of tanks in the yard, had one of his helpers wade into one; after some effort he lifted up a baby peixe-boi weighing, I should judge, about fifty pounds. I was interested to see that the freshwater species differs a good deal from the saltwater dugong which I saw in Ceylon. The peixe-boi has a rounded rather than a bifurcated mouth and its eyes are smaller. Both have streamlined mermaid shapes and seen through deep water must have given many an ancient sailor pause.

Schwartz told us a curious thing about hunting on the rivers. He said the black water rivers seldom provide much game while the muddy rivers invariably do. He explained this by saying that the black rivers are older and hold less food for the fish and other aquatic wildlife, while the newer streams, which tear away their banks, are full of nourishing tidbits.

Asked about the attitude of the Indians, he said in some cases they have become very hostile due to the hunters who kill the game and leave the Indians no meat. He said that the Indians on the Anaua River, a tributary of the Rio Branco, which is itself a tributary of the Rio Negro, recently wiped out a hunting party of fourteen men and have gained such a reputation for ferocity that no hunters will now enter this river. The hunters were killed by arrows, and he showed us a sample of the big six-foot arrows of this tribe. No poison is used; the arrow shot from a powerful bow is quite lethal enough. The mouth of the Anaua is only about three hundred miles from Manaus, but the government has not been able to punish the tribe. In fact, several Indian Agents, men specifically sent out to protect the aborigines, have also been killed.

Manaus today does not enjoy the high prosperity of the rubber boom of the 1890's but neither is she today the ghost city which the travel people in America seem to think. Even the opera house, which used to offer Caruso and Jenny Lind to the rubber barons when it opened in 1896, is now used again, although for much more modest recitals. The building, which is pure rococo and has a vast amount of style, is approached by a formal garden in the middle of which is a fountain supported at the base by the prows of four bronze boats named for the four continents. Happy cherubs ride in each boat.

In the early morning we heard a great thrashing around on the pier to which we were tied up and going on deck found the crew hauling up a ten-foot anaconda which had been discovered stalking rats. I was impressed with the thickness of the snake if not with his length. It looked quite capable of gulping a stevedore or a passenger. The snake made no effort to bite its assailants but it took five men to wrestle it into a crate. Later in the morning the captain sighted a manatee drifting alongside and we saw its streamlined form turn slowly in the dark water.

There are only 400,000 people in all of Amazonas and half of them live in the towns. Manaus, with a population of 150,000, is the magnet for the diverse inhabitants of the hinterlands and the river is always full of all kinds of craft bringing people into the city and taking them away. There are Brazilian river steamers loaded to the gunwales with produce and humanity; the latter spend most of their time in hammocks and the three decks look like a cocoon factory. There are monterias, the long, thin canoes which can navigate far up the little rivers, and squat wood-burning "African Queens" with a pair of pink panties flying from the flagpole and a dozen children draped about. The river children must learn to swim before they walk for a great deal of their life is spent on the river. Even the market is a floating one with a permanent fleet of huge catfish lying below the scows waiting for scraps or the unwary youngster.

By far our most rewarding effort in Manaus was a visit to the headquarters of the Missoes Salesianos Prelazio do Rio Negro where the missionaries have a museum of the Indians of the Rio Negro and its tributaries. Sister Lucia, a voluble Italian nun, aided by Joseph, a boy who did the murals in the museum, gave us a fascinating tour of the displays. We saw the artifacts of the "white Indians" discovered by Father Antonio Goes in 1952 on the Rio Cauaburi on the border of Venezuela. Blue-eyed and with strangely European faces, these Indians believe in an afterlife, for they provide for the dead with bowls of farinha. They also have a devil in the form of a drumlike object which, when blown, gives out a deep and sinister note. It is kept under a waterfall and any woman seeing it is sure to die. The dead are kept in a wooden coffin for eight days and then burned. During the ceremony the elders of the tribe wear curious funeral costumes consisting of tapa cloth tops on which are painted faces. Grass skirts complete the outfit. The drums of the white Indians are hollow decorated logs with four holes in them. The holes make different tones and good news is sent on two of them and bad news on the other two. A communication system similar to that used on many of the African rivers is still in operation on the Rio Negro. The arrows of the Cauaburi Indians are six feet long and tipped with bone. They also make delicate bone flutes and handsome ornaments out of the teeth of big caymans and jaguars. Yellow and blue feathers, probably from macaws, are fashioned into headdresses and girdles.

The boards on which the Indians grind their mandioca roots to make farinha are studded with animal teeth or sharp stones and a story is told of one such board which found its way to a curio shop in Georgetown, British Guiana, where it was purchased by a discerning Englishman who took one look at the stones and immediately started inquiries. He finally narrowed down his search to a trader who operated on the headwaters of the Rio Anaua and learned from him that the Indians from whom he bought such trifles were dangerous. Nothing daunted, the Englishman, who was gone for eight months, returned racked with fever but happy. His whiskey bottle was full of diamonds.

With considerable regret we left the good ship *Veloz* at Manaus and arranged to fly to Iquitos, Peru, a distance of 1,300 miles, in an ancient Catalina amphibian of Pan Am of Brazil. Not only did we have to save time but I wanted to see what the rivers which make up the Amazon look like from above, and also to stop at many of the little ports which the ship does not bother with. The main river is no longer only called the Amazon but becomes the Solimoes, a stream aided and abetted by a great number of tributaries such as the Rios Purus, Coari, Japura, Tefe, Jurua, Jutai, Ica, Itacoai, Javari, and Napo. All of these have people living on their banks and I hoped to learn more of the fauna of Amazonas and the adjoining selva or forest of Peru. The lands east of the Andes which include the jungles make up 60 per cent of the nation's total area, but hold only 6 per cent of its population.

As we droned up river to Iquitos—we left Manaus at eight in the morning and did not arrive until six at night—I reviewed our Brazilian exposure and came to the conclusion that virtually nothing can be done to make the game laws stick in an area as large and as sparsely settled as the Brazilian Amazon. How can the law distinguish between the Indians who kill giant otters because they are hungry and really need meat and the trader who simply slaughters for a profit? An effort can certainly be made to limit the export of black alligator skins and the internal sale of turtle meat and eggs, but only if Rio de Janeiro is willing to put teeth in the regulations, and nothing in Brazil today leads one to believe that the government is going to embark on unpopular legislation simply to save creatures without votes. Dedicated scientists like Dr. Dalcy Albuquerque of the Goeldi Museum in Belem, and even animal buyers like Schwartz of Manaus are not without influence in their fields, and fully realize the danger signals. A campaign to tell the public of the threat to their national heritage would certainly help. I promised to discuss this in the capital with the Minister of Agriculture and others.

The first thing we noticed about Iquitos was the cleanness of the streets. Unlike those of Belem and Manaus where filth accumulates in the broken pavements and papers seem never to get picked up, the thoroughfares of this jungle city were spotless. The same smart appearance applied to the police and army. Of course, getting paid regularly may have something to do with it. By common consent the best source of information on wildlife in the town was Leo Baumer, a Swiss who had lived in Peru for twelve years and for the past four had been exporting tropical fish and animals from Iquitos. An engaging young man who was interested in his work, Baumer said the rivers near Iquitos were so denuded of all kinds of fish by poisoning that there was a real possibility that some of the rarer species might be wiped out. Two kinds of poison were used; Barbasco which is made from a root, and Huaca which is made from a plant. Both types are unfortunately easily available in the jungles. The fish poisoned by Barbasco may not die immediately but always do eventually. Baumer said he can always tell when his tropical fish have been caught in a river which has recently been poisoned because the fish die in a few days. The fish poisoned by Huaca do not float on the surface like those affected by Barbasco, but sink to the bottom, and only a small number of those destroyed are caught by the fishermen.

There is a severe penalty for poisoning fish—two years in jail—but

Baumer had never heard of anyone being charged with the crime while he had been living in Iquitos. In order to convict, proof must be furnished to the police, and this proof never seems available. Hundreds of fish, obviously poisoned, come into the Iquitos market every day but the culprits are never apprehended. There were rumors that some of the police themselves were involved in the nefarious business. Barbasco is sold commercially as an insecticide and it might be possible to license this business so that no one except the legitimate exporters be allowed to possess it.

Baumer took us around his establishment where millions of tiny fish swam in basins and tanks. He showed us the Neon Tetras, the favorite of tropical fish fanciers in the States, which give off a phosphorus-like glow in the dark; the yellow-and-black striped Leoporinis; the Head-standers, little fish which always swim at a 45-degree angle, and the Knife and Pencil fish. He showed us fish which were about to die and said that just before they expire they assume their most brilliant colors.

His small menagerie included a mussarama, that most useful and friendly of all snakes, which goes about killing other snakes—including all the poisonous varieties. Like the king snake in America it will take on any of its cousins small enough to be swallowed. He also had some big boas and anacondas. Questioned on the size of the latter, he said he had personally never seen an anaconda or a boa bigger than five meters or fifteen feet.

There is no protection for any animal in the Selva or jungle territory of Peru. The only creatures having legal protection are the paiche, a huge river fish which cannot be exported out of the Department of Loreto, which includes the Selva, and crocodiles under one meter in length. Everything else can be shot at any time and in any numbers. Mrs. Margery Smith, an American who has lived a long time in Peru and runs a shop specializing in Indian artifacts, told me that jaguar skins brought $80.00 each and even little ocelots were worth $40.00 in the local skin market. Baumer said he had handled only seven giant otters in the past three years and doubted there were many left in the Peruvian Amazon.

Throughout my Amazon Journal I have referred to saurians as "alligators," the term used by most English-speaking Brazilians and Peruvians. Strictly speaking there are no alligators in the Amazon. The only two species in the world are the ones we have in the southern United States and those which inhabit the rivers of southern China.

The South American "caymans" consist of two species of crocodiles, one of which lives in the Orinoco and the other in the Amazon. The alligator differs from the crocodile in that the former has a shorter and broader head. The alligator also has an enlarged set of teeth which fit into a pit in the upper jaw rather than into a notch as they do in a crocodile.

Dr. Joseph Davis of the Bronx Zoo gave me a picture of an appealing little pearl-gray animal with black markings and a pink nose and ears which goes by the honorific name of *Caluromysiops irrupta,* or, in more easily understood language, the black-shouldered opossum. The Zoo owns one of these small marsupials which was found scurrying around a street on the outskirts of Iquitos, and Dr. Davis very much wanted another if one was obtainable. When I showed the picture to Baumer he recognized it immediately and said that he was the collector who had sent the Zoo the first black-shouldered opossum. He added that they are rare but he believed he could find another. Mission completed.

The editor of *El Oriente,* the daily newspaper of Iquitos, told me that he wanted a piece on conservation and the article, kindly translated into Spanish by Mrs. Smith, duly appeared. The local impact was probably minimal. I talked to a good many people of various classes and the attitude was that since life is none too easy for humans why should they worry about animals, fish or birds. My interest in the preservation of crocodiles and turtles made even less sense to them. The argument that a valuable economic asset will soon vanish if action is not taken produces little reaction. Today there are still crocodiles to be killed for their skins and turtles to be eaten, so why worry about tomorrow.

Sixty-five miles down the Amazon from Peru's jungle capital of Iquitos, the little Rio Manati adds its modest contribution to the great yellow flood of the main river. Few people live on the Manati which meanders for some hundreds of miles—more than six days canoeing, say the Indians—toward the borders of Brazil. There are four villages of the Yaguas Indians, the clearings of some half-caste Peruvians and the establishment of Anthony Wong, an energetic Iquitos businessman who occasionally takes paying guests who want to see the jungles without benefit of a tourist atmosphere. We met Tony Wong through Nicole Maxwell, an American girl who was studying the medicinal herbs used by the Indians, and the three of us boarded Tony's outboard motor boat in the bright dawn and set off down the river.

The Amazon at Iquitos is a rivulet compared to its ten-mile width on its lower reaches, but it is still a mighty river, and we passed raw scars in the bank where whole groves of big trees had been ripped away and sent hurtling downstream. Occasionally we saw the wood-burning scows which run up the lonely rivers, but more often the canoes of the inhabitants of the little thatched huts which every mile or so break the green walls of the jungle.

The sun was directly overhead and the river had turned to molten silver when we suddenly veered to the right into the Manati and, after chugging up it for a few miles, came into land at the log dock of Tony Wong's jungle hacienda. A crowd of naked brown children and a gorgeous macaw, who answered to the name of Waco, greeted us gleefully. The children wanted candy but Waco was quite willing to eat my fingers. The establishment consisted of a main guest house with screened rooms, a shower, toilet, and good but somewhat heavy food. There were numerous servants who smiled and sputtered in Spanish.

The next morning we took a hike through the surrounding jungles with Wong's factotum, an old half-caste who knew a great deal about the forest and its secrets. He stopped at numerous trees and shrubs and explained their uses. There is the catawa tree from which poison for the blow guns is made. So dangerous is the sap of this tree—if it gets in the eye, one goes blind—that the Indians seldom cut it down, preferring only to tap it when they needed to arm their darts. He pointed out the machacuy bush, whose berries and leaves are pounded into a paste which relieves toothache, and a variety of other useful and dangerous herbs which make up the witch doctor's medicine chest.

Nicole Maxwell, who has written a book about jungle medicine called *Witch Doctor's Apprentice* which received favorable reviews from medical men as well as the literary critics, believes that there are a number of herbs which would be of great value to modern medical science. On one of her expeditions into the bush she found a plant which prevents internal hemorrhages and one which prevents conception indefinitely. From the Mainas Indians she secured specimens of plants which produce abortion and others which induce fertility.

We passed a good many assorted ants and the old man pointed out the red fire ants whose bite is not only painful but infects rapidly if scratched. He showed me a scorpion scuttling away under the leaves, and on the scarlet flowers of an aerial plant called a Bromeliad the big furry body of a tarantula. We found no armies of the dreaded esala, the big soldier ants whose legions are feared by everything that lives in the jungle except the insect-eating birds. My journey was not without its unpleasant reminder. Just after we got back to camp I felt a fiery sting on my leg, and looking down saw a three-inch centipede crawling slowly across it. I brushed the brown furry mess off with a sweep of my hand and as a result was badly bitten in both places. Nicole rose to the occasion and stopped the pain almost immediately by an application of tobacco and alcohol (external).

I learned that game was not scarce on the Manati and that the Indians got all their meat from hunting. They use long, heavy blow guns from which they shoot with remarkable accuracy five-inch darts tipped with poison. They can hit a small animal at 100 feet, and a large one such as a tapir at twice that distance. They also hunt monkeys, peccaries, the various big rodents, and a variety of birds. The Yaguas evidently do not poison the streams with Barbasco because we saw a number of men fishing with lines, an idle gesture if the river had been poisoned. Most of the catches consist of various species of piranhas, none of which are colored like those I caught on the Orinoco tributaries in Venezuela.

The Manati has its own tributaries and we took a long ride in our canoe up the Rio Paparo, a narrow dark stream over which hangs the primeval jungle. Great hardwood trees, a hundred feet and more high, reach their branches across the water while the aerial roots of tree ferns and the ropelike tendrils of climbing vines form a screen above. There are brilliant sapphire and yellow butterflies and sometimes the flash of kingfishers and other brightly colored jungle birds. The hanging nests of orioles are sometimes found in the deep jungle but these yellow and black birds seem to prefer the haunts of man and almost every clearing along the river has its colony.

Back in Iquitos I held a series of talks with people who knew the jungle and had ideas about conservation. Two of these were profitable. I learned from Mrs. Murilla Segond, a Belgian who taught at the University of San Cristobel de Huananga, that there was a move to create a national park near Iquitos. Sparked by a local tycoon named Joaquin Abenzur, the scheme involved a reserve of some 10,000 hectares (20,000 acres) but a location had not been decided on. A possible area would be the land between the Napo and Putumayo rivers where patrolling would be made easier. The idea had the tentative approval of President Beluande, with whom Mrs. Segond had discussed it, but was bogged down in the Senate. The real catch, of course, will be enforcement. The army has so far always failed to implement the conservation laws and there is no reason to believe it has reformed. If a department could be set up under another ministry with its own wardens, the future would look brighter.

The possibility of proclaiming a game reserve on an island in the Amazon was considered but all of the Peruvian islands are flooded during high water. In Brazil, a project to set aside Banhan Island in the lower Amazon is under consideration.

From Iquitos, the capital of the jungle Department of Loreto, to Pucallpa, the jumping off town for explorers and missionaries, is a matter of five days by fast steamer on the Rio Ucayali, but in the DC3's of the Peruvian Air Force the journey takes only two hours. True, the service can bog down entirely when the rains turn the dirt fields to acres of mud, and February is the height of the rainy season, but the bush pilots of the Selva have had a lot of practice in negotiating some of the world's most rugged flying. There are no clearings large enough to land in and the planes either make their destination or vanish in the green morass of the jungles and rivers. Aside from these two towns and the river hamlets, the vast area of some 50,000 square miles is inhabited only by Indians and there is a wide divergence of opinion as to how tame or how wild these primitive people are.

The dedicated members of the Summer Institute of Linguistics, to give the organization its full name, make many modern explorers look a bit silly. Instead of spending a few months in the bush, panning a few thousand dollars worth of gold, then writing a book about how brave they are, the 460 men and women live with the tribes and devote their lives to inventing writing forms for 175 of the 590 tribal tongues they have found in eight Latin American nations. To see how the Institute functions we spent two days at the Institute's Peruvian headquarters some twenty miles from Pucallpa. Under the able leadership of Eugene Loos, some fifty linguists were working with thirty-two tribes, ranging from the Quechua of the high Andes, who number over five million to the little remote tribes of the jungle Selva, like the Cashiba, who have only a few hundred members. The compilation of Indian tongues requires the teacher to be taught by the pupils. First, a member of the tribe must be found who knows a little Spanish or Portuguese, and working from that base the linguist develops the Indian vocabulary. The Institute's linguists work in pairs and women can go places where men would be in trouble. When two young women arrived in the Shapra tribe the chief told them that if they were men they would assuredly be killed. The reason given was fear that the Indian women would be taken away. The Indians have few possessions and their wives rank high among these.

After a vocabulary has been developed by the linguists, a dictionary and primers are printed at headquarters and the Indians of the tribes are taught to read. The bright ones are also taught to teach and are brought into Pucallpa for courses. We visited various classrooms and were immensely impressed with the interest and activity of the students. One class was studying geography, another learning to play the flute, and a third working on history. On the walls were prints of Bolivar, San Martin and other Peruvian heroes. These classes are taught in Spanish which the Indian teachers have to learn in addition to their own language. There was an excitement in the room that I have never felt in my own schools. "When paper begins to talk," said the linguists, "a new world opens up for the Indians and for us it is an exciting breakthrough." Later comes the reading by the tribes of the passages from the New Testament and as a result some dramatic changes in attitudes. In addition to languages the Institute's members teach hygiene and agriculture, and even enable Indians to practice democracy. In Peru one cannot vote without documentary proof of citizenship and before the linguists helped them to register the Indians had no such proof.

In order to maintain the far-flung chain of stations—boats would take months—the Institute has a fleet of aircraft. There are two big Catalina amphibians, some Cessnas and a new Helio with an amazingly low landing speed. About half the planes are fitted with floats to land on the rivers. Every team has a short wave sending and receiving set.

By any standards the Institute has the widest possible coverage of the Peruvian jungles and I spent a lot of my time at headquarters questioning the linguists about the wildlife. The pacarana, the giant rat, is now extremely rare but I found several linguists who had heard the tribes with which they worked speak of these big rodents. Evidently they do not live in the Selva proper but on the foothills of the Andean slopes. Allen's *Extinct and Vanishing Mammals of the New World* says of them: "The Pacarana reminds one of an immense rat well advanced in development toward a bear." It is said to be of a peaceful and phlegmatic disposition, a combination of leisurely movement and supreme good nature, in fact about every characteristic that makes it easy to find and destroy. The Indians value the pacarana as food and hunt them mercilessly.

I also made inquiries about strange and new animals. In the last century and a half an astonishing number of new species have been discovered. Harold Coolidge found the kouprey in Indochina, the pygmy hippo was reported in Liberia, the komodo dragon came to light in the Dutch East Indies, and from the Ituri Forest of the Belgian Congo came the okapi. New birds such as the Congo peacock, the cahow of Bermuda and the notornis of New Zealand have also been classified. Furthermore, there are still living fossils like the coelacanth, the crocodile, and the tortoise, and it is not beyond reasonable doubt that species new to science may still linger in the vast and little-known jungles of the Amazon Valley.

The Indians are still superstitious but when the Institute's planes first started landing on the remote rivers, some of them believed a report that the planes were run on a kind of oil distilled from the flesh and blood of their people. None of the Institutes's linguists, however, have been killed as have the missionaries of other organizations. A few tribes at first refused to cooperate, convinced that the linguists planned to steal their language away from them. The first teams of linguists were trained in 1934 and now, over thirty years later, the methods and approaches are so well worked out that it can almost be predicted how soon a new tribe will begin to show interest in the program.

Legends of half-human jungle men persist among the Indians, and from time to time white men have agreed. In 1917 François de Loys, a Swiss geologist, while exploring the Sierra de Parijaa, a range of mountains on the Colombia-Venezuelan border, saw two tall monkeys which defecated in their hands and then threw the contents at him. He shot what turned out to be the female of the pair and photographed her. She looks a bit like a spider monkey but is much larger and has no tail. The Motilone Indians who live in that area said they had seen these "jungle people" often. Even the famous scientists Alexander Von Humboldt reported in 1799 that he had heard of "a hairy man of the woods, called a Vasitri" which lived on the Upper

Orinoco. The animal collectors in Iquitos whom I asked about the tales said that there is a very big monkey named Maribunda which has a strangely human cry and appearance.

While the "Hucamari" or spectacled bear, is the only member of the bear family reported to be extant in South America, I heard several reports of a small jungle bear which lives in the Selva. The spectacled bear is found only on the arid slopes of the Andes above 5,000 feet but there is just a chance that there is a little bear or bearlike creature in the jungles which has not so far been classified. None of my imformants could give me detailed descriptions. They said the "bear" weighed about fifty pounds, had a black coat, and is seen at twilight, indicating a nocturnal animal.

But none of these ghostly animals could be confirmed by the linguists. The largest snake any of them had ever heard of was an anaconda of six meters and reports of jungle men and jungle bears were put down to the superstitions of the Indians. I did establish that some ten years ago there was a manatee in Lake Yarina, the lake which the Institute overlooks, but this unfortunate creature was dynamited along with some fish. So scarce are the manatees now that most of the people I asked about them had never heard of them.

In Pucallpa, a dusty little river town of some 20,000 persons, without paved streets, sewer or water supply, I asked questions of the skin dealers and found that giant otter pelts are extremely rare and black crocodile bellies very expensive. The local jaguar and ocelots have long ago been shot out and the skins which they now buy have come long distances down the rivers.

Pucallpa's future may be far greater than its appearance promises, for the town is the terminus of a road over the Andes, and when and if this becomes surfaced and can be used all year round, the products of the Selva, which used to have to go down the Amazon to the Atlantic and then around to the Peruvian port of Callao on the Pacific, can reach Lima in a fraction of the time over a fraction of the distance. A pipeline over the mountains for the oil and another for natural gas are being engineered. When these links are forged, Iquitos, irrevocably tied to the waterways, may well wither on the vine.

ELEVEN

Peruvian Journey

PERU IS REALLY three countries: the steaming jungle of the Selva, the icy peaks of the Andean Cordillera, and the deserts bordering the Pacific. By land the journey from Pucallpa on the road over the Andes to Lima takes three days of bone-shattering bumping but the transition is logical. By the Faucett DC3 the journey is only a matter of two and half hours but the change is almost too quick to grasp. One takes off on the dusty dirt strip, rises over the matted green morass of the jungle through which coil the muddy rivers, and climbs slowly but surely toward the distant white peaks. At 10,000 feet the passengers are told to start sucking on the oxygen tubes —these old DC3's are not pressurized—and by the time the pass is reached the plane seems to be barely moving in the rarefied atmosphere of 18,000 feet. On either side of the pass rise the jagged sides of mountains, for the Andes here average over 20,000 feet and it seems as if we are flying in a menacing valley whose walls may at any moment become so narrow we can never get out.

But the plane does get out and soon afterward soars down over the brown barren hills to the blue basin of the Pacific. At the Lima Airport my good friend Ambassador John Jones met us and took us to his embassy residence. For the first time in nearly a month we had hot water to bathe in, safe water to drink, and a dry cool climate to live in. Even the animals and birds are different. In my mind's eye the fate of the mountain tapir becomes a more immediate problem that that of the manatee; and the Andean condor gets more attention than the umbrella bird.

118

According to Dr. Albert Giesecke, Secretary of the Comite Nacional de Proteccion a la Naturaleza, whose members include the foremost conservationists in Peru, the vicuña was in very bad shape. Despite strict laws against killing them and selling the skins, the Indians of the high Cordillera, tempted by prices as astronomic as $100 for a single pelt, continued to poach these little animals. There was no estimate of the numbers of wild vicuñas remaining, but the prices paid for their fur indicate that they are extremely hard to find. There were several small herds of tame ones—I had myself photographed with one of these large-eyed, fleecy-coated, even-toed ungulates—and the species is probably not in danger of extinction, but one can never tell when inbreeding will produce changes in an animal or even make it incapable of reproducing. The vicuña I met was gentle but had a disconcerting habit of spitting at me when I stroked it.

Few of the vicuña skins were sold in Peru on account of the stiff fines but there were no laws against selling them in Bolivia and a regular traffic went on there. Efforts to persuade the Bolivian Government to do something about this have so far come to nothing. The position may well be that no government can today enforce game laws among the hungry and communist-agitated Indians of the high Andes. Johann Jakob Tschudi, a Swiss diplomat and naturalist, who was stationed in Peru from 1838 to 1842, was one of the few Europeans who described a vicuña hunt during their days of plenty. A group comprising one man from each of eighty villages assembled in a remote part of the mountains and made a circle of stakes at intervals of about twelve feet. The stakes were then connected by a rope to which was fastened colored rags which fluttered in the wind. The men then drove the vicuña into the cul-de-sac and closed the entrance. The poor beasts feared to jump the snapping rags and were rapidly dispatched with bolas consisting of two heavy stones and one light one, tied to elastic thongs made of vicuña guts. The bola is a very lethal weapon in the hands of an expert, who can throw the stones farther than a lariat.

In the days of the Incas vicuña were regarded as royal animals and only the nobility and the priests were allowed to wear garments made of its fur. We saw the rooms in the ruins of Pachacamac where the Virgins of the Sun used to weave the vicuña's delicate wool into gorgeous vestments for the ruler.

The vicuña is a smaller edition of the alpaca, which is a smaller edition of the guanaco or wild llama. All are members of the camel family and originated in North America. They range from the Argentine Patagonia to Peru but stay only in the highlands, preferring the ranges above 14,000 feet. Both the llama and the alpaca have been domesticated and are used for beasts of burden as well as a source of wool.

Another resident of the high Cordillera is the chinchilla, a squirrel-like little animal with a coat that enraptures women and may well bring about its extinction. A wild chinchilla wrap in New York, if available at all, may sell for $50,000. Except in captivity the Peruvian chinchilla, known as the royal chinchilla, may now be extinct. Again, price tells the sad tale. In 1900 the skins were $6.00 a dozen and by 1930 had risen to $200 each. Since then the rewards have been so high that the Indians hunt them with dogs and weasels and only in the virtually inaccessible peaks may they still survive. There are three races: the Peruvian, which commands the highest price; the Bolivian, which comes cheaper, and the Chilean, which is the least expensive. Chinchillas take 111 days to whelp and have only three litters a year. The Incas appreciated the silver and black coats of these little mountain animals and gave them protection. It seems an ironic commentary that wildlife flourished under the protection of absolute rulers while it faces extinction under the "enlightened" republics.

Dr. Giesecke himself is something of a rare creature. A member of the staff of the American Embassy in Lima for the past thirty-three years, the fine old gentleman has invaluable knowledge of the country and its people. Before joining the staff he was president of Cuzco University, took General Pershing on a tour of the Inca ruins, and helped Hiram Bingham, the discoverer of the last Inca stronghold of Machu-Picchu in 1911. He did a great deal of excavation work at the site of Pachacamac and took us on a tour of these interesting diggings. He has always taken a keen interest in conservation and has been editor of the *Boletin,* the publication of the Comite Nacional, since it first appeared in 1944.

Spreading the light on conservation is part of my job and one of the best ways to do this is through the columns of the local press. Pedro Beltran, owner of the big Lima daily, *La Prensa,* invited us for lunch at his hacienda some fifty miles down the coast from the capital. "Montalvan" is a producing cotton estate of some 1,500 acres and, before the Beltrans bought it, it was the ancestral home of the O'Higgins family, whose foremost member was the liberator of Chile. One hears a lot in

North America about the exploitation of the South American peasants by the "Patrones" and when we were invited by Senora Beltran to see the workers' quarters I did not expect to see the model housing which was shown us. Each of the seventy families on the estate will have, when the project is finished, a six-room house which will include a bath, kitchen, and patio for animals. Forty such units have already been erected and the rest are under construction. Except for the cost of excess electricity the workers pay nothing. Relations are obviously good and we got smiles in the village street. The main house, part of which was built by the early Spaniards in the sixteenth century, has great charm. In the cellar is a wooden stock into which the feet of the recalcitrant Indians were locked, and in the gardens are bronze baths on which are engraved the names of the ladies who owned them and the dates. In 1778 a lovely named Dolores splashed in one handsome tub.

The best place in any city to begin one's wildlife detective work is the museum, and at the Museo de Historia Natural I found the director, Dr. Ramon Ferreyra, pleased to see me and eager to help. Questioned as to Peru's national parks where wildlife is ostensibly preserved, Dr. Ferreyra said that there are today only two such parks—Cutervo, or San Andres as it is sometimes called, and the Cueva de las Lachuzas. But neither the Cutervo, which extends to some 6,250 acres in Cutervo Province, nor Cueva, which is only a tiny reserve of 78 acres, are patrolled by wardens. Anyone who wishes to break the law can enter and shoot in the Cutervo and the only safeguard for the rare birds of the Cueva is the nearby presence of the Tingo Maria Agricultural Station. The guacharo, a very rare bird, still survives in this little park. The bird is evidently a carrier of some sort of mycosis or "parrot fever" for Dr. Ferreyra came down with the disease and was in bed for several months after handling the droppings. He assured me that every effort is being made to keep the guacharo, a medium-sized hawklike bird with handsome brownish yellow plumage, from joining the pavo de monte which became extinct in 1877.

In sharp contrast to these two modest wildlife reserves Peru has proclaimed more than 12½ million acres of forest reserves. There are sixteen of these, almost all of which are in the jungle country of the Selva. There are none on the forested eastern slopes of the Andes where some of the country's rarest animals and plants are now under increasing pressure from man. Dr. Paul C. Hutchinson, a botanist from the University of California and director of that university's present expedition to the Andes, told me that the vicious cycle of roads, people, goats and erosion are having a tragic effect on these high forests. When he made an expedition there in 1957 he discovered a new species of cactus. Later he returned to the area where he had found the cactus and discovered that it had been entirely wiped out by goats.

Dr. Hutchinson was able to give me some useful information on rare animals. He said that the mountain tapir, a large edition of the jungle species, can still be found in the vicinity of Huancalanca, a town in northeast Peru in the 7,000-foot altitude range. He added that Charles Cordier, a Swiss animal dealer, was then preparing to go to this area in order to trap mountain tapir. On the Pan American highway at the Porculla Pass, the lowest in the Andes, Hutchinson heard rumors of oso de antejos, the spectacled bear, which were sometimes hunted and killed by the local Quechua Indians.

At this point in our talks we were joined by Dr. Hans Koepcke and his wife, Dr. Maria Koepcke, two German naturalists from Hamburg University who are working in the museum and have done a considerable amount of field work in Peru. I asked if anyone had ever seen or heard of a bear in South America other than the spectacled bear. Dr. Ferreyra said he thought there might be a smaller species and showed us a stuffed example. The two Germans immediately said that this was simply a young spectacled bear and closer examination convinced the director that they were right. Dr. Ferreyra is not a zoologist and was quite willing to admit his weakness in that field. Dr. Maria Koepcke said that she had seen the skin of a mountain tapir offered for sale by Indians in the foothills of the Andes and later on the same trip when she had gone down to an area near Pucallpa had seen the skin of a giant otter offered for sale for 1,500 sols ($60.00). The Indian who offered it said he killed it on the Rio Pachitea, a tributary of the Ucayali.

All three of the experts agreed that the wild chinchilla is now virtually extinct in Peru. One of the last strongholds of these little animals was in the vicinity of Lake Titicaca. A few may still be found in Bolivia.

The Andean condor, which I had heard in New York was growing rarer, seems to be in pretty good shape. These great vultures are seen frequently in the high Andes and even come down often to the coast to attack young sea birds on the beaches. At the Beltrans' one day one of the guests said he had seen a condor swoop down near the road where a cow had died. One of the biggest birds in the world, the condor has a wing span of ten feet and can fly at great altitudes. The pilots of the planes flying over the mountains fear them as they are apt to hit them in fog.

All agreed that the vicuña is in bad shape and that, unless the government makes some effort to protect them, the wild species is doomed. In addition to shooting and trapping them, the Indians often poison the water holes.

Peru has a few game laws but no one seems to know what they are and I had difficulty in getting any information on them. Obviously, if the men who take the greatest interest in conservation don't know the laws how can one blame the simple Indians for not knowing them? Furthermore, there is no enforcement. Not even the national monuments such as the Inca ruins have guards.

I found no information in the Museum on the Peruvian guemal, the little mountain deer of the high Andes. Known locally as a "taruga," the deer seems to be nearly extinct in Peru but may still be found in Chile. There is no specimen in the museum.

The pacarana, or giant rat, was also not represented in the museum and none of the experts knew much about it. I have come to the conclusion, however, that the pacarana and other rare animals are often called by different names which mean the same thing. In questioning the Indians and peasants of the Selva I took along a child's coloring book with pictures of the various animals to avoid this confusion.

I found that the plan to proclaim a game reserve near Iquitos is still bogged down in the Senate and that it will probably not amount to much anyway, as there is no provision for enforcement. I also found out that the rumors in Iquitos of the impending issuance by the central government of a new and complete set of game laws was, to say the least, premature.

Peru's failure to implement wildlife conservation is particularly unfortunate in that she was one of the first of the Latin American nations to ratify the 1948 Convention on Nature Protection and Wildlife Preservation in the Western Hemisphere.

Off Peru's rocky coast runs a fabulous river of cold water in which teems one of the world's great fish concentrations. Known as the Humboldt Current, the fifty-mile-wide stream of icy water from the Antarc-

tic is the home of millions of anchovies which thrive on the sea plankton and themselves form the food supply of larger fish and the guano
birds, those aerial alchemists whose droppings have made the fields of
Peru fertile since the days of the Incas. Left alone, this ecological cycle
would have continued to benefit mankind through the ages, but twenty
years ago an enterprising fisherman discovered that he could make
more money catching the anchovies and selling them as fish meal
than he could netting the larger fish. The result was an amazing
growth. From a total catch of only about 200 tons in 1944, the industry
now exports 1¼ million metric tons of fish meal a year with a value of
more than $120 million. This is gravy for the fishing industry which
invests in fast boats, electronic devices to find the anchovies, bigger nets,
and boasts that fish meal has surpassed cotton and copper as Peru's
leading export.

But one man's meat may be another man's sorrow and the ever-
increasing hauls of anchovies mean that there are fewer fish for the
guano birds, and consequently less fertilizer for Peru's agriculture.
Since 1956, when 330,000 tons were gathered from Peru's 48
guano-producing islands and 16 promontories, the total has dropped
to 150,000 tons, indicating a net decline of more than 50 per cent
in the number of guano birds. Not only do the birds die of starvation
because there are fewer anchovies to feed on but many become entangled in the fishermen's nets and drown.

To show me the guano birds Dr. Giesecke arranged for Luis
Gamarra Dulanto, chief of the technical staff of the Guano Administration, to take me on a tour of the promontory of Punta Salinas, some 72
miles north of Lima, where there is the largest concentration of guano-
producing birds left in Peru. We started at six in the morning and by
the time we had driven down the coastal road, which is a stretch of the
Pan American highway, the sun was shining on the Peruvian ocean
which, due no doubt to the plankton of the Humboldt Current, is not
the conventional blue but a greenish gray.

About a million and a half birds live on the rocky point of Punta
Salinas and anyone who has never seen that many birds packed into an
area of about 25 acres has no idea how dense bird-density can be.
Every effort is made to keep them safe. A wall cuts off the point so that
foxes and other predators cannot get in and the guards have long shotguns for the condors which float down from the Andes seeking a breakfast of scrambled eggs. Eighty-five per cent of the bird population of

the point consists of Guanay cormorants while the balance is made up of Peruvian boobies and Peruvian pelicans. The cormorants' guano-producing abilities far surpass that of the other two species, the nitrogen content being 15 per cent as against 13 per cent for the booby and only 10 per cent for the much larger pelican.

By walking very slowly we were able to approach within a few feet of the solid mass of cormorants and one inquisitive youngster pecked at my shoes. The adults have white breasts like penguins, and when they are breeding a red circle appears around their eyes. This does not disconcert Mrs. Cormorant who is identified as willing by a similar scarlet badge. The young, immature birds have gray breasts and no red lights around their eyes. All of the young had hatched and the nests were reduced to mere outlines in the guano-covered ground. Many of the young birds, however, had not developed enough to fly out and dive for food and were still being fed by their parents. Both the male and female bring food to the children, who get it by sticking their long beaks into the mouth of the parent bird and picking out an anchovy. The cormorant's long neck makes a good receptacle for carrying fish and I had often admired the ability of these birds to catch fish for their masters in China. A leather collar kept them from swallowing the catch but every fifth fish was given them so that they would not lose interest.

So valuable was the "Guanay" bird to the Incas that they decreed the death penalty for anyone who mistreated them or the "Piquero," the booby. The pelican or "Alcatraz" was not so much admired. In the days of the Sun Kings virtually all of the population of Peru was engaged in agriculture, and without fertilizer the nation would have starved. Even today 60 per cent of the people depend on farming for their living, and since there is only one nitrogen fixation plant which produces at a high cost only a fraction of the country's needs, the guano industry is still extremely important. More than a billion sols worth of crops are raised yearly with guano fertilizer.

Cormorants seemed to me to show a great deal of affection in constantly seeking to rid each other of lice and clean up each other's feathers. Mr. Dulanto, who feels about the birds much as a cattleman does about his best milking cow, says that they rear an average of two and a half young with each year's mating and have a life span of seven years. The sea gulls, who often steal eggs from the cormorant nests, live forty years.

The guano birds face other dangers besides predators and avaricious fishermen. About every seven years a deadly current from the tropics called "el Nino," the child, floods south and heats up the cold water of the Humboldt Current to a point where marine life perishes and hydrogen sulphide bubbles up from the sick ocean. The whole ecology is immediately shattered; dead fish litter the beaches, starving guano birds totter up the streets of the fishing villages, and man prays in the little churches for an end of "Callao Painter" so called because the decay-filled sea turns the white paint of the fishing vessels brown.

Since 1909 when the Peruvian Guano Administration was formed by the government, there has been an effort to conserve the birds and regulate the extraction of guano so that it does not exceed the limitations of nature. But those who know most about the industry fear the undisciplined drain on the anchovy and have begun to put considerable pressure on the government to regulate the catches, particularly near the guano islands and points. There is, in fact, a law that denies fishermen the right to cast their nets within two miles of these bird sanctuaries but it is not observed. Enforcement, the same problem that defeats conservation efforts in the Selva and in the Andes, is militating against the guano birds.

Nevertheless, the guano birds do receive a great deal of protection from man and the revival of the colonies from a guano-producing low of 70,000 tons in 1909 to a high of nearly a third of a million tons in 1956 was the result of strenuous conservation efforts. Other wildlife of the Peruvian seas has not been so fortunate. The Peruvian diving petrel, a compact bird with a black back and a white breast, makes its nest in burrows where it lays a single snow-white egg. Fishermen like to eat the plump young and frequently reach down the burrows and take them out. They also eat penguins which are becoming as scarce as the diving petrels. Neither of these birds enjoys any protection.

The sea mammals are also in a bad way, according to Dr. Erwin Schweigger, an authority on the Peruvian marine life. There are two species of sea lions on the Peruvian coast—the common or rough-coated "chusco" and the fine-coated fur seal. Both must be hunted under license but undisciplined kills have depleted their numbers to a point where the annual take has fallen from 100,000 skins in 1941 to 20,000 this year. The sea otter is so rare that it is seldom reported.

An island sanctuary for all of Peru's dwindling marine life would be a good idea and at a round table conference held to acquaint me with these problems, it was proposed that the island of Sangalla, near the south coast city of Ica, be proclaimed as such a refuge. It is not a guano island and has no economic use, but is patronized by the seals, diving petrels and penguins. There is also a land snail there that occurs no place else in the world.

Peru catches whales but does not belong to the International Whaling Convention so that her kill is in addition to the quotas awarded to Britain, America, Russia, Japan, and Norway and the other subscribing nations. Luckily, the giant blue whale, whose reduced numbers may well put it into the vanishing species category, seldom comes this far north, but I was told that five blue whales were taken in 1963 by one of the three whaling stations which Peru operates. Most of the whales killed are "cachalotes" or sperm whales, which come into the warm waters near Paita, a port in northern Peru, to feed on the octopus. According to the government report more than 2,000 whales are killed annually off the coast, and since Peru insists on a Territorial Sea or closed area of 200 miles, no other nation can send their whaling ships along the coast where most of the whales congregate. So close are they that no factory ships are needed and the Peruvian killer boats simply dart out from the Paita and the two other ports, and kill their 30-ton quarry, and tow it back to port where the carcass is cut up and reduced to oil. Sperm oil is valuable because its viscosity is not affected by temperature changes and there is ready market for it for engine lubricants. It is also used in cosmetics, detergents and shoe polish, not an aristocratic fate for the noble creature immortalized by Herman Melville. Evidently there is no more discipline in the whaling industry than there is in fishing and the catches are getting smaller. The females and young are easily recognized as they are much smaller than the bull whales. Supposedly protected, they are in fact often killed.

Thanks to a personal letter, written in my behalf by Prince Philip of England to Fernando Beluande Terry, the President of Peru, the chief executive gave a dinner for my wife and me at the palace and lent a most sympathetic ear to the wildlife problems faced by his country. In our travels for the World Wildlife Fund we have talked with a good many chiefs of state but this is the only one who has expressed his interest in such a personal and complimentary manner. Also present at the dinner were the Prime Minister and the Foreign Minister, the

American and British Ambassadors, and men directly interested in conservation such as Dr. Giesecke and Philip Benavides.

An architect who was educated at the University of Texas and speaks good English, Mr. Beluande is without any doubt Peru's most traveled President both abroad and in his country. He told Irene, who sat on his right, that he had made many journeys on balsa rafts down the rapids of the rivers which run out of the Andes into the Selva. Many of these have never been mapped or thoroughly explored, and he came on strange Indians who were not dangerous but easily could have been.

When the President asked for my impressions of the conservation picture in Peru I told him frankly that there is a great deal to be done, but that a number one priority should be the safeguarding of the vicuña. I recommended that a national park for them be proclaimed in the Andes and that adequate measures be taken to guard the sanctuary. I added that Peru's only sizable park is in the lowland jungles and that none of the animals of the mountains have any protection. I cited the spectacled bear, the Peruvian guemal, the mountain tapir, and the pacarana as animals which are becoming extremely rare and the chinchilla as a species which in its wild state may well be extinct in this country.

I was particularly pleased with the President's reaction, as conservation in Peru is not easy to sell to the man in the street. Of the eleven million people, about half are illiterate and most of these are the Indians of the jungles and the Andes where a large proportion of the game is found. One of the President's favorite schemes is to build a road along the eastern slope of the Andes to open up the timber and agricultural resources of this vast area. It is important that a wildlife reserve be proclaimed before easy access is made available. I think it will also be wise to teach the settlers something about erosion.

One of the guests, Philip Benavides, a member of an old Peruvian family, was acquainted with both of my principal directors, Princes Bernhard and Philip, and is a keen conservationist. He told us that he planned to raise a public subscription for a zoo—Lima had none—and later to start a Peruvian branch of the World Wildlife Fund. Like so many of our most generous subscribers, he is a hunter himself, and during his diplomatic career shot birds in England and the Continent. Land for the zoo has already been donated by the government and Benavides believed that the running expenses, above the sums donated by private individuals, could be raised by fees for game licenses and big game fishing permits. He wanted to start a Zoological Society to act as a nucleus for these conservation efforts and he will undoubtedly ask many of the members of Comite de Proteccion a la Naturaleza to join it.

In order to develop further the plan for a game reserve in the Andes, Dr. Giesecke assembled a group of wildlife experts for a round table discussion. I told them briefly of the objectives of the World Wildlife Fund, and then asked their opinions on endangered species in Peru and what action they thought could be taken.

Dr. Hans Koepcke said that in his opinion, and all of the seven conservationists agreed, the best place to proclaim a reserve would be the Parina Cocha in the southern Andes. He pointed out that the most important animal to preserve today is the vicuña and a 50,000-hectare tract at this 12,000-foot level would be suitable for this purpose. In addition a rare species of flamingo, Darwin's rhea, a small member of the ostrich family, and various wildfowl would also profit from this refuge. He mentioned the "taruca" and I found out that this is the Peruvian Indians' name for the guemal which I had previously supposed was nearly extinct. The guemals, although legally protected during their breeding season, are hunted hard all year round and are now dangerously scarce.

Other members of the forum said that the spectacled bear is not as rare as I have been led to believe and in certain areas they can still be found in moderate numbers. The mountain tapir, however, due to its great size (the males are almost as big as donkeys) and gentle disposition, has been hunted to the verge of extinction. Unfortunately, neither the mountain tapir nor the spectacled bear would flourish in the Parina Cocha park as the altitude would not be suitable for them.

Dr. Maria Koepcke said that animals and birds are not the only form of wildlife threatened in Peru. The introduction of rainbow trout from America into the waters of Lake Titicaca has resulted in the rapid decline in the numbers of some of the indigenous fish. The "umanta," a useful food fish, has vanished completely, undoubtedly devoured by the voracious rainbows, while the "boga," a carplike fish and the "sucha," a catfish, have declined drastically.

Rainbows were introduced into the rivers of the Cerro de Pasco copper company properties in 1925. Up to that time no trout existed in Peru and there was some doubt if the imports would thrive. An initial shipment of 200,000 fertile eggs from the U.S. Bureau of Fisheries suffered heavy losses en route—the only means of transportation in those days was by ship—700 survived and were planted in Lake Junin where they promptly disappeared. Then one day several years later, a 12-pound rainbow was caught in the Mantaro River, a stream that flows out of Lake Junin. Since then the Peruvian government has stocked many of the icy streams that originate in the high Andes and Peru today offers some exceptionally fine fly fishing.

Next to my conversation with the President, the most important official with whom I talked conservation was Henrique Torres Llosa, the Minister of Agriculture. A young and hard-working minister, Mr. Llosa has his hands full with the major problems of land distribution but was quite willing to take time out from a busy schedule. I pressed the idea of an Andean reserve for vicuña and the Minister said he was interested in the idea and would be glad to consider it seriously if we would submit a plan to him.

The net of it was that Dr. Giesecke and the experts of his conservation society promised to draw up for the minister a bill proclaiming a tract of land in the Parina Cocha area. Proposed legislation to give some protection to the guano birds, by enforced laws prohibiting the fishermen from catching anchovy too close to the islands and promontories where the guano birds live, should also be given the Minister.

The future of conservation in Peru, in fact, rests entirely on enforcement. Unless a force of trained and dedicated wardens can be developed, the mere proclaiming of land is useless. The Cutervo National Park was founded in 1961 but it exists only on paper. If the government will not supply the fund to patrol these parks and bodies of water, the money will have to be raised privately and Mr. Benavides' scheme of soliciting the help of the rich men may be the only alternative. After all, Ducks Unlimited, which did so much to save the wildfowl in our own country, was primarily financed by a few industrialists who liked to shoot.

TWELVE

Chile

IN JULY OF 1833 the *Beagle* dropped anchor in the harbor of Valparaiso and Charles Darwin, having ridden on horseback up to Santiago, said of the climate: "I did not cease from wonder at finding each succeeding day as fine as the foregoing. What a difference does climate make in the enjoyment of life. How opposite are the sensations when viewing black mountains half enveloped in clouds and seeing another range through the light blue haze of a fine day." The climate of the capital of Chile has not changed; one can bask by the pool on the roof of the Hotel Carrera and admire the snow-capped chain of the Andes, for Santiago lies in a valley almost 2,000 feet above the sea. Only Caracas has as sunny and imposing vistas.

Darwin also noted that Chile had an aristocracy of wealth and wrote that "It is said that some few of the great landowners possess ten thousand pounds sterling per annum; an inequality of riches which I believe is not met with in any of the cattle-breeding countries eastward of the Andes." Today, one hundred and thirty some years later, 75 per cent of the land is still owned by 5 per cent of the people. One hacienda near Santiago extends to 618 square miles. But the "humble ones" are leaving the country and crowding into the cities where they live in vast slum belts called "callampas" or mushrooms. The contrast between the houses surrounded by rose gardens and shade trees of the residential districts and the shacks of the slums are beginning to be reflected in the voting. Chile has reduced illiteracy to less than 30 per cent and the great mass of her 7.6 million people want a better life.

Santiago's zoo, attractively located in a series of terraces on the hill of San Cristobal, has a good variety of animals and birds from all over the world. An Alaskan brown bear and an American bison almost rub shoulders—the cages were too small and none too clean—with an African lion and an Indian tiger. But the fauna of Chile are hard to find. There is a pair of strange little animals called Quique O Kiki which look like a miniature, mixed version of badger, mongoose and skunk; a pair of pumas from the Andes; a sleepy sea lion from the Chilean coast; and a small herd of guanacos, or wild llamas. Birds found in Chile are not much better represented. There were a few of the rare James flamingos; a cage of tricahue, a beautiful, bronze-green, almost extinct parrot; and a brooding condor, whose three-foot-square cage barely gave him room to turn around. To have soared over one of the world's great mountain ranges and end up in a chicken coop must be hard.

On one of the highest terraces I found a paddock containing a pair of goats (*Capra hircus*) from the Juan Fernandez Islands, made famous by Daniel Defoe, who based *Robinson Crusoe* on the adventures of a Scot named Alexander Selkirk who was stranded on one of the islands for four years and four months (1704–09). Some 400 miles west of Valparaiso, the islands have a large population of wild goats and 333 inhabitants. A considerable part of the area of the Juan Fernandez Archipelago, 45,750 acres, has been proclaimed a national park and is administered by the navy. The Easter Island National Park of 42,500 acres is also run by the navy.

On the books Chile has nineteen national parks and twenty-six forest reserves but they are not sanctuaries for wildlife or timber in the sense of parks in North America or Europe. In 1935 a law was passed which authorizes the President to establish settlers on 80 per cent of the agricultural land which exists in the parks and forest reserves.

Chile signed, but has not yet ratified, the 1948 Convention on Nature Protection and Wildlife Preservation in the Western Hemisphere. In 1949, however, the government promulgated an official decree creating the National Committee for the Protection of Wildlife which consists of 25 members of various agencies and institutions interested in conservation. Of both these gestures more later.

My first call was on our ambassador Charles W. Cole. He is a wildlife observer and said the Chilean condor is shot and is growing rare. The puma is under heavy pressure from hunters and he visited one hacienda in the south where forty were killed in a single month. He said the Chilean lakes and rivers still offer some fine fishing for both brown and rainbow trout but commercial fishing by the natives, especially where the fish can be sold, is taking a heavy toll. Most rivers are too fast for netting but dynamite and unslaked lime are used in the pools.

There were only a handful of wildlife experts in Santiago and one of these was Alfred W. Johnson, an American who was born in California and has spent fifty years in Chile. He is a co-author of *Birds of Chile,* the only standard work with color prints. During a long lunch he told me about the James flamingo, which my fellow board member, Roger Tory Peterson, asked me to inquire about. Johnson was a member of the party which "rediscovered" the James flamingo in 1957 after it was lost to ornithologists for sixty-eight years. This grayish-white bird with pinkish breast and red legs is evidently not as near to extinction as Dr. Peterson thinks. According to Johnson, there are today about 8,000 birds living in a salt lake just inside the Bolivian border in the high Andes. Egg stealing by the local Indians, which Dr. Peterson said was so prevalent during the time when he visited these birds on the Yale-Life expedition of 1959, still goes on, but on a rational basis. Johnson said the Bolivian government has licensed the neighboring tribe to take the first eggs laid—the females lay only one at a time— and leave the fourth to produce the chick. This must take some careful counting but seems to be working because the James flamingo population is not declining.

There are only six species of flamingos in the world and three of them are in South America. Their diet is made up of "diatoms," a tiny form of animal life which exists in the heavily saline water. The birds build their nests about a kilometer off shore and Johnson said getting to them is tricky as the lake lies over a volcano and there are volcanic vents in the lake bottom into which one can fall. The altitude is 16,000 feet, and despite the hot water from the volcano, the lake freezes nearly every night. The James flamingo was named after Mr. James, a British businessman, who financed the expedition which first discovered the species in 1880.

Alfred Johnson, although primarily an ornithologist, was also interested in other Chilean fauna and said the huemal, the little Chilean deer, was growing scarce in the southern forests. Chile is 2,800 miles long but the railway runs only to Puerto Montt, about half way between Santiago and Punta Arenas, the Chilean town just across the Straits of Magellan from the island of Tierra del Fuego. It is in this wild and sparsely settled area that the deer can still be found. The guanaco, or wild llama, seemed to be holding its own. There were also some wild vicuña on the border of Bolivia.

"The National Committee for the Protection of Wildlife" was completely unknown to Johnson who said he had grave doubts if it still exists. He also did not put any stock in the so-called "national parks" and said they existed only on paper. There were no defined boundaries and no wardens. Johnson believed, however, that a national park could be sold to the President and his ministers. He suggested Campana, a bell-shaped mountain that lies between the cities and has a valuable ecology of wildlife on its various altitude levels. It was owned by a single estate and could probably be purchased cheaply by the government. I told him I would be willing to discuss the proposition with the government.

Julio Philippi Izquierdo, Foreign Minister of Chile, was not only an astute public servant but had a deep concern for the conservation of his country's wildlife and, more important, was prepared to do something about it. He told me during a long and interesting interview in his office at the Ministry that he was planning to proclaim one of the big islands in the south as a sanctuary and see that it was adequately protected. The move could not come at a more crucial time for the future of Chile's rare fauna.

Henry E. Gardiner, the manager for Chile of the Anaconda Copper Company's vast holdings, told me that only once in fifteen years of shooting and angling in Chile had a Carabinero asked him for his license. True, Chile still offers some of the best dove shooting in the world and down in the forest areas of the south there are still plenty of deer, mostly European exotics which have crossed the Andes from Argentina. But Chile's indigenous animals such as the vicuña, chinchilla, and two species of deer are growing more rare every year.

The primary reason Chile's parks were ineffective as sanctuaries was the presence of people, and one of the most important reasons for starting a game reserve on one of the southern islands would be that most of them are completely uninhabited and the nature of the terrain is such that they will never offer much inducement to colonists. Furthermore, fires which annually destroy thousands of acres of valuable timber as well as the habitats of the birds and animals, would be less likely to occur on an uninhabited island. The Minister was most anxious that we should see this wild and beautiful part of his country and wired the Governor of the Province of Magallanes to give us a conducted tour when we arrived in April in Punta Arenas.

My talk with the Minister was warmly applauded by the small band of conservationists who have been working for years to get the various governments to make some concrete efforts in behalf of conservation. Dr. Rodulfo A. Philippi, a cousin of the Minister and a director of the National Museum of Natural History, was delighted when I told him of my conversation at the Foreign Ministry, and said he was prepared to make a vigorous follow-up on this promising lead. He added that time was of the essence as there were only six months remaining until the next elections and no one could tell what a new government might do. Certainly, with all the other problems facing Chile, wildlife was not among the top priorities.

Dr. Philippi received me in the director's office of the museum where there was a bust of the first Rodulfo Philippi, a German who came to Chile in 1851 from Berlin and became the nation's best-known naturalist. Both Foreign Minister Philippi and Dr. Philippi were related to him. The Museum, which was started in 1870, had some unique examples of ancient taxidermy. It was sometimes difficult to ascertain exactly what the original animal was, but with the expert guidance of the director I was given a thorough tour of Chile's indigenous fauna. I was interested to learn that the huemal, the Chilean deer, has two species: one, quite large, which is found high in the Andes between the snow line and the beginning of vegetation, and the other, the small deer of the southern lowland forests. The male huemal of the mountains has antlers while both the male and female of the small species have tiny prongs. Contrary to other information I had received from less informed sources, Dr. Philippi said that the mountain species is rare and should be protected along with the vicuña which is found at the same high altitudes. The little southern deer, however, which is known as the "pudu" is still fairly common in the wild areas of the south. Both the huemal and the condor appear on Chile's coat of arms.

Dr. Philippi confirmed Mr. Johnson's opinion that the James flamingo was in no danger and added that in addition to the 8,000 birds living in Bolivia there were at least 5,000 on the salt lakes of the Chilean Andes and maybe others on the Argentine side.

Probably neither the vicuña nor the mountain huemal would thrive in the low altitude of an island sanctuary and a reserve will eventually have to be established in the northern Andes for them. Dr. Philippi felt that if the island reserve was a success it would be easier to establish other parks elsewhere.

In my talks with the officials of the Ministry of Agriculture—unfortunately the Minister himself was away from Santiago—I found out that a belated effort was being made to tighten enforcement. The fine for failure to purchase a hunting or fishing license was 100 escudas, about $25.00, as against the former nominal penalty of $2.00. The licenses themselves cost about $1.50 each but the revenues from this source and from the fines did not go to the Fish and Game Department; they were merely added to other national income. The fishing season lasts eight months, from September to April, and the hunting season is also generous.

Fernando Mujica, director of the Hunting and Fishing Department of the Ministry, said that he had a staff of 40 inspectors scattered around the country, whose job was to check on game and fish, as well as an appointed non-paid group of 150 honorary wardens who were supposed to aid wildlife enforcement. But only the Carabineros had the power of arrest and since conservation was the least of their many duties, they seldom went out of their way to enforce it. Not long ago a gang of poachers mounted a machine gun in a jeep and slaughtered a whole flock of vicuñas. The news soon filtered down to the capital—the skins were undoubtedly sold through Bolivia—but no arrests had been made even though the poachers were well known in their district. The ramifications of family relationships in all probability protected them. There were rumors of cases where the Carabineros themselves had been involved in illegal taking of game and fish, but by and large the corps had a good reputation and bribery was almost unheard of.

It is not easy to get much of an idea of Chile's wildlife when one is based for a week in Santiago but, thanks to Mr. and Mrs. Alfred Johnson, we spent a day driving to the coast where we visited the private wildfowl refuge of Senor Subercasseux some miles from the port of San Antonio. The road to the sea runs along a fertile valley of vineyards and cattle ranches. There are more mounted men than cars and many of the little compact Chilean horses show a good deal of Arab blood. The "Husaso" or Chilean cowboys ride with long stirrups and longer bits while their spurs glitter in the sunlight.

The reed-bordered pond was full of wildfowl. There were more than a dozen handsome black-necked swans, surrounded by a fleet of coots with butter-yellow bills. Three species of grebe, the great, Roland's and pied-billed, swam happily around with a single pair of chiloe widgeon, the only true ducks we saw. Above the pond soared a score of brown-headed Patagonian gulls, and as we watched them a rare traveler dropped from the sky in their midst and landed near us. It was a yellow-shanks, a bird from Arctic Canada. On a spit of land we saw a spurwing plover and swimming in the reeds a pair of cormorant. On the shore sat five "tique," the little brown carrion hawks.

Mr. Johnson told me that there are today two species of Chilean birds whose future is questionable. The "torcazo," a pigeon, has New-castle disease, the same virus that attacks chickens in the States, and is seriously reduced in numbers. The other endangered bird is the "per-diz," really a tinamou but called perdiz by the Spanish after the red-legged partridge of Spain. The perdiz is nominally protected but is actually shot all the time.

Ambassador Cole told me that while fishing in the high Andes he saw a beautiful little black and white duck which evidently lived on the stream. Mr. Johnson, it developed, knew a lot about it and said it is called a torrent duck, after its habitat on the reaches of fast-flowing rivers, and is found all the way from Tierra del Fuego to the 13,000-foot level of the Andes. The male has a black and white striped head and black and white body, while the female is a rich brown. She lays three to four eggs and her nest is so cleverly hidden that it took the Johnsons twenty-eight years to find one. Only after three hours' work on a hole in a cliff where they thought the bird had disappeared did they find the nest. The torrent ducks feed only on the larvae of the stone fly and allocate their hunting grounds so that only a single pair can be found on a particular reach of a stream.

Another curious and interesting duck is the South American black-headed duck, a parasitic species which lays its eggs in nests of coots, glossy ibises and even perhaps in those of carrion hawks. The question puzzling ornithologists is, who raises the chicks? How would a carrion-eating mother hawk feed the offspring of fish- and vegetable-eating ducks?

A third mission might well be to find out something about the

Meganic plover, which is restricted to the Straits of Magellan even though most of its relatives cover two continents in their migrations. Mr. Johnson and Mr. Goddard classified the species in 1952.

As we progressed farther south we expected to meet some ducks seen on the Eastern shore of Maryland but they would have other names. The widgeon is the pato real; the pintail, the pato jergon; the cinnamon teal, the colorado; the little ruddy duck is the pato rana; while the red shoveler is the pato cuchera.

THIRTEEN

Argentina

WHEN THE *Beagle* sailed into the broad estuary of the Rio de la Plata on the 17th of July, 1832, Buenos Aires was a town of 60,000 and Montevideo a village of 15,000. Game was everywhere and Darwin described a hunt with the gauchos when the bag included ostriches, wolves, deer, foxes, pumas and cavies. Today the capital of Argentina has more than seven million people and there is little game outside the national parks and the great estates. Furthermore, the wildlife of the parks faces a dire threat for there is a group in Congress which would remove the parks from the control of the federal government and leave them to the tender mercies of the various provincial authorities, where local politics would soon make a shambles of the sanctuaries.

The men who run Argentina's 4½ million acres of parks are fighting hard and so far they have been able to stave off the evil day of a show-down vote in the Congress, but the enemies of conservation, under the dreary old dodge of giving the people more fun, control formidable blocks of votes, particularly in Buenos Aires and the other cities. In 1961 a bill providing for the handing over of the parks to the provinces was passed by the Chamber of Deputies but was killed in the Senate.

On the side of conservation are the members of the National Parks Board, a group of eminent citizens which includes representatives of the Ministry of Agriculture, Ministry of Education, scientific organizations and recognized authorities in the field of recreation. Funds are provided by the National Congress. The present budget of 130 million pesos, about $100,000, only allows for 50 wardens and is quite inadequate for the policing of the nation's dozen parks. Any decrease from today's minimum budget would be sure to be reflected in increased poaching.

I was given a thorough briefing on the parks and the wildlife picture in general by Andres R. Biaggini, president of the Board, and the members of his staff. All are very worried about the possibilities of the parks being taken over, and expressed the urgent wish that I take up this matter with the President of Argentina and the Minister of Agriculture. They also felt that the international interest in conservation will be helpful in promoting the local effort. To circulate this view, I gave a press interview about the World Wildlife Fund and the story was carried in the leading papers.

The second largest country in South America, Argentina extends 2,150 miles from the sub-tropics on the Brazilian border to the icy wastes of the "uttermost parts of the earth" at Tierra del Fuego, and includes the habitats of some diverse animals and birds. Largest and most spectacular of these parks is the Nahuel Huapi National Park in the Andes on the Chilean border. In the park's nearly two million acres are found two rare Andean deer, the huemal and the pudu, as well as the guanaco and vicuña. There may also be a few chinchilla. Up on the Brazilian border is the Iguazu National Park in whose 137,500 acres of forests are found jaguar, ocelot, tapir and capybara. At the other extreme of the country is the Tierra del Fuego National Park of 162,000 acres where there are some wild guanaco and numerous birds.

Asked about the position of rare fauna, Senor Biaggini told me that they have only scattered information on the lesser known animals and birds and would be very much interested in the possibility of obtaining the services of a wildlife expert from the United States who would make a survey for them. I said that if after visiting the parks I also felt that such a survey would be worthwhile I would be glad to forward a project along this line to the directors of the Fund for consideration.

If it were not for my old friends in the diplomatic service and particularly the ambassadors, the job of rounding up and interviewing people would have been much harder. Rob McClintock, our Ambassador to Argentina, invited us to stay with him during our week's visit to

Buenos Aires, and he and his charming wife Elena did everything possible to make this time pleasant and profitable.

The man specifically responsible for looking after us in Argentina was my old friend Alexis Wrangel, who was a member of Rob's staff. Alexis is the son of General Wrangel, the famous White Russian leader who battled the Reds to the bitter end. With Alexis I called on Walter Kugler, the Secretary of Agriculture, and had a frank talk about conservation. Although not a sportsman himself, the Secretary was well aware of the importance of conservation and was interested in my mission. He did not think that the group of politicians who wanted to return the parks to the provinces would be successful. He agreed with me that the ratio of wardens to parks was unrealistic but said that it was hard to get money for projects which were not yet self-supporting.

As I talked with more people about conservation in Argentina I found more criticism about the parks. Most of the scientists felt that the introduction of exotics, such as European red deer, was a bad policy, and it was an even worse one to allow hunters to go into the parks and shoot them. They pointed out that the annual invasion of hunters was bound to disturb and frighten the indigenous game. The scientists were also very much against the government policy of allowing timber interests to cut trees in the national parks. The lumberjacks poached and were also none too careful about forest fires. In some places there were people living in the parks.

The hunters who were equally keen about conservation saw it differently as regards the exotics. They said that for all practical purposes there was no fauna in most of the parks and that the huemal and pudu, the two species of Argentine deer, were extremely scarce. Furthermore, the hunters tended to regard the scientists as spoilsports and seldom cooperated with them.

In an effort to get these two groups together I asked that a conference be arranged by Mr. Biaggini, the chairman of the park board, where we could discuss conservation freely and try and arrive at a common approach. Representatives of 32 organizations ranging from the editor of *Pets* to the faculty of natural sciences of the University of Buenos Aires showed up. Among the most interesting was Dr. Edwardo V. Moreno, son of the Father of Argentine Conservation, Dr. Francis P. Moreno, who was a friend of Theodore Roosevelt and is mentioned in the latter's book as being one of the few men he knew who had been attacked without reason by a puma. The conference lasted about two hours and at times the air was thick with accusations and counter-accusations, most of which were translated for my benefit.

I spent a day each at the natural history museum and at the zoo and was sorry to find that both have poor representations of Argentinian fauna. There are no mounted specimens of either the huemal or the pudu deer in the museum and no live ones in the zoo. The museum, however, does have several pudu skins for study. The bird collection at the museum is a good one and Dr. William Partridge, who was recommended to me by Roger Tory Peterson, was most helpful in showing us around and giving us his views. He said both species of ostrich are getting scarce and that the smaller one, Darwin's rhea, is now extinct in many districts of Patagonia. Ostriches are killed for their feathers which are made into dusters to wipe off cars, as in Africa where wildebeests are killed to make fly swatters of their tails.

I had been under the impression that a guanaco is a wild version of the llama. Actually, while closely related, they are two different animals, and in the zoo I saw for the first time vicuñas, llamas, alpacas and guanacos in the same pen. Dr. Enrique Saporit, director of the zoo, said that the guanacos while nominally protected are shot all year round. He also said that the nutria, and the Patagonian hare, a strange creature with short ears and the hind quarters of a little deer, are also being shot out. The Cervo de la Pantano, a small splay-footed deer found in the swamps of the La Plate estuary, is now becoming so hard to find that the zoo has none although the habitat is only a few miles away.

Like the parks, the zoo suffers from an extremely small budget. Revenues from game licenses and fines are not turned in to the game department to foster conservation but simply added to the general income. I found that a hunting license costs less than a dollar and most people don't bother to get it.

The booted and spurred cavalry guard of the Casa Rosada, the Pink Palace where the President of Argentina conducts his nation's interests, snapped to attention and presented drawn swords; a functionary bowed and we were ushered into the main hall and upstairs to where, in a long room, Dr. Arturo Umberto Illia, the country doctor

20. The author with tapirs, Belem, Brazil

21. Harpy eagle, Brazil

24. Guano birds, tightly packed on the beach at Punta Salinas, Peru

25. Guano birds

26. Bachelor seal, Isla de Lobos, Uruguay

27. Upland geese, Falkland Islands

28. Gentoo penguins, Falkland Islands

30. Macaroni penguin and chick; king shag and rock-hopper penguins
     in background

29. Gentoo penguins, Falkland Islands

31. Black-browed albatross and chick, Falkland Islands

32. Sea lions, Falkland Islands

33. Yellow-billed teal, Falkland Islands

34. Pair of Johnny rooks and tussock bird, Falkland Islands

35. The author with a 3½ pound brown trout, Falkland Islands

who was Chief of State, welcomed us cordially. White-haired and dignified, the President had a kindly smile and a flattering manner of giving the man he talked with his complete attention. He had, of course, been briefed on my mission and asked pertinent questions. I told him that I could not report accurately on conservation in his country until I had seen the parks for myself and he made me promise to return to Buenos Aires and inform him personally after my field trips. At the same time he issued an order that every facility be given us.

Following my talk with the President I went to the capitol where I was received by the Speaker of the House and five other deputies and senators. In the last analysis these were the men who could really do something about conservation, as they made the laws and voted the funds. I gave a short summary of what we are trying to do in the Fund and my initial impressions of conservation in their country. I made the following points:

1. No shooting should be allowed in the national parks.
2. No more exotics should be released in them.
3. No lumbering should be allowed in the park forests.
4. People living within the boundaries of the parks should be resettled outside.
5. The present budget of only $100,000 should be increased.
6. Revenues from game licenses and fines should be allocated to the parks for additional wardens, as there are now only 50 guards for 4½ million acres.

Since most of the land of Argentina is privately owned and such game laws as there are stop at the gates to the estancias, the choice of conserving or destroying wildlife is largely a private matter. To see one of the great estates that makes a point of saving the game, Irene and I accepted with pleasure the invitation of Manlio Olivari whose estancia lies about a hundred miles due south of Buenos Aires in the heart of the Pampas.

In my travels only the steppes of the Ukraine in Russia compare with the Pampas. Both are boundless plains of rich earth but the vistas of the steppes are often unbroken by a single tree and the pastures of the Pampas are dotted with groves of eucalyptus and ombues whose leaves glisten in the sunlight and lend welcome shadows to the plains. We passed herds of Herefords, Shorthorns and Aberdeen Angus with occasionally a few sheep. Crops of corn, wheat, and barley alternated with the green pastures. As one drives deeper in the Pampas the houses become fewer and only the gates of the big estates are seen.

"La Vigilancia" runs to some 10,000 acres and used to belong to the famous General Rosas who ruled Argentina with an iron hand for many years until he was deposed in 1852.

Olivari was the most gracious of hosts and no sooner had we said we wanted to ride than four horses were saddled. He kept an Arab stallion to serve his mares and the ranch's herd of 175 head included some very good-looking mounts. My horse, a gray gelding of mature age named Lucero, carried me with verve and comfort. Irene rode a bay named La Silfide, while Alexis Wrangel bestrode a big brown. Our host, dashingly clad in black boots, white polo breeches, and red silk sash around his middle, rode a handsome buckskin. One of the gauchos came with us to open the gates.

Olivari's policy of allowing no shooting paid off in the enjoyment of seeing wildlife. We flushed dozens of perdiz, the large and small game birds that are called partridges but are really tinamous. On the Rio Salado we found flocks of patos which looked like teal, as well as glossy ibis, coots and cormorants. The fishing was evidently good for the birds dived often and always came up with small silver fish. A flock of twenty ostrich was sighted. We passed many groups of chimangos, the little brown hawks who sit in grave conclave all over southern South America. Lapwings rose from the water holes and screamed at our intrusion. In winter there are black-necked swans and geese.

There were many European hare on the estancia which were imported and have now spread all over the Pampas. Other small mammals on the ranch were armadillos and a ferret-like creature that kills the chickens and sucks the eggs. There were many gray foxes and some wildcats.

Olivari had a hard time with poachers. He had threatened to shoot them and has virtually forced the local police to take action. Despite these continuous efforts, a great deal of illegal shooting goes on in the countryside, and as many of the great estancias have absentee landlords it often goes unchecked. The larger species of the perdiz is now virtually extinct in most of Buenos Aires Province. Even egrets and coots, worthless as food, are shot.

FOURTEEN

The Falklands

As THE LITTLE steamer *Darwin* bucked her way through the wind-tossed wastes of the South Atlantic we took to our heaving bunks and read all we could find about the Falkland Islands. Opinions about them differ. When the ship's namesake, Charles Darwin, visited them on the *Beagle* on March 1, 1833, he found them somewhat short of enchanting and wrote laconically: "After the possession of these miserable islands had been contested by France, Spain and England they were left uninhabited. The government of Buenos Aires then sold them to a private individual who likewise used them, as old Spain had done before, for a penal settlement. England then seized them and the Englishman left in charge was murdered. A British officer was then sent, unsupported by any power; and when we arrived, we found him in charge of a population, of which rather more than half were runaway rebels and murderers." The Chief Engineer of the *Darwin* put it more succinctly: "The Falklands," he said, "is a dump." Sir Ernest Shackleton, the polar explorer, said he was colder in Port Stanley, the capital of the islands, than he had been at the South Pole.

But the Islands have their supporters as well as their detractors and a large percentage of these are found among the 2,200 people who make up the population. Known as "kelpers"—to distinguish them from foreigners—the native-born Falklanders, who number about 1,000, have a fierce devotion to their barren islands and certainly do not approve of Darwin's description of them. "An undulating land with a desolate and wretched aspect, which is everywhere covered by a peaty soil and wiry grass of one monotonous brown color."

The Falkland boosters point out with geographic accuracy that the islands occupy the same latitude south that London does north and that the average rainfall is about the same. They seem to forget, however, that London has the advantage of the Gulf Stream and even with it is seldom advertised as a place to go for sunshine. In the matter of wind, however, there is a pretty general agreement. Lying 1,000 miles south of Montevideo, 550 northeast of Cape Horn, and a bare 800 miles north of the Antarctic Circle, the islands get the full fury of some of the worst storms in the world.

Despite these climatic deterrents the Falklands are rich in birdlife and it is for this reason that we left the sunny pampas of Uruguay and boarded the *Darwin* at Montevideo.

A tight little ship of some 1,700 tons, the *Darwin* was built in 1957 by Goole of Lincolnshire expressly for the Montevideo-Falkland run. Her owner is The Falkland Islands Trading Company which occupies about the same position as the Honorable East India Company did in the early years of Britain's relations with the sub-continent. In fact the Falkland Islands Company is relatively more pukka because it owns about half the land and half the 600,000 sheep. The company is a limited one and has its headquarters in London. The managing director's son, a self-assured young man named William H. Young, went out on the *Darwin* with us to take over as resident manager.

We had to be careful not to mention our trip to the Falklands while in Buenos Aires. Argentina claims the islands, which she calls Islas Malvinas, and to make sure everyone gets the point she issues stamps showing them as part of the mother country, and has even appointed a "Governor" who lives in Tierra del Fuego with bags packed ready to dash to Port Stanley the minute the British leave. But the islands have been a Crown Colony since 1832, and, barring a revolution, will probably continue to be one for the foreseeable future. The day is almost here in fact when the Empire on which the Sun Never Set will be entirely reduced to bits of land too small to want to be independent.

The story of the Falklands' only large mammal is a sad one, and particularly so in that there is now nothing the World Wildlife Fund can do about it. The Falkland fox, sometimes wrongly called a wolf, joined the dodo bird when the last one was shot at Shallow Bay, West Falkland, in 1876. There was no reason for this for a gentler member of the canine tribe it would be hard to find. Darwin reported that gauchos killed them by holding out a piece of meat and knifing them while the trusting foxes nibbled the offering. Although the existence of these foxes, which were an entirely separate species from any known on the South American mainland, was known as early as 1690 when Captain Strong reported them, it was not until 1839 that a real effort was made to exterminate them. In that year the New York fur trader, John Jacob Astor, sent a vessel to the islands to buy up all the skins she could and thousands of foxes were slaughtered. The only skins now preserved are four which Captain Fitz Roy of the *Beagle* gave to the British Museum, and from them we know that the Falkland fox stood about fifteen inches and had a soft, thick coat of rich brown fur with a white belly and white lower jaw.

The Falkland fox kept down the upland goose, a voracious grass eater which competes with the sheep for the pasturage, so that with the passing of the native species, foxes were imported from the Argentine. These soon became so prolific that they attacked the lambs and had to be shot. They are now found only on Weddell and Beaver Islands. Hares were introduced on the East Falklands and rabbits on the West.

There are three kinds of penguins; the rock-hopper, jackass or Magellan, and gentoo. The rock-hopper is the commonest, the jackass has the most peculiar cry—like a jackass—and the gentoo is the handsomest. Other birds which nest on the islands are the black-browed albatross, the Dominican gull, dolphin gull, rock shag, several petrels, and the thin-billed prion, an attractive blue-gray bird. Kelp geese and black-necked swan are also found along the shores.

Sea mammals are represented by the southern sea lion which breeds on some of the small islands; the sea elephant, that mammoth member of the tribe; and occasionally the leopard seal, which can gulp a penguin like a peanut. The fur seal, which was exterminated by Mr. Astor and his ilk, is making a comeback.

Some of the smaller whales are still seen near the Falklands but the whaling station which was built on New Island in 1908 was abandoned in 1916 when the whale-catching company moved to New Georgia. I was told on the *Darwin* that the price of whale oil is now so low that only the Japanese and Russians are currently operating in the Antarctic and that the station on New Georgia has been rented to the Japs.

There are two useful books on birds of the southern seas: *Birds of the Ocean* by W. B. Alexander, and *Birds from Britannia*, by H.R.H., the Duke of Edinburgh. I balanced both on my knees as the *Darwin* skidded through the waves and attempted to recognize the birds which wheeled and sailed across our wake. A day out from Montevideo I saw a brace of Pintado petrels or Cape pigeons easily told by their checkered sooty-brown coloring. The next day there were five of these species and the following days, four. The conclusion is, of course, that at least two of these birds accompanied us on the whole thousand mile trip, but Alexander says that this is not necessarily so. He believes the number of birds vary from day to day and even from morning to evening on the same day. On the other hand he cited the claim of a certain Lieutenant Weld of the Royal Navy, who said that a Cape pigeon with a piece of red ribbon around its neck followed a ship he was in for 1,500 miles.

The albatrosses are more difficult to identify but I think that the one I saw was a wandering albatross as it was mainly white with black tips on the wings. It had a wingspan that looked to me to be more than ten feet, and the sailors called it a Molly-hawk. There are thirteen known species, of which nine are found in the southern oceans, and the one most seen by the *Darwin* is the black-browed albatross. Long distance flyers of great endurance, an adult albatross was marked with a ring on the Kergulen Islands in 1914 and was captured three years later near Cape Horn, a distance of 6,000 miles.

I found the Duke's book, (written and illustrated during his world tour in 1956,) valuable for its excellent photographs, most of which he took himself, and for the drawings by Commander A. H. Hughes. The Duke touched at many of the out-of-the-way islands that I have also visited, such as St. Helena and Tristan da Cunha and Ascension. He spent three days on the Falklands where he photographed Magellan penguins, logger ducks and dolphins.

Contrary to all predictions we arrived at Port Stanley on a still and sunny day. True, the air had the nip of Scotland but the skies were blue and the only ripple in the harbor was the wake of a pair of logger ducks who sailed out to meet us.

Our genial host, Sir Edwin Arrowsmith, K.C.M.G., the Governor of the Falklands, met us on the dock and drove us to Government House in what he described as a London taxi, but which is just as comfortable and even a bit more modern looking than the ancient Rolls Royces which serve to convey Her Majesty's governors in many of the island colonies which I have visited.

About half the population of the islands live in Stanley in neat tin-roofed bungalows with gardens in front and little enclosed greenhouses on their front porches. The British could make flowers grow on the moon. There are a good many cars but only twelve miles of roads. They all stop a few miles out in the "camp" as the country is called, and the best way to get around is by jeep or on horseback. Most of the sheep herding is done mounted, and the islands have some useful horses which one sees grazing on the Stanley pastures along with some cows and a sprinkling of sheep. The latter, on which the economy of the islands is entirely based, are found on both of the larger islands, the East and West Falkland, and on many of the 200 smaller islands. It takes about five acres to graze one sheep.

Labor is a problem. The young people of the Islands tend to emigrate and about half the work force has to be recruited from abroad. Many of these men come from Scotland and must sign a five-year contract. Starting wages are about $100 per month. The great trouble is girls. There are few on the sheep stations and most of those in Stanley like their urban life and have no wish to depart for the camp. The population, far from increasing, as it is in almost every country in the world, is actually declining. The 1953 census showed a total of 2,230 persons and the census of 1964 revealed a total of 2,132. But those who stay on in the Islands have long lives. We learned from Dr. Stuart Slessor, when we inspected the hospital with Lady Arrowsmith, that the average life expectancy in the Islands is between 70 and 90 and the babies are so healthy that almost none have to be admitted. There are four doctors on the Islands, giving the population one of the highest ratios of doctors to potential patients in the world.

The Falklanders are all extremely loyal to the Crown and speak of the time when the Duke of Edinburgh was on the Islands as "Duke time." They may well be the last satisfied colony in the British Empire.

The Chief Constable, K. W. Gray, M.C., whom we met on the dock when we arrived, has a force of six constables and doubles in brass as Gaoler, Immigration Officer, and Sanitary Inspector. His primary duties are not onerous, for in 1963 there was only one prisoner who served fourteen days. In case of invasion there is the Falkland Island Defense Force, a voluntary organization armed with rifles. There are also two saluting cannons on the green and a variety of retired muzzle loaders. Out in the camp are some heavier pieces.

Escorted by Bykie Anderson, a Kelper who has never been off the Islands, and mounted on Prudence, a mare of mature age, I rode up onto the common behind Government House and over the hills to the other side of the island where we could see the silver inlet of Port Harriet and beyond it the gray-blue reaches of the South Atlantic. In a valley lay an old Spanish corral seven feet high and built of nicely fitted stones. There were only a few birds about on the moors. We flushed a snipe and once I saw a small thrush. That there used to be much more birdlife is attested by the *Historical Journal* in which Dom Pernety wrote under the date of February 3, 1764: "In the evening our sportsmen returned loaded with geese, bustards, ducks, teals, and a black and white bird (probably king shag). The boat was almost full of game and the night obliged us to throw into the sea a great part of what we had procured in the day."

Bykie told me that he likes penguin eggs and that most people on the Islands eat them. In the old sailing days the crews needed fresh meat and the slaughter of the penguins was terrible. According to M. B. R. Cawkell's book, *The Falkland Islands,* the penguin oil collected by four schooners in 1857 necessitated the killing of half a million rock-hopper penguins. By 1870 the king penguin was virtually exterminated for its rich oil and handsome skin. It returned to the Falklands in 1945 and is now breeding in a place so secret that I cannot reveal it even to the Directors of the World Wildlife Fund.

The favorite game of the Islanders is the upland goose, whose flesh is delicious and whose eggs are equally palatable. So numerous are the upland geese that on some farms they are clubbed to death during the molting season to prevent them from competing with the sheep for the pasturage. There is also a small ruddy-headed goose, called a Brent goose, and very rarely one sees an ashy-headed goose.

The upland geese are too numerous and too tame to afford much sport but the Paraguay snipe is a game bird worth bagging. Some of these fast little snipe live all the time in the wetter parts of the camp and others are migrants from South America. There are also a variety of ducks of which the yellow-billed teal is the most common. The crested duck, known locally as the gray duck, is protected. The Chiloe widgeon, the yellow-billed teal and the rarer cinnamon teal all breed in the Islands. Migrants from Patagonia include the brown pintail and the red shoveler, but according to the experts they are all accidentals. Unfortunately, the ducks are often shot indiscriminately. Luckily both the flesh and the eggs of the kelp goose are inedible so that the beautiful snow-white gander and his multicolored consort are common. Irene and I saw several pairs floating in the bay in front of Government House.

In order to acquaint us with the people on the Islands most interested in conservation, Sir Edwin and Lady Arrowsmith gave a cocktail party for us the day after our arrival. Among these were S. A. Booth, the Senior Assistant Master of the Stanley School, Ian I. Strange, the manager of the Falkland Islands Company Mink Farm, and H. Bennett, Registrar of the Supreme Court.

The next morning Ian Strange took Irene and me to Kidney Island and gave us our first real taste of roughing it in the Falklands. It was a gray day with a thin drizzle falling and a damp chill in the air, but we were dressed for it and set off in the little government launch *Alert* soon after breakfast. Leaving the dock we chugged under the bows of the old three-masted barque *Fennia*, that was so battered when she rounded the Horn in 1927 that her Finnish owners sold her along with her cargo of coal to the Falkland Islands Company. She is now used for wool storage. A fleet of logger ducks escorted us into the outer harbor and under our bows played a pair of Comersons' dolphins, while over our heads wheeled a flight of Dominican gulls. Ian told us that these gulls have multiplied in recent years, undoubtedly due to a steady diet of mutton. Some 200,000 old sheep are killed each year and the carcasses are left for the scavengers. Some farmers, in fact, accuse the Dominican gulls of hastening their meals by attacking the eyes of old and ailing sheep.

Kidney Island, which lies near the mouth of Port William Harbour which is really the outer extension of the bay on which Port Stanley is located, is almost entirely covered with tussock grass, a ten-foot-high mass of vegetation that furnishes excellent fodder for cattle and horses but makes the job of progressing through it somewhat tougher than the jungles of Indochina. Furthermore, the grass was soaking wet and by the time we had battled it for an hour we were too. But there were rewards. We found and photographed Magellan penguins, called jackass penguins because of their peculiar bray. I did not believe a bird could sound so much like a four-footed animal until we stepped on one in the tussock grass and picked it up. Throwing back its sleek head and opening its long bill, the penguin gave birth to a set of ass noises that was wonderful to hear. When we set him down he followed us down to the shore and sat on a rock ten feet away while I photographed him.

Another tame bird is the tussock bird, a little wrenlike creature which shows no fear of man and took crumbs from me. In the kelp beds near the shore four sea lions reared their heads and played a game of tag in the shallows. Ian said that there are also occasional fur seal and sea elephants on the Island. On a set of jagged rocks off the beach I photographed a pair of kelp geese who posed with the greatest composure next to a black-browed albatross, and for contrast a tiny Cobb's wren. A night heron, looking glum, sat off by himself. Around the bend we found a colony of king shags, or cormorants, and near them a giant petrel and a covey of little South American terns, which I understand breed locally.

There are no sheep on the island and the Governor told me that legislation is now pending to set it aside as a permanent nature reserve. Ian has a list of another eleven islands that are deserted and would make good refuges. He is particularly interested in Beauchêne Island, which lies 150 miles southeast of Port Stanley and is a breeding ground of the rare caracara, a small falcon or carrion hawk which is known locally as Johnny rook. Ian believes it also breeds in Tierra del Fuego and asked me to see what I could find out about this when we went there on our return from the Falklands. The caracara has no natural enemies but is shot, as all hawks or flesh-eaters are shot, by the sheep herders.

On the way home we ran close to the cliffs on the eastern side of Kidney and saw masses of gentoo and rock-hopper penguins sitting on the almost vertical rock face. Pink-breasted gulls hovered over the boat and a giant petrel came sailing down the wind. We were back by three for a hot bath and a stiff shot of Sir Edwin's good whiskey.

Sir Edwin was personally interested in conservation and told me that in addition to Kidney Island he was going to recommend that some of the Jasons, a remote group of islands on the extreme western rim of the Falkland archipelago, and some others be proclaimed as sanctuaries. All such recommendations, of course, must be approved by the Legislative Council.

The weather during our stay in Stanley was good to us and on a cloudless afternoon we drove with L. Picton, the Superintendent of Public Works, to the lighthouse on Cape Pembroke. Built in 1853 the old light is the southernmost beacon in the world and is still guiding ships into Port Stanley. The keeper, Fred Bernsten, told me that his 105,000-candlepower light can be seen 16½ miles at sea. But there are few ships stopping at the Falklands these days. Once a month the *Darwin* makes her run to Montevideo and an occasional whaler touches in on her way back or to the grounds off South Georgia, but the log, which has been kept every day since 1913, shows a steady decline of traffic. John Pearce, the keeper the year before the First World War, noted on September 14 that he had sighted a square rigger beating in to Port William Harbor. There is a notation that His Majesty's ships put into Port Stanley after the battle of the Falklands. If the British had not won this engagement the Islands would certainly have been invaded and occupied. On the way back from Cape Pembroke we stopped at York Bay and photographed several hundred gentoo penguins on the white sands. Irene, by moving quietly, got within a few feet of them.

The little De Haviland Beaver turned her nose into the wind, roared across the choppy waters of Stanley Harbor, and sailed up into an azure sky. As guests of Sir Edwin, Irene and I were bound for the Island of West Falkland, a day's sea voyage from Port Stanley on East Falkland, but only an hour by plane. Below us lay a vast and empty land dotted with black lakes and laced with winding streams. The pilot, Jim Kerr, pointed out stone runs, strange rivers of rock left by the ice age, and the Governor beamed down on the Malo and San Carlos rivers, two of his favorite trout streams. We flew over small flocks of sheep and once I saw scrawny cattle, probably descendants of the wild ones whose ancestors Darwin chased more than a hundred years ago. But not until we sighted the tiny settlement of Port San Carlos did we see human habitation.

We left the mail at the lonely jetty of Port San Carlos and, taking off again, flew across Falkland South which divides the two main islands of the archipelago. To the west dark clouds banked in the sky and we were reminded that if the weather closed in we might be marooned on West Falkland. Not that we minded. Brown trout were introduced into the rivers of the Islands years ago and fish of more than ten pounds have since been taken.

Our first stop was at Port Howard where Douglas Pole-Evans, the manager of the Waldron Company's 142,000-acre farm, had invited us to spend the weekend and fish the Warrah River. After a sumptuous lunch of mutton and vegetables—the sheep stations raise virtually everything they eat—Pole-Evans took us for a conducted tour of the settlement, the administrative and processing center for the company's 38,000 sheep. He showed us the shearing room where a good man can strip a sheep with electric clippers in less than two minutes and clip the wool from more than 300 sheep in a nine-hour day. Grades range from superfine to extra coarse and with today's prices at 83 pence per pound for the best at the London auction, wool is very profitable. It takes 36 men to handle the flocks and about half of them are on five-year contracts from Great Britain while the rest are locals. With their sheep dogs and eight horses each, the shepherds live a lonely life out on the range, coming into the main camp only occasionally but being supplied weekly with food and any mail which comes in on the *Darwin's* monthly trip from Montevideo.

Pole-Evans is a good conservationist and told me that aside from the upland geese, which have to be kept down because they compete actively with the sheep for the pasture—ten geese eat as much as one sheep—he sees that the game laws are observed. No seal are shot on the stations along coast lines but in the past there have been rumors that illegal sealers from the mainland have been operating in Falkland waters. He did not think that any of the local wildfowl are in any danger of extermination.

Not only the upland geese menace the sheep. When a ewe is "cast," that is, falls on her back and is unable, due to her flat coat of wool, to get back on her feet again, turkey buzzards and skuas, known as sea hens, peck out her eyes and often her tongue as well. Some of the gulls are also carnivorous. The fire bird makes its nest by burrowing in the ground and one can have a nasty tumble if a horse breaks through into one of these carefully concealed holes. A bounty is paid on the upland geese—30 shillings for every 100 bills.

From Port Howard we flew in the same little Beaver—there are only two operating in the Islands and their importance cannot be exaggerated—to the village of Goose Green on the east coast of East Falkland where we were met by Mr. and Mrs. Thomas Gilruth, whose guests we were to be for another three days of viewing the Islands' wildlife and perchance taking a few of its trout. Gilruth, who was retiring in May after 32 years in the Falklands, was the Camp Manager of the Falkland Islands Company, the combine which owns half the land, half the sheep, and produces about half of the five million pounds of wool shipped yearly from the Colony. Next to Barton, the Resident Manager of the Company at Stanley, Gilruth holds the most important commercial job on the Falklands. He is also a fisherman, a hunter and a conservationist. In front of his house I saw a flock of upland geese which well knew they were browsing on the only safe lawn in the Islands.

"Darwin," the hundred-year-old house where the Camp Managers live, has a setting of austere beauty. In front lies Choiseul Sound, and beyond, the green rolling hills of Lafonia. Behind the house the pastures are ringed by old turf walls that were built more than a century ago by the gauchos to keep in the cattle. Cattle are still raised on the Company's stations but only for internal consumption, and to eat down the rougher parts of the pasture which the sheep won't tackle.

The plain where the river winds its way was full of upland geese, many so tame that I passed within ten feet of them while wading the stream. I flushed two covies of snipe which appeared to be somewhat smaller than the European species. Tiny yellow and green siskins darted over the tussocks and once, floating in a big pool, I saw a pair of teal.

The weather, which had been exceptionally good to us during our first thirteen days in the Falklands (there were only three completely rainy days), suddenly turned stormy. The barometer fell to the lowest point recorded in ten years and a howling gale blew up from the Antarctic. Flying home—a mere half hour's hop in the Beaver—was out of the question and the Governor called Stanley to arrange for a relay of Land Rovers to take us across the sixty miles of peat bog and pasture that separated Tom Gilruth's house from the capital.

Known as the Government Track, the only trail across East Falkland Island leads a haphazard and winding course. Often we had to cross rivers by fords and the Governor, looking like Moses leading the children of Israel across the Red Sea, would stalk ahead in his high fishing boots and sound the depths. A wilder country would be hard to imagine. A stinging rain, driven by the cold winds, whipped across the hills and even the sheep huddled in the valleys with their backs to the

storm. We passed the lonely sheep stations where the shepherds sometimes do not see another human being for weeks on end and, if not
married, have for company only their border collies and the thick-
coated horses.

We started at nine and by noon had reached the hospitable settlement of Fitz Roy where Jim Clements and his wife and daughter gave
us double whiskeys and a hearty mutton lunch. At seven that night,
after a journey of ten hours, we reached Stanley. We had averaged six
miles an hour.

If the proposed bill is passed by the next session of the Legislative
Council, and there seems no reason to doubt it will be, the Falkland
Islands will have powers to set aside seventeen small islands and some
20,000 acres of land on the two main islands as wildlife refuges where
no stock can be grazed and no shooting will be allowed. This is a personal achievement for Sir Edwin, who conceived the idea of the sanctuaries and persuaded the Council members to go along with the plan.
Most of the islands are Crown land but several of them are privately
held and have been offered as refuges by their owners. The importance
of this conservation program cannot be underestimated, for, even in
such remote islands as the Falklands, species such as the Falkland fox
have already been exterminated and others such as the caracara, or
Johnny rook, have been drastically reduced in number and may well
be facing extinction. Happily, Carcass Island, a breeding place of the
caracara, is one of the islands which will be declared a reserve.

At the same session another bill revising the game laws will also be
submitted. Under it there will be a closed season between August 1
and the last day of the following February, when it will be illegal to
kill or take any wild animal or bird. Exceptions will be some common
species which attack the sheep, and game birds which may only be
shot between March 1 and July 31.

While considerable work has been done on the birds by visitors
such as Dr. Pettingill of Cornell, and local ornithologists, almost no
specialized attention has been given to the mammals such as the sea
lions, sea elephants, and fur seals. Ian Strange, with whom we visited
Kidney Island, plans to make such a study and I recommended to the
World Wildlife Fund that we make him a modest grant to extend the
scope of this important work.

I had hoped to gather some useful information on the blue whale
but found that since Britain had laid up her pelagic fleet little can be
learned in the Falklands. South Georgia and the South Sandwich Is-

lands are both dependencies of the Falklands and come under the authority of the Governor. Farther south he wears another hat as High Commissioner of the British Antarctic Territory, a vast wedge-shaped slice of the south polar regions that includes the South Orkney Islands, the Palmer Peninsula (Graham Land) and tens of thousands of additional square miles on the frozen continent. Argentina and Chile claim some of this Eskimo pie and the United States takes the position that no nation has the exclusive right to sovereignty there. I am pleased to report that, by agreement among all nations with bases in the Antarctic, it has been proposed to ban all hunting except for survival purposes.

Equal in size to all of Europe and most of Australia, the Antarctic is one of the world's great continents. Only one per cent is exposed rock while the rest is covered with a cap of snow and ice which in places is two miles deep. The total area is more than five million square miles, and the air which moves over this vast ice-box has a direct effect on the weather of the southern half of the world. It is because of this that some nations now have scientific stations there. Who would grudge these lonely watchers the odd penguin or seal?

Until recently only a handful of men had braved the central plateau which lies from six to nine thousand feet above sea level. In 1908 Shackleton manhandled his sledges up the Beardmore Glacier and traveled across the polar plateau to within 98 miles of the South Pole. To save the lives of his party he had to turn back with the goal a few days away. Three years later Amundsen and Scott set out from different bases, using dog teams, and both reached the Pole, Amundsen on December 14, 1911, and Scott on January 18, 1912.

Sir Edwin has visited the British bases in the Antarctic and has taken some excellent photographs of the seals, penguins and whales that inhabit this frozen world, but his interest in conservation began many years ago when he was a district officer in Bechuanaland in South Africa and used to make long journeys across the Kalahari Desert. Later he served as the principal officer on the island of Dominica and became an authority on the birds there. He was Governor of the Falklands from 1957 to 1964 and traveled to virtually every inhabited and many uninhabited islands of the 202 which make up the Falkland archipelago.

On the theory that the more people know about the aims of the World Wildlife Fund the better, I made an effort in all of the countries which we visited in South America to see that the local press carried a full account of my mission. The Falklands, however, only has a monthly news sheet which is devoted mostly to social and sporting events. News and announcements are read over the Government radio and most of the Colony's homes keep their receivers tuned in permanently to the Stanley announcer. Everything goes in the clear and once we listened to a shepherd out in the West, telling the doctor in Stanley what was wrong with him. He said, "If I were a mutton the hurt would be where the thick chops start."

W. H. Thompson, the Colonial Secretary, used the radio as an educational medium and in this capacity interviewed me on conservation. The fifteen-minute exchange was taped and broadcast on the popular Monday evening program. It is safe to say that virtually all of the Islanders old enough to understand listened to it.

In conclusion I would like to sum up my impressions of the Falkland Island fauna and what I think should be done about preserving it. Sixty species of birds breed there and sixteen of these are endemic, while many others rely on the islands as their main breeding areas. Three species of mammals breed in the Falklands, of which the fur seal is an endemic species.

Three species of birds, in my opinion, should be given special protection. The most important of these is the previously cited Johnny rook or caracara, which Ian Strange feels has declined to a point where it is endangered. The king penguin, as I noted earlier, is just beginning to come back and the site of the breeding ground must be kept a secret. The relatively rare macaroni penguin is very similar to the common rock-hopper and often breeds in the same rookery, where its eggs are subject to collecting along with those of the rock-hopper.

Very little data is available on the mammals. The last census of sea lions was made by Hamilton in 1934 and since then the numbers of pups born on the islands are said to have decreased drastically. The last elephant seal count was made in 1953 by Laws, who estimated that no more than 1,000 pups were born each year. The fur seal position is even more obscure and some of the data, such as the report made of seal on Beauchêne Island in 1962 by H.M.S. Protector, is incorrect. An up-to-date survey is badly needed.

Lastly, aside from the importance of giving sanctuary to rare species, is the value of preserving some of the unspoiled islands as reference areas where ecological studies can be made.

FIFTEEN

Uruguay: The Purple Land

IN A MECHANIZED world there are few nations left where the horse is still man's primary means of locomotion. But livestock cannot be herded by motorbikes and since Uruguay's economy rests solidly on her 24 million sheep and 8 million cattle, the gaucho and his trusty steed are in no danger of joining the dodo in oblivion. Montevideo is certainly full of motor cars, but outside the capital and the larger towns traffic is more apt to be four-footed than wheeled, and it is a pleasant sight to see these horsemen, often accompanied by their dogs, move the herds along the broad borders of the roads. Stocky of build and wearing a broad-brimmed black hat, an embroidered jacket, baggy trousers and short leather boots, the gaucho makes a fine figure of a man, and is well aware of his importance to the nation and himself.

W. H. Hudson called Uruguay "The Purple Land" and in the evening, when the shadows are starting to stalk across the green pastures, the land does take on a mauve tint. Much of Uruguay is flat and treeless, like the pampas of Argentina, but some of the coastal lands are rolling and there are scattered plantations of eucalyptus and palmetto palms. These low hills and valleys absorb some color as the day dies. In contrast, the whitewashed haciendas stand out sharply against the vistas and seem to bid the stranger to ride up to them on the avenue made by the trees.

Accompanied by Dr. Alfredo Delgado, Director of the Department of Wildlife and Fisheries in the Ministry of Agriculture, my wife

159

and I and Larry Garges, commercial attache of our embassy, paid a two-day visit to the Santa Teresa National Park, 300 kilometers from Montevideo and situated only a few miles from the Brazilian border.

Santa Teresa takes its name from an old Portuguese Fortalezia and because even ancient forts are the special interest of the military, the whole 8,000-acre reserve is run by the Ministry of Defense, although the bastions themselves take in only about an acre. This odd state of affairs has resulted in some overtones that have little to do with conservation of wildlife. There is a spacious retreat where the President of the Republic (and ostensibly tired generals) can rest in comfort, an aviary which contains an assortment of non-indigenous birds, and a greenhouse full of odd and interesting plants. There are also various goldfish pools, walks and other ornaments which attempt to improve on nature but do not always succeed. Other sections of the park are utilized for pasture for government-owned cattle.

The only area we saw which could really be called a wildlife refuge was a small pond known as Laguna Pena. I noted a drowsy nutria among the lily pads, placidly munching aquatic plants, while on the bank his big cousin, the carpencita or capybara, enjoyed a leisurely meal of sedge grass. The nutria is a rodent which looks like a cross between a rabbit and a rat and has a fur which is highly valued for wearing apparel. Some 60,000 nutria go into coats yearly but their numbers do not seem to diminish. They are nominally protected during the breeding season. The carpencita is also a rodent, but from its appearance the rat seems to have achieved the impossible and cohabited with a hippopotamus. Weighing upward of a hundred pounds, the carpencita has little defense and is now rare in Uruguay. The guazubira, Uruguay's only indigenous deer, was not represented.

Birdlife on the pond was somewhat richer. A pair of black-headed swans admired their graceful profiles in the dark water; a snowy egret stood like an ivory statue on the bank, and a flock of coots and grebes made sport in the shallows. The only remarkable bird was a southern-crested screamer which did not shatter the silence by so much as a sigh. Walking back to the cars, I saw a red oven bird, whose curious nest does look like a primitive clay oven.

The birds of the countries which bound on the great River of Silver were the delight of W. H. Hudson, and his *Birds of La Plata*, although written nearly a hundred years ago, is still the standard work for the area. He lived in the Argentine until his early thirties and knew the rich birdlife of the pampas as few others did. In his autobiographical book, *Far Away and Long Ago,* he says that his interest in ornithology began when he was a small boy and carried on all through his life. He had a fine ability to make his readers see the birds he wrote about and refused to let his accounts become technical. He hated collections of dead specimens and the sight of a caged bird made him angry. He was not, however, against wildfowl shooting and in his youth supplied his father with a daily bag of partridges and ducks.

When we visited an estancia bordering Laguna Negro, a fifty-square-mile lake that adjoins the Santa Teresa Park and should in fact be part of it, we saw a great many birds that Hudson so well described. Most common was the spurwinged lapwing, known locally as the teru-teru from its insistent cry. Largest and handsomest of the plovers, the lapwing is a brave bird and will aggressively defend its nest against all comers. Despite being shot at and plundered of its eggs, the lapwing refuses to leave its territory and I have seen it rise in noisy protest when a dog approaches. The birds pair for life and while the female is sitting on the eggs, the male keeps guard and warns her with a low cry if danger approaches.

A fairly rare bird in Uruguay is the crested cardinal, which we saw early in the morning when its beautiful coloring was particularly effective. The upper plumage is gray and the under surfaces white, but the bird's chief glory is its vivid scarlet crest. Another bird with a fiery head which we sighted was a federal, a bird that is popular with people as a cage-bird, and we saw on a fencepost a tiny prisoner in a wicker cage. I wish I had released it. A third redhead seen on the trip was the churrinche, the scarlet tyrant. The old birds migrate from the Plata area when they feel the heat of January but the young do not leave until the end of April. Hudson said this was one of the strangest facts he had ever encountered in the migration of birds.

The only game birds we saw were an occasional "perdiz," the Spanish for a tinamou; a small flock of blue-winged teal; and a single large duck which looked like a mallard. Although we heard no shots, we did see several men on the roads with guns and there is no doubt that a good deal of illegal hunting goes on. There are only fourteen game wardens for Uruguay's 72,172 square miles and they have no power of arrest. Enforcement is left up to the local police who may or may not be effective. There are game laws and shooting licenses can be purchased for a very nominal price; but the set-up is hardly one to discourage poaching.

During an excellent dinner of clams and steak and a good local white wine, I had a long talk with Dr. Delgado and the two officers from the Department of Agriculture who accompanied him. Garges, a keen amateur ornithologist, translated. I told them that for all practical purposes, Uruguay has no game park in the sense of a sanctuary for wildlife. Santa Teresa is really nothing more than a tourist attraction. If, however, the management of the park should be transferred from the Ministry of Defense to the Ministry of Agriculture, a good deal might be done with the area. First, the cattle operations should be eliminated; second, the area of sanctuary could be greatly increased by incorporating Lake Negro, and lastly, the park needs adequate policing. As civil servants, my companions did not wish to take a position but all appeared pleased when I said that these would be my recommendations to the President of the Republic.

But I did not have a rounded picture of the conservation situation in Uruguay until I called on Dr. Diego Legrand, the benign botanist who is Director of the Natural History Museum in Montevideo. The facts are grim. Already the puma, the fox (warrah), the swamp deer (tatu), and the anteater (coendu) have ceased to exist within the borders of the nation. True, these are also indigenous to neighboring countries so that they are not extinct species, but as far as Uruguay goes they are finished. Others, like the lutra or otter, the procion or raccoon, and the capybara are rare, especially in the north where the people eat them.

The survival pattern among the birds is not so alarming. The only endangered species, according to the museum ornithologists, are the perdiz grande, or big partridge, and the cisne cuello negro, or blackheaded swan. Both species are nominally protected under the existing laws but both are also shot by almost everyone whenever possible. Virtually all the land in Uruguay is privately owned and since the tiny staff of wardens have no authority to enter, what is or is not shot is entirely a matter of conscience, or more probably knowledge, of the estancia owner.

I was fascinated to learn that one of the ornithologists at the museum is writing a paper on the black-headed duck, the shiftless parasitic species which lays its eggs in other birds' nests and leaves to the luckless foster parents the rearing of its young. My friend Johnson in Santiago has already written a piece on these irresponsible wildfowl, and I told Eugenio Gerzenstein to get in touch with him.

Why most Uruguayans (and for that matter most Latin Americans) shoot everything that moves would make an interesting sociological study. About half the nation is of Spanish descent and half of Italian. Both races come from ancient lands where the fauna, except on the private estates of the nobility, has long ago been exterminated and perhaps because of this they equate democracy with the right to kill at will. In Mexico many years ago I asked a man why he had killed a hawk—in this case a perfectly innocent hawk which fed largely on mice—and he replied that he shot it because it was flying away.

His Excellency Luis Giannattasio, President of the Republica Oriental del Uruguay, took time out from a busy schedule to listen to my story and give his attention to the cause of conservation in his country. An able and industrious politician of about fifty, the President graduated from the Massachusetts Institute of Technology in America and speaks good English. My appointment with him was made by the British Ambassador, Sir Norman Brain, but our ambassador, Wymerley Coerr, accompanied me on my call.

I told the President of my pleasant trip to the Santa Teresa National Park and my admiration for the Uruguayan countryside. I also told him that it seemed somewhat illogical for the Ministry of Defense to be in charge of the Park while the Ministry of Livestock and Agriculture, which is responsible for wildfowl, has no say in the administration of it. I added that the park had no facilities for waterfowl and by the addition to it of Laguna Negra, the 50-square-mile lake which it borders, this would be accomplished. Furthermore, since the lake is government property anyway, it would cost nothing to proclaim it as part of the sanctuary.

The President's reaction to this was predictably neutral but I felt that he understood and was sympathetic to the problem. He was also not unaware of the importance of the good publicity which results from conservation measures. I stressed the point that other South American nations are now making efforts to save their fauna and cited the cases of Peru and Chile which are seriously considering the founding of large-scale sanctuaries.

The next day I called on Wilson Ferra Aldunate, the Minister of Agriculture, and repeated my opinions. A strikingly handsome man of middle age, the Minister proved an engaging gentleman. Before going into politics he was a big land owner and is thoroughly familiar with his country's animals and birds. He told me that he did not think that the Ministry of Defense would mind giving up control over the Santa Teresa Park providing they kept the old fort, rest house, aviary, and other buildings. He also said that he did not think there would be any problem about annexing the lake. I felt pleased as I left him. It looked as if Uruguay at long last would have a park in the sense of a sanctuary. Of course promises are one thing and accomplishment another, but our embassy people—I was accompanied on this call by the Agricultural Attaché, Burckhardt—felt that if the Minister gave his word he would follow through.

The educating of young people in the importance of conservation is a vital part of any over-all effort to save wildlife, and through the kindness of the British Ambassador, who gave a luncheon for me so that I might meet many of those most concerned with the subject, I had a good talk with Dr. Fernando Oliu, Under Secretary of the Ministry of Public Instruction. He told me that an effort is being made in the primary schools to teach the children about wildlife but that a good deal more could be done. The teachers themselves need training in this and a course in it should become part of the curricula of the teachers' college.

At the Faculty of Humanities of the University of Montevideo, I had a conference with a group of scientists keenly interested in conservation. Among these were Dr. Legrand, Dr. Parietti of the Zoological Gardens, and Mr. Klappenbach, head of the Wildlife Department of the Museum of Natural History. These men felt that the government should consult them more on wildlife matters and should provide more facilities for field study. They were pleased to hear of my talks with the President and the Minister of Agriculture, and only mildly cynical as to the results. Like all scientists they are wary of politicians and because of this are seldom able to put over their points. I found on this South American trip that the best way for conservationists to put pressure on the politicos is to form a committee which contains sportsmen as well as scientists and includes at least one well-known businessman who can mix easily with the ministers and get across ideas to them. Such a man in Uruguay might well be Diego de Arteaga, a well-known cattle breeder and big game hunter.

There is one mammal in Uruguay, however, that is adequately

protected. This is the seal and to see them at home we drove down to Punta del Este, where we boarded a government launch, and after an hour chugging across the blue waters of the bay, arrived at Isla de Lobos, the Island of the Seals. Two species, the fur seal and the sea lion or hair seal, have their habitat on the island and when they are all there every square foot of the ten-acre island, except the area occupied by the lighthouse, is crowded by 110,000 seals. Isaias Jimenez, the director of SOYP, the government agency which controls the sealing operations, came with us and told us about his charges. There are roughly 80,000 fur seals and 30,000 sea lions and approximately 28 per cent of the total are killed for their hides yearly. He showed us the corral where the seals are driven to be slaughtered in July and August. The fur seal skins are worth $30.00 after processing in Uruguay, and $70.00 in the U.S.A. On a girl's back the price may be as high as $125 and it takes six skins to make a coat. The Fouke Company of St. Louis takes the entire kill.

But these sordid statistics seemed far from the thoughts of the happy company we saw sunning themselves on the rocks and leaping off into the breakers. The impression was one of a highly urbanized community with some members sleeping, some loving, some tending the children, and some just playing. The females have only one pup a year. Most of the young ones were able to scamper around but some were still nursing and a young mother whose baby was hidden in a cave refused to leave it when I advanced to photograph her. Only the male seals are slaughtered as one bull reigns over a numerous harem. I found a blind female, lying in a cleft of the rocks, which I was able to approach up wind without frightening her. I learned that the cataracts often disappear after a time.

On a secluded bay of the island there is a colony of very old bulls who have been driven from their harems by younger and lustier males and have gathered together like members of some ancient and highly respectable club to pass their last days in comfort and quiet.

1965

East Asia and the Pacific

SIXTEEN

Pomarea of Tahiti

IT TOOK HIS Majesty's ship *Bounty* ten months to sail to Tahiti in 1788 and by the time Captain Bligh and his weary crew raised the purple headlands of these distant islands they had built up some great expectations. Today the journey is easier, and the expectations are lesser. Eight hours after one leaves Los Angeles airport, the islands appear as green dots in a dark blue sea, and a few minutes later a rather plump, fully clothed native girl hangs a wreath of tiare blossoms around one's neck, and one has arrived at Papeete, chief city of Tahiti. Tahiti is the chief island of the French colonial possessions known as the Society Islands.

Bligh's mission was to collect breadfruit plants for the West Indian islands and our mission, in addition to selling the government on conservation, was to find out what we could about *Pomarea nigra nigra*, who is not a coal black princess, but the Tahitian flycatcher, a small and extremely rare bird. The American Museum's Whitney Expedition of 1931 collected a specimen and Dr. Dillon Ripley saw several when he climbed high into the upper Papenoo Valley in 1937, but since then reports of *Pomarea* had been ominously lacking.

We arrived, however, on a Sunday morning when scientific exploration, and in fact any variety of effort, is frowned on. Papeeteans take Sunday so literally that little moves besides the wind in the palms. In the late afternoon when the rains, which fall almost every day in January and February, had abated and the land was glistening green we drove to the house of William Robinson, an American writer, sailor and amateur ornithologist, who makes his home in Tahiti when he is not sailing the seven seas on his brigantine, *Varua*. Asked about *Pomarea* he said he did not recognize the description but that it is quite possible that the bird still survives in the remote valleys of the interior. So difficult of access are some of these hidden valleys that he doubts if more than a dozen people now living in Tahiti have ever been to them or even heard of them. For the birds whose habitat does not protect them from man, the future is grim. Robinson knew of no laws protecting any birds and no sanctuaries where they cannot be hunted. Boys with .22 rifles pick off the few remaining doves and herons and even the sea birds are not safe.

In fact, the only two birds I saw on our first long drive along the coast were chicken hawks and myna birds, both of which are not indigenous to the islands. The saga of how these exotics got to Tahiti is a study in futility. Vanilla does not pollinate itself, so wasps were introduced to do the job. The wasps did not comply and spent their time stinging people. Myna birds from India were then brought in to devour the wasps but soon developed a liking for less prickly bugs. Finally hawks were imported to keep down the myna birds, but the hawks found chickens easier to kill and better to eat. Result is that there are now lots of wasps, lots of myna birds, lots of hawks, and almost no indigenous birds. Rats and cats brought in by the early whalers undoubtedly started the decline of the island's bird population but the few survivors have certainly been helped toward the status of the dodo by these voracious newcomers.

According to Greenway's excellent book *Extinct and Vanishing Birds of the World*, six of the twelve species of land birds confined to the Society Islands are now extinct and five other species have disappeared from the island of Tahiti, but are still found in ever declining numbers on the smaller islands. A sea bird (*Pterodroma rostrata rostrata*), which is a species of petrel, has also vanished from Tahiti but is still found on the outer islands. This petrel may have been the bird that James Morrison, the boatswain of the *Bounty*, mentioned in his diary as being good to eat, although no sea birds I have ever heard of are. Among the vanished species are a parrot, a shorebird, a starling, a pigeon, and a ground dove.

On Monday, the first working day of our Polynesian exposure, we made our way to the Musée de Papeete where we were received by Henri Jequier, the Director of the Museum, and Miss Aurora Natua, the principal curator whose gamut runs from anthropology to ornithology. A large woman with kindly eyes, Miss Natua was immediately interested in my mission and promised to help. She said there is no law protecting the surviving birds of Tahiti and was enthusiastic about my suggestion that I try to get the Governor and the Assembly to pass such an ordinance. She felt that a general law protecting all birds, both land and sea, would be well worthwhile even though she doubted if there would be any money for enforcement. Agreeing with Robinson, she said there is a good chance that *Pomarea nigra nigra* still survives in the remote upland valleys. She personally has never seen this little black flycatcher nor is there one in the small collection of bird skins on display in the museum.

Robinson dined with us and promised to introduce me to an influential member of the Assembly who could follow through if I succeeded in interesting the Governor. Robinson has been a moving figure in the campaign to eradicate filariasis, the mosquito-born disease of the lymph glands which, if unchecked, eventually produces elephantiasis for which there is no known cure. Thirty years ago a third of the population was infected with filariasis and even today there are occasional new cases, but degeneration to elephantiasis is now rare. Venereal disease is still rampant but can, of course, be cured if treated early enough.

Of the many books about Gauguin, the only one he wrote himself is *Noa Noa*, the record of his first trip to the islands in 1891. He was disappointed by the inroads of European culture in Papeete, but in the remote village where he settled he found the natives unspoiled and wrote this about them: "On Tahiti the breezes from the forest and sea strengthen the lungs, they broaden the shoulders and the hips. Neither men nor women are sheltered from the rays of the sun nor the pebbles of the seashore. Together they engage in the same tasks with the same activity or the same indolence. There is something virile in the women and something feminine in the men. This similarity of the sexes make their relations easier. Their continual state of nakedness has kept their minds free from the dangerous pre-occupation with the 'mystery' and from the excessive stress which among civilized people is laid upon the 'happy accident' and the clandestine and sadistic love. It has given their manners a natural innocence, a perfect purity. Man and woman are comrades, dwelling together almost without cease, in pain and in pleasure, and even the very idea of vice is unknown to them."

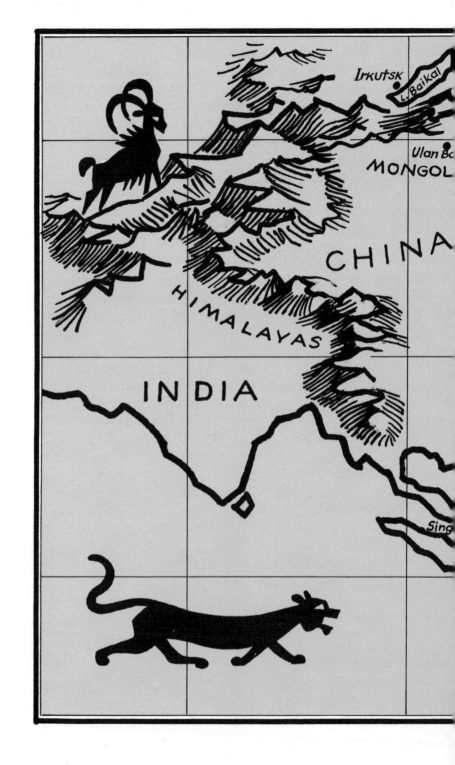

So far, any connection between Gauguin and *Pomarea nigra nigra* has been somewhat obscure, but if my readers will bear with me a bit longer they will be surprised at the link between this unhappy man of rare talent and the little bird of great rarity.

We left early one morning to take the coastal road around the island, see as many birds as we could, and make local inquiries about the elusive flycatcher. Aurora Natua was our pilot and a better and more knowledgeable one it would be impossible to find. She knew the names of every flower and tree, every bird and every important historical site. Again and again she would ask the driver to stop and present Irene with tiare blossoms, butterfly lilies, the flowers of the orchid tree, and huge aromatic gardenias. She named the trees; ironwood with feathery foliage, mangoes, wild hibiscus, Tahiti chestnut, breadfruit, guava, kopak, and wild banana (whose fruit cannot be eaten without cooking). She pointed out the sites where Robert Louis Stevenson in 1888 worked on *The Master of Ballantrae;* where Zane Grey lived when he caught his record black marlin; and where Rupert Brooke stayed when he wrote his sketches of the islands.

We saw our first bird when we crossed the Vaitepiha River, some seventy kilometers from Papéete. Aurora called to the driver to stop and pointed out Te 'uriri or the wandering tatler, which migrates all the way from Alaska. Next we saw the reef heron stalking sedately along the black sands which ring the north coast of the island. Swooping among the coconut palms which leaned over the boiling surf, we saw white-capped noddys and white terns. Twice in the lovely botanical garden in the District of Papeari, some 55 kilometers from Papeete, I heard the low crooning call of a dove and Aurora told me it was Te 'u'upa, the Tahiti fruit dove.

Near the garden is the new Gauguin Museum, a complex of interestingly designed buildings which house reproductions of many of the artist's best known paintings as well as exhibits of contemporary life at the time Gauguin lived in Tahiti. There were old photographs of Tahitian girls swathed in missionary Mother Hubbards, undoubtedly the master's models before he undraped them. I learned that there are some 640 extant paintings by Gauguin of which about two-thirds are in private collections. Somerset Maugham bought two panels for about $20 and today they are worth tens of thousands.

We had finished our tour of the Museum when the Director asked me what was my main reason for being in Tahiti. I told him about

Pomarea and he said that one of his caretakers was a great hunter who knew a good deal about the island's forests and the birds which are found there. Aurora then asked the man if he had ever seen Te 'otatre, the native name for the Tahitian flycatcher. He replied immediately that he did and proceeded to describe it in detail. Aurora, controlling her excitement admirably, asked him many more questions and told me she was completely satisfied that the man, Ernest Ferrand, has seen at least four Tahitian flycatchers in a valley belonging to a Miss Charlotte Goltz in the district of Papeari. His last hunting trip had been in December and he found them about four kilometers from the coast where the valley starts to rise into the mountains.

Despite the good news that the Tahitian flycatcher still survives on the island and may in fact be more numerous than anyone suspected, there is no question about the across-the-board decline of all of the indigenous species of French Polynesia and particularly of those species found on the more heavily populated islands of Tahiti, Moorea, and Bora Bora.

Nothing can be done about the natural enemies but something can be done about protecting the birds from man and with this idea in view, I enlisted the support of such interested people as Aurora Natua, William A. Robinson, Henri Jequier, Director of the Papeete Museum; and others. It was the consensus of our opinion that a law protecting the birds of the islands against shooting, trapping, and raiding of the nests for eggs, should be introduced into the Assembly.

Through George Gray, the newly appointed consul of the United States to French Polynesia, I met Jacques Drollet, leader of the Opposition in the Assembly, who is very much interested in conservation and told me that he is a member of a commission which has been appointed to recommend regulations governing fishing and shooting. He agreed with me that clauses dealing with the protection of birds other than ducks and wild chickens, the only two species that are considered game, should be included in the commission's report, and said that he would support such clauses in the debate. He thought it was most important that I discuss conservation with the Governor who was new to the job and whose stand on many matters was not yet known.

The flag at the Palace was at half mast when I paid my call on His Excellency, Jean Sicurani, the Governor of French Polynesia. But aside from this tribute to Sir Winston Churchill, there was nothing quiet about the office of France's chief administrator in the South Seas. Secretaries shuttled in and out, visitors were lined up and the old building which has housed French governors for the past century had taken on the hum of progress. Ushered into his air-conditioned office by an aide, I was immediately impressed by the charm and ability of the new Governor. A handsome fit-looking man of about fifty, Sicurani had arrived in Papeete only a week before and was already making his mark in the colony.

We talked first of places of mutual interest such as Cambodia and French Africa and I learned that the Governor has had a long career in the French Colonial Service. Finally arriving at the purpose of my mission, I was pleased to see that he immediately saw the point in preserving the rare birds of Polynesia. I had had prepared a list of these for him with the French, English, Tahitian and scientific names of each of twenty-nine sea and land birds that Miss Natua felt should have immediate legal protection. He asked me to write him an official letter stating my views and promised to see that it would be studied in the near future with a view to the fastest possible action by the Assembly.

The Governor's mandate, which covers an area larger than all Europe, in addition to the Society Islands, includes the Gambiers, the Marquesas, the Tubuais, and the Tuamotus. Some of these are tiny coral atolls and some are forest-covered volcanic islands, but almost without exception they fail to pay their way. There is no income tax in French Polynesia and the only local revenue is derived from export and import duties. These seldom balance the budget and France pays the difference. Curiously there is no tipping on Tahiti, making the island and Russia the only places I know that deplore this bothersome practice.

The editor of *La Dépêche*, the daily newspaper, became interested in my mission and wrote a good piece about it which appeared in the same edition as an article about an American psychologist from Texas, who was studying the local lepers. The point seemed to be that at least a few Americans come to Tahiti for serious reasons.

Flying from Tahiti we passed over many of the 322 coral-ringed islands of the Fiji Archipelago. Only 106 of these are inhabited by the half million islanders and most of these live on Viti Levu, where the capital of Suva is located. Sugar is the principal export and Indian laborers brought in to work the cane have multiplied to a point where they outnumber the native Fijians. Like the Tamils in Ceylon, and the Chinese in Tahiti, this creates frictions—of which more later.

The Red Book, that bible of endangered species issued by the savants of the International Union for the Conservation of Nature, in Motges, Switzerland, lists only one bird for the Fiji Islands and the data on this rarity is scanty. Macgillivray's petrel is a large, distinctive and uniformly sooty-black petrel, known only from a single specimen captured on Ngau, a little island in the Koro Sea some fifty miles west of Viti Levu. The only scientific reference given is W. B. Alexander whose *Birds of the Ocean*, 1954, I have found to be most useful for all of the seven seas, and even this basic source of sea bird lore is completely stymied on this elusive petrel.

Our primary purpose in coming to Fiji, however, was to see what was being done about protecting all rare birds and from my inquiries in America, it appeared that many of the indigenous species are today suffering, as they are on all the Pacific islands, from the deadly grip of rats, cats, and man.

After reporting to Tom Hill, the genial and helpful American Consul, my first call was on Bruce Palmer, the Curator of the Fiji Museum. An anthropologist who also takes a keen interest in birds and animals, Palmer said he had heard about the World Wildlife Fund and was pleased that I had come to Fiji. As I suspected, the indigenous birds were under pressure but, unlike Tahiti, laws have already been passed giving them a certain amount of protection, and a reserve is in the process of being set up at Taveuni Island. Palmer had also been instrumental in appointing Robin Mercer, a local banker, as "honorary ornithologist" of the Fiji Islands, a post that might well be imitated in other countries where there are no government funds available to employ one.

Mercer, an attractive young New Zealander, is engaged in writing a handbook on the birds of the Fiji Islands which his wife is illustrating. The only other artist to paint Fijian birds is another New Zealander, William Belcher, who did a series of watercolors in 1926. An effort is being made by the museum to get these pictures reproduced.

Mercer told me that there is a law on the books which nominally protects all the birds not classified as game birds, but since few of the islanders know the difference between the various species, the prohibition really extends only to those birds whose size does not make them a tempting target for the hunters. The hunting season opens May 1 and lasts one month. The daily bag is five pigeons but few observe this limit.

In addition to rats, which arrived without invitation, there are mongooses, brought in to control the rats which severely damaged the coconut and the sugar cane plants. Like so many efforts to upset the balance of nature, the mongoose importation turned out to be as great a pest as the rats, for the mongoose also likes eggs. Another reason given for the mongoose invasion was to keep down the Pacific boas, a large constrictor with a liking for chickens. There is one poisonous snake on the islands, a species of banded crate, but it is very rare. The only indigenous four-legged creature is the banded tree iguana, called "vokai" in Fijian.

I am pleased to report that the bird banding program of the Smithsonian Institution had received a good deal of publicity in the Fijis. Hill had handbills of the program mimeographed and sent to all of the inhabited islands. Anyone seeing a bird with a colored plastic leg streamer is requested to report to the Smithsonian the name or a description of the bird wearing it, color of the streamer, date seen, and latitude and longitude of location of sighting.

The program, aimed at increasing our knowledge about the migrations of sea birds, has already led to the capture and banding of more than 300,000 birds of 28 different species in the Central Pacific. Most of the birds are marked with aluminum leg bands but 60,000 now have the streamers. Some of these birds such as the wandering tatler, which I saw in Tahiti, have flown all the way from Alaska and there are others which are known to make 10,000 mile migrations but whose regular travels are unknown or poorly understood.

Sad to say, no one I talked with in Suva had ever heard of either the Macgillivray's petrel or Pritchard's megapode, a much more common sea bird that according to the Red Book is still found on the Island of Niuafobu in the Tonga group, half-way between Samoa and Fiji. This does not mean that both of these birds do not survive; it merely means that no one with any ornithological knowledge has bothered to seek them out. The last important scientific expedition to Fiji and, in fact, to most of the islands of Polynesia and Melanesia was the American Museum Whitney Expedition in 1931. The only specimens in the Papeete Museum are those donated by the Expedition and if Mercer had not collected and prepared some specimens himself, the gifts of the Expedition would today be the only ones on display in the Suva Museum.

As I mentioned above, more than half of the population of the Fiji Islands is Indian and even though some of them laugh at the idea, there are evidently a good many who believe in aphrodisiacs of a non-scientific variety. For some reason which I have not been able to fathom, the blood of the pigeons found on the islands is thought to have such power.

In an era when colonialism is blamed for all the ills of mankind and when the merest hint of gratitude toward the former colonial powers is considered black heresy in the enlightened halls of the United Nations, it was a relief to find a set of remote islands whose inhabitants are proud to be a British Crown Colony. Almost unique among the lands on which the sun never used to set, the Fiji Islands enjoy, and have made it quite clear that they wish to continue to enjoy good government, a stable administration, and British standards of justice.

There is, of course, a good deal of internal self-government with the population's three main groups—Fijians, Indians and whites—each represented by six members in the Legislative Council. The fact that 220,000 of the total population is Indian, 185,000 Fijian, and only about 20,000 European and part European, had not—so far at least—led to agitation for a more representative division of the chamber.

Brought in as indentured labor to work on the sugar plantations, the Indians, as they have in so many lands, have multiplied exceedingly and usually bemoaned their lack of political power in their adopted homes. There is, in fact, a small party of Indians in Fiji which has protested in the United Nations but the great majority of the Indians have nothing to do with it. The Indian members of the Legislative Council, and those enjoying other positions of trust in the government, are as loyal subjects of the Queen as one can find anywhere.

Fulcrum of this delicate balance wheel which is British rule in Fiji is the Governor, Sir Derek Jakeway, a career Colonial Office officer who has had a good deal of experience in the remnants of empire. He served in British Guiana, Sarawak, and Nigeria and did so well that he was awarded one of the very few posts left where Her Majesty's governor can still call the tune. We lunched with Sir Derek and Lady Jakeway in the old rambling Government House which is a copy of the

Museum in Colombo, Ceylon, and talked of mutual friends as well as birds and what to do about them.

Although not a bird-watching expert, Sir Derek was interested in conservation and assured me that he was anxious to cooperate in any efforts to improve the protection of the island's rare species. He showed me the Ordinance of December, 1923, which lists some sixty land and sea birds as fully protected. The list, however, gives only the English names which means little to the Fijians and also the scientific names, making it sometimes a matter of dispute as to which bird is actually which. I suggested that as a basic start to a new look at bird conservation on the islands, a survey be conducted to see what birds are becoming rare. And as a prelude to this survey, I suggested that some government help be given to publishing Robin Mercer's illustrated booklet on the less common indigenous species.

Later in the day, I made some suggestions to The Honorable H. M. Scott, Speaker of the Legislative Council, who is a successful Suva lawyer and amateur ornithologist. With the Speaker and the Governor sympathetic, the chances of action were greatly improved, but there was still the matter of funds and no one was optimistic about much monetary support.

Grand old man of conservation at Suva is certainly Herbert W. Simmonds, who at 88, was still hale and hearty and walked up his garden lawn faster than I could follow him. Formerly the government entomologist, Dr. Simmonds eradicated the house flies on Viti Levu by introducing a beetle from Zanzibar which laid its eggs in the house flies' larvae. He also introduced a toad which ate up the slugs which used to make walking on the island's lawns a squashy business. Dr. Simmonds has been the moving figure on the formation of the 9,000 acre sanctuary on Taveuni Island.

Not only the birds are growing rare in Fiji. Gwen Watkins, the Acting Conservator of Forests, told me that the cowry tree, one of the finest hardwoods on the islands, was being cut to a point where its very existence may be threatened. 80% of the land belongs to the Fijians and by law must remain so but there is no law against timber cutting even when it threatens the industry. Watkins would like to see tree sanctuaries dotting the timber reserves and from a bird standpoint also such untouched habitats would have value.

The strong British feeling that the land belongs to the indigenous population has also led to the support of the Fijian hereditary chiefs who exercise a good deal of unofficial power in their own bailiwicks. Two of the six Fijian members in the Legislative Council are elected by the Council of Chiefs.

Fiji's economy rests on two basic crops; sugar, which last year brought in $32 million and copra, which was worth about $5 million. The increasing population, however, makes the opening of new land and the improvements in agricultural techniques imperative.

Tourism is becoming a major industry but a good deal remained to be done to make Suva and other towns of the main island competitive with Hawaii and even with Tahiti. There is, however, a great inducement in the duty-free status of imports to the islands. Some articles made in Japan, such as good cameras, are actually cheaper in Suva than in Tokyo because of the lower overhead.

Big game fishing is becoming an attraction and a 268 pound black marlin was recently boated off Korolevu Beach. A world record wahu of 118½ pounds was also caught and a 170 pound sailfish. Inland fishing is for the rugged few but Mercer told me that he takes his light canoe far up the rivers and has had great sport with the native perch which sometimes run up to three pounds. As in Tahiti, rainbow trout were tried in the mountains but the water was too warm for them and today there are none left.

Not every phase of life in the Fiji Islands is bright. There is no across-the-board compulsory education and while most children get a little if their parents can afford it, the standards are low and the gap between the well-educated and the average person is wide. Segregation, practiced not by the government but by the Indians and the Fijians themselves, makes the problem more difficult. By and large, the Indians get better education because they want it more. The Fijians have their own schools but secure in the knowledge that they own the land, they do not study hard. There are almost no Fijian doctors or lawyers.

There is very little intermarriage between the Indians and the Fijians and little between the half-whites and the darker races. But relations between the whites and the other races are good. There is none of the sullen animosity that one sees so often now in the emerging nations of Africa. The Fijians smile broadly at everyone and it is possible to have close and lasting friends among them.

Like all British colonies, Fiji has its clubs but the old days when most were pure white have passed and even the arch-conservative Fiji

Club has a few Fijian members. Other clubs, such as the Yacht Club, are fully integrated with Indian as well as Fijian members. Some of the resentment against the Indians felt by the British is based on the fact that very few of them volunteered to fight in the last war while the Fijians did so in droves. One received the Victoria Cross.

On my last day in Suva, I addressed the Rotary Club on the subject of conservation and gave an interview to the Fiji Times.

SEVENTEEN

Way Down Under

THE BIG TEAL jet had barely lumbered off the Nandi runway on Viti Levu in the Fiji Islands and pointed her long nose toward New Zealand, 2,000 watery miles to the south, when I heard above the whine of the turbines the measured and sonorous tones of a gentleman of distinction in the seat behind us. The Right Honorable Keith Holyoake, Prime Minister of Her Majesty's loyal Dominion of New Zealand, was traveling with us and proved an engaging companion. I have met a good many men in public life and not all of them seem to be able to talk to one person at a time. Mr. Holyoake has this gift combined with considerable personal charm. Just now he needs both attributes for his majority in Parliament is so slim that he must sometimes have to concentrate on a few recalcitrant members to keep his government. I told him of our interest in his country's wildlife and he seemed genuinely pleased that we should come so far to try to help the birds and animals.

At the Auckland airport we were met by our Consul General, David Wilson, and driven through miles of Victorian architecture to the White Heron, the city's only modern hotel, where our ambassador to New Zealand and Mrs. Herbert B. Powell, were also staying. A former four-star general with a long and distinguished record in the armed forces—he was sitting on the Yalu when he heard on the commercial radio that the Chinese had started to invade Korea—Powell likes New Zealand and is doing a good job here. The Powells and a few of their friends have bought an island off Georgia where they have established a refuge for birds and game. Both are keen conservationists and were very pleased to learn about our mission. The support of our ambassadors has always been an important factor in my wildlife efforts and when I find one who takes a personal interest as well, it makes the job even pleasanter.

February is midsummer in New Zealand with the rose gardens blooming and the lawns a velvet green. The houses are mostly ugly, but shaded and decorated by verdure, they look better than they would otherwise. With E. G. Turbott, Director of the Auckland Institute and Museum, we drove through the sunny streets to that impressive building which houses both New Zealand's war memorials and the museum. The latter is a private institution and not a civic enterprise.

Turbott, a lean, quiet-voiced New Zealander, with a vast amount of knowledge about the natural and man-made history of his country, gave us a vivid picture of both in his two-hour conducted tour of the museum. Starting with the twelve-foot tall Moa, the fabulous flightless giant of a bird that existed in great numbers before the landing of the island's first human inhabitants, the Maoris from Polynesia at the beginning of the Christian era, he explained that even though the largest species of the Moas were certainly exterminated before the arrival of the whites in 1840 a smaller variety certainly existed until very recent times. He cited the tale of an old New Zealand woman, now in her nineties, who claims to have seen a two-foot Moa when a child.

In these times, said Turbott, there are three indigenous birds whose future is uncertain. First the kakako, a big greenish-yellow bird, which looks like a cross between a canary and an owl, and is found only in very limited numbers in the Milford Sound area on South Island. One clue to its presence is its deep booming cry but unfortunately it does not give tongue often. The bird is nocturnal and lives in a burrow. Even though it still has wings, it has lost its breastbone, that keel indispensable to flight. Second, the native thrush, also found in the rugged heavily-forested areas of South Island; and third, the famed takahe or notornis, found in the inaccessible Fiord land at the tip of South Island. He feels, however, that the notornis has received so much attention and so much effort had and was being expended toward its well-being that its survival is not as uncertain as that of the other two species. He added that until an adequate survey is made, no one will really know how many of these rare birds are actually there. It is possible that there may be other pockets of these birds, or even other birds, in the remote vastness of South Island. (New Zealand's geography consists of two islands, North with an area of 44,280 square miles, and South with an area of 58,093. Both are about 500 miles long and the total area about equals that of Great Britain.)

That New Zealand can still hide an unknown bird of fair size is strikingly proved by the story of the takahe. Although the Maoris mentioned the moho or takahe, there were no bones available and the legend was shelved until 1847 when Walter Mantell obtained, near Waingongoro in North Island, a skull and some bones. The bird had a breastbone and could not, therefore, be a kiwi or a moa. Professor Richard Owen named the bird *Notornis mantelli.*

In 1849, sealers on Resolution Island off South Island found a large bird in the jaws of their dog. With a dark blue and violet head and neck, olive spotted with brighter green on the wings, metallic blue on the primaries and purplish blue on the chest and sides, and brilliant red beak and legs and feet, the bird was a wonder to behold. By great luck, Walter Mantell bought the skin. In 1850, a Maori caught a second takahe on Secretary Island. Then the bird vanished for 30 years, but in December, 1879, one was caught by a dog in the Province of Otago, sent to London and auctioned. The Germans outbid the British Museum by 5 pounds and got it. Next clue was an incomplete skeleton in 1884 and a complete one in 1892 near Lake Te Anau. The country was marshy and covered with thick brush. A dog got another in 1898. In 1948, Dr. Geoffrey Orbell of Invercargill trapped two takahe near a small lake 3,000 feet in the mountains near Lake Te Anau.

Today there are said to be between 50 and 100 of these rare birds in two colonies in neighboring valleys. They produce only one young a year. The Wildlife Division of the Department of Internal Affairs maintains a center at Mount Bruce, about 120 miles from Wellington, where two pair of notornis are in captivity. The center also has the only kakako in captivity. Four other kakakos from whom it was hoped to breed died.

Far less rare but just as strange are the kiwis, a large flightless bird with hair-like dark brown plumage, and nostrils at the end of its beak. A relative of the extinct moas, the kiwi is the only bird that finds its food by scent, and since its habits are nocturnal, it is hard to find. Only one genus of kiwi, *Apteryx,* survives today, but its common name has passed into trade and now graces shoe polish and other important appurtenances of our culture.

Before the advent of the Maoris the only land mammals on the islands were two species of bat. The Maoris introduced the dog and the Polynesian rat and the white man later introduced just about everything else. Some of these exotics, like the myna bird from India, multiplied mightily but probably have not affected the indigenous species. There is no question, however, as to the evil effect of European rats, cats, and dogs. The flightless birds could not escape.

In most cities we made it a point to visit first the museum and second the zoo, thereby getting a broad picture of what was and what is. Although New Zealand's indigenous wildlife is light on mammals, it has some ancient forms of reptiles which still survive, and at the Auckland Zoological Park we were given a close look at the tuatara, a "living fossil," which resembles a small scale Komodo dragon. Unlike the lizards, it has ribs over the abdomen. The "third eye," for which the tuatara is famous, cannot be seen, but if the skin between the eyes is cut open and peeled back, one finds the primitive vestige of a pair of eyes which are reputed to be able to distinguish light from dark.

Thanks to Derek Wood, the Superintendent, we were able to handle a kiwi, a much heavier bird than I expected, and were shown the tiny residual wing which is only an inch long and has no feathers. The kiwi's only defense is its strong legs and claws with which it can inflict a dangerous wound.

Wood appeared nervous and told us that he was expecting a giraffe colt. He said we could not witness the birth but could see it on a closed TV circuit which had been set up by the local station. Repairing to the elephant house we watched the mother giraffe, surrounded by a number of cameramen, veterinaries, and other assorted helpers, prepare to have her baby. I could not help thinking she might have had it with more ease if left alone.

The search for rare animals attracts some famous men and not the least of these is Sir Edmund Hillary, the conqueror of Mt. Everest. We spent several hours with Sir Edmund and his wife at the home of her family, Mr. and Mrs. James Rose. Sir Edmund led the expedition whose report effectually scotched the existence of the yeti or Abominable Snow Man, at least in the area around Everest where it was reported to have been seen by many generations of monks and village people. The so-called yeti skins preserved in the monasteries proved to be skillfully molded pieces of wild goat skin. Sir Edmund believes that the legend is kept alive by views of the Himalayan blue bear, a rare carnivore which often stands on its hind legs when startled.

Sir Edmund also headed an expedition to Tasmania to look for the "Tasmanian Tiger," the wolf-like marsupial which although very rare is believed still to exist in the densely wooded portions of the island. The expedition made a long trek on foot across the area where the tiger is said to linger but saw neither tigers nor tracks of them. The tiger used to be plentiful in Tasmania and from 1877 to 1909 a bounty of 10 shillings a head was paid for them. In 1930, they were accorded partial protection and in 1936 full protection. Recently, there have been reports of sightings and it is on account of these that we decided to go to Tasmania during our visit to Australia. Sir Edmund kindly showed me his file on the tigers and gave me the names of a number of key men to look up in Hobart.

His Excellency Sir Bernard Fergusson, Governor General of New Zealand, virtually inherited his post. Both grandfathers and his father represented the Crown in the Dominion and there seems to be no reason to believe that Sir Bernard's seven-year-old son will not some day be stationed in Government House. A tanned, energetic man in his mid-fifties who keeps his monocle well screwed into his eye and talks fast and well, Sir Bernard obviously likes his job with the New Zealanders. During the war he served with distinction in Burma and was afterwards at allied headquarters in Paris. Well-informed on the wildlife situation, he said he would do everything possible to make my trip profitable and started by phoning the various ministers in Wellington whose departments concern the various phases of conservation.

This was a lengthy chore as no less than eight government departments figure in one way or another in the wildlife picture. From all I was able to gather, each was doing a good job but there could not help but be costly duplication as well as opportunities for a conflict of authority. Recognizing this multiple overlapping, the Government of New Zealand, in 1962, appointed the State Services Commission with a view to proposing an independent branch which would take over and run all phases of conservation. The Commission reported and recommended that such a branch be set up but had not yet stipulated under which department it would be placed. Logically it should probably be under Internal Affairs in the same relationship which our Fish and

Wildlife Service has to the Department of the Interior. Internal Affairs already had a Wildlife Branch which could easily be expanded to take over the allied functions of the other departments. For instance, the Department of Lands was responsible for the national parks, flora and fauna reserves and scenic reserves; Forestry was responsible for all forests and control of all noxious animals except rabbit control and introduction of exotic animals; Science and Industrial Research took care of animal ecology and mammal research; Maori Affairs was charged with private fisheries; and the Department of Works had soil conservation and river control. I had a good talk with Kenneth Miers, Deputy Controller of the Wildlife Branch.

In addition to the State Services Commission, a private organization known as the Nature Conservation Council was also established in 1962 to make suggestions on improving conservation in the Dominion. Chairman of this Council was Dr. R. A. Falla, Director of the Dominion Museum.

Dr. Falla was away during my visit, but I did spend a very profitable and interesting time with John Seabrook, an Auckland businessman, yachtman and conservationist, who, along with Dr. Falla and Professor J. T. Salmon of Victoria University, Wellington, was one of the leading figures in the conception of the Nature Conservation Council. As of then, no definite decisions had been reached and since the Council's proposals will eventually have to be presented to Parliament it may be some time before action can be expected, but with men like Seabrook on the conservationist firing line, I have no doubts as to the ultimate victory.

The possibilities of a New Zealand Appeal, along the lines of the British and American Wildlife Appeals, did not look very favorable. This is not because the New Zealanders do not care as much as anyone else about wildlife, but because there is no policy of tax deductions for this kind of giving. Several leading lawyers, with whom I discussed the matter, told me that it would take a revision of the existing tax schedules to exempt gifts of this kind. Some people I talked with also felt that since New Zealand has no indigenous animals and only three indigenous birds which are in danger of extinction, it might be hard to raise worthwhile sums for conservation efforts which would only supplement the measures now being taken by the government. As in all welfare states, the New Zealanders rely heavily on their government to handle most problems affecting the national good. There are few really rich people who can afford to make large gifts to conservation and the middle class, which makes up most of the country, pays so much out for cradle to grave benefits that it has little left for charity, especially when not deductible for taxes.

But perhaps even more important than either of these reasons was the growing uneasiness in the Dominion over developments in South East Asia. Commodore R. E. Roe, the Royal Naval officer commanding the New Zealand navy, felt strongly that New Zealand must spend a great deal more money on her defenses. He told me that he believed that New Zealand and Australia are entering a dangerous era where their way of life may well be tested. Red China has 800 million people against 2½ million in New Zealand and 12 million in Australia.

The two events which shook the average New Zealander most deeply were the fall of Singapore and the British effort to get into the Common Market. The Battle of the Coral Sea saved them from the Japanese and De Gaulle's refusal to let England into the continental trade club saved their preferential ties to the old country, but the New Zealanders have neither forgiven nor forgotten although they are very loyal to the Queen.

They do not, in fact, return to England very often and as the years go on they have become more and more insular. There is a built-in dislike of serving. The taxi driver opens the front door and expects his paying guests to sit next to him and discuss any subject he chooses to bring up. Some of these vehicular debates are amusing and some are dull. The service in the restaurants is slow until near closing time when plates are whipped away in seconds after they appear. Evidently the help want their meals at a civilized hour so the guests are forced to eat between 6:00 and 7:30.

Overbalancing these shortcomings, however, was a genuinely friendly people who in our case went way out of their way to make our visit pleasant. The New Zealander is shy and it is harder for him to appear outgoing than it is for an American or an Australian, but everyone we met made us feel that they were glad to have us and sincerely wanted us to like them and their country. We were very lucky in having a series of introductions from my brother-in-law, Colonel James Pettus, who served in our Embassy in Wellington and made many good friends there.

New Zealand's internal airways system is excellent and the hostesses, as if realizing the shortcomings of most other serving people, do their best to be charming and helpful. In the lounge of the Auckland airport, a pretty young thing came up to us with a map and pointed out the places we would fly over en route to Wellington.

In the absence of the ambassador, we were welcomed by Ruth Bacon, the deputy chief of mission and one of the very few women who have top jobs in our Foreign Service. Without help from the Embassy, we would never have gotten into a hotel. Despite an avowed desire for tourists, New Zealand has a totally inadequate number of rooms available and the greatest pressure must be applied to get one. At both Auckland and Wellington we stayed at the White Heron Lodge, modern, motel-like caravanserais with much better food and service than the average hotel.

The Dominion Museum in Wellington has a good bird collection and we were given a tour of it by Count Frederick Charles Kinsky, a Czech, who escaped some years ago from his communist-run country and has now become a New Zealander. He showed us that New Zealand has a greater number of shags than any other country, there being some 15 species and sub-species. The islands are rich in four species of penguins among which I recognized my friend the rock-hopper which also visits the Falklands. There are two mounted specimens of the rare notornis, and a reconstruction of the giant moa. Dr. Falla is said to believe that smaller moas may still survive in the rugged country of South Island.

Among the huge specimens of mounted trout and sea fish I saw a ribbon fish, whose flat, silver, twenty-foot body has a band of bright scarlet running along the dorsal fin from the head to the tail. If ever there was a basis for a sea serpent it is certainly the ribbon fish.

The typhoon which we just escaped in Fiji finally caught up with us on Lake Okataina in central New Zealand, and whipped to white-capped waves the normally serene blue surface of that lovely body of water. A pair of black shags tore past and vanished in a solid wall of rainwater; the pongas, graceful tree ferns, bent almost double in the gale, and our sturdy boat bobbed like an animated cork. Then, as suddenly as it had come, the squall passed and a brilliant rainbow arched over the lake.

Okataina is only one of a complex of lakes that make up the Rotorua-Taupo districts of North Island. In addition to fishing, for which the lakes are justly famous, the Chinese pheasants, California quail, and bobwhite abound in the area. Like the fish, however, all of these are exotics and one must look hard to find the indigenous species. In the swamps between Lake Rotorua and Rotoiti, our host, Stanley James Blackmore, pointed out a bittern, a handsome shy bird whose feathers were in such demand for fishing flies that the government has had to put them on the protected list. Another reasonably rare bird he showed us was the tui, a beautiful little bird with blue plumage and a silver gray neck. Under its throat hang two little tufts of curled white feathers which look like earrings. The Otaheitian word for such female decorations is tui. William Wales, Captain Cook's astronomer, described it in 1773 and remarked on the sweetness of its song.

According to the Maori legends it was a bird, the long-tailed cuckoo, which led those intrepid explorers to New Zealand. A chief named Kupe, after arriving at Tonga from Tahiti, saw in a dream a land lying far to the southwest and was led to it by a koekoea, the Maori name for this migrant which yearly flies across thousands of miles of ocean between the Melanesian Islands and New Zealand.

Rotorua is the center of Maori culture and there are more Maoris living here than any other district in New Zealand. One can still see handsome Maori carvings but sad to say, some of the work sold as Maori is done in Germany and not by German Maoris either. Through Peter McIntyre, one of New Zealand's best artists, we met Michael Pomare, the son of the late Sir Maui Pomare, one of the leading chiefs of the Maori. Pomare is the name of the last kings of Tahiti and the New Zealand branch of the family claims to have inherited the name from the Maoris who came in one of the six great canoes which arrived in New Zealand in 1350. Young Pomare and his mother have a house full of fascinating objects and pictures. They showed me the feathers of the huia, the sacred bird whose tail plumage could only be worn by the paramount chiefs, and many of the green stone axes and tools with which the ancient Maoris carved their woodwork. I was a bit startled when he produced two long bones which I thought must be walrus ivory. A closer inspection revealed them to be human femurs, a grim reminder that the Maoris not so many decades ago liked an occasional meal of "long pig."

Young Pomare is a farmer who knows a good deal about the history of his people and sketched for me the really vast extent of Polynesia in the world's greatest ocean. One apex of this triangle, whose sides are four thousand miles long, is Hawaii and the others are Easter

Island and New Zealand. He did not point it out, but a full century after the last of the great Polynesian migrations in the 14th century, the peoples of Europe were afraid to venture beyond the Pillars of Hercules into the Atlantic. The Polynesians were in fact the greatest explorers in history and, in many instances, they followed the path of the birds. Their voyages from Tahiti to the Hawaiian Islands were on the same course as that flown by the Pacific golden plover and the rare bristle-thighed curlew.

Not all the anthropologists believe that New Zealand was first populated by migrants from Tahiti. Some think that the earliest migrations came from the Solomon Islands and that these followed the migrations of the shining cuckoo which flies from the Solomons to New Zealand for its breeding season. Another bird which the Maoris may have used is the bar-tailed godwit, which flies from Siberia and Alaska to the southwest Pacific as far south as New Zealand. Stan Blackmore remembers when godwits were on the game license but, since 1941 they have been fully protected. It is believed in New Zealand that the Russians still shoot these little birds in Siberia.

For short distance navigation, the Polynesians used the frigate or man-o-war bird. Disliking to alight on the ocean, these wise birds will fly to the nearest land but failing to see any, will return to the ship. The Vikings were said to have used shags for similar reconnaissance.

Many species of big game have been introduced in New Zealand and have increased so rapidly that government hunters have to be employed to keep the herds down. No license is required and there is no limit on the bats. Moose, wapiti, red deer, sambar, mule deer, sika deer, chamois and tahr can all be shot by anyone who has the desire and the energy.

All of the animals and fish are exotics. The first deer were introduced in 1850 and came from the deer park of Windsor Castle, most famous and ancient of the royal preserves.

The success of the red deer importations led to even more exotic introductions. In 1867, Axis deer from Ceylon were brought in and sambar from the same source in 1875. Moose were shipped from Canada in 1900 and Sika deer from the private herd of the Duke of Bedford. Natives of Manchuria and Japan, the little Sika flourished in their new home, especially on the South Island. The Duke also sent New Zealand six Himalayan tahr, or wild goats, which provide fine sport in the Southern Alps. Chamois from Switzerland also do well in the mountains. Bharal or blue sheep were imported from Tibet in 1907 but do not seem to have propagated.

Only six degrees north of the Falkland Islands in latitude, South Island of New Zealand is the second most southerly inhabited island in the world. And the barren sheep-dotted mountains which one flies over on the rough journey to Queenstown have much in common with the austere hills of the British colony off the east coast of South America. The little airports consist of lonely sod runways which are only accessible by daylight as they lie deep in peak-surrounded valleys. We were late starting from Christchurch, and by the time we flew through Lindis Pass the sun had sunk behind the snow-capped Southern Alps and dark shadows had begun to blanket the valleys. The lights of Queenstown were just beginning to glimmer when we dropped through the clouds over Lake Wakatipu and spiraled down between the peaks to a landing. Our relief at arriving on solid ground was only a little dimmed by the fact that the Mount Cook Airline had neglected to put our baggage on board. The kindly manager of O'Connel's Hotel sent us dinner in our room even though we arrived long after seven-thirty when most hotel dining rooms in New Zealand seem to close down.

South Island is nearly 14,000 square miles larger than North Island, but it contains only a minority of the population. Aside from Christchurch, Dunedin, and Invercargill, the towns are little more than sheep stations. Queenstown, however, got its start from gold mining in the 1850's and even though its population has declined from 7,000 to about 2,000 it still has some pretensions and with the help of tourism, may yet equal its importance of the last century. Flanked by "The Remarkables," a 7,000 foot range of mountains which were dusted with snow on the night we arrived, the little town has a spectacularly beautiful setting. The old hotels which used to cater to the gold miners have, with two exceptions, been pulled down and the atmosphere of the frontier has passed into history; but a few old timers still pan for dust in the mountains.

Our purpose in coming to South Island was only, incidentally, to see the sights. We still had a number of birds, listed as rare by the Red Book of the International Union for the Conservation of Nature, to check on and hoped to be able to talk with Dr. Orbell, discoverer of the notornis who makes his home at Lake Te Anau.

I looked for but did not find the blue duck. I had read about this curious duck in *Waterfowl of the World,* the duck-fancier's bible by Peter Scott and Jean Delacour and my notes revealed that the blue duck of New Zealand has no obvious similarity to any other ducks and is one of the most puzzling of all waterfowl. According to local people I consulted, the blue duck is not common but is seen occasionally in the forest areas.

The New Zealand sheep farmers live close to the land and I found we could pick up a great deal of useful information from them, particularly in the public bar of the Garston Inn where we stayed. I asked about the Paradise duck and was pleased to hear that they are still fairly common in this area of South Island. Captain Cook was the first European to note these ducks and wrote of them in 1773: "We found here five different kinds of ducks, some of which I do not recollect to have seen anywhere before; the largest as big as Muscovy duck with a very beautiful variegated plumage, on which account we called it the painted duck. Both male and female have a large white spot on each wing." Actually, the Paradise is not a true duck but an intermediate between ducks and geese. Scientifically, it should be called the New Zealand shelduck.

Paradise ducks are listed as one of the three game species which can be shot in New Zealand but they are extremely wary and at the start of the two months shooting season avoid the haunts of man.

New Zealand wildfowl listed in the Red Book as in danger of extinction include the Campbell Island flightless teal. Lying 500 miles south of South Island in the icy waters of the South Pacific, Campbell Island is today seldom visited. Years ago sheep were run there and a few buildings to house the shepherds were erected. J. A. McLeod of Castle Down, Dipton, Southland, was one of these shepherds and I asked my friend McKnight to question him about the birds there.

About the same distance east of South Island lies the Chatham archipelago where a number of rare birds are reported to survive still. Among these are Forbes' parakeet, which were reported to number about a hundred in 1962. Five species of New Zealand snipe also inhabit the Chathams but very little is known about them. The New Zealand shore plover holds out in very restricted numbers in the Chatham group as does the Chatham Island pigeon. Shooting and trapping are listed as the reasons for the decline of both birds. Another race of this bird which used to inhabit Norfolk Island, now a popular resort for New Zealanders and Australians, has become extinct. The Chatham Island tui is believed to be more common. I talked with several fishermen who had been to the Chatham Islands recently but none had the faintest clue about the birds beyond the fact that they saw some flying about. Sheep are still run on the Chathams and there is also a weather station there.

From Garston we drove to Fiordland, the remote and rugged southwest coast of South Island where the government in 1953 established a 3,023,100 acre National Park, one of the largest in the world and twice the area of New Zealand's eight other national parks. It is in the Murchison Mountains of Fiordland that the takahe still survives. Fiordland is also the last refuge of the kakapo or owl parrot; the New Zealand wren; the South Island kokako and the South Island piopio.

It is a drive well worth taking. The road, paved for about half the four hour trip, runs first through sheep country, laced by bright brooks and brooded over by dark treeless mountains on which grows silver tussock. The little towns, much like those of our West, are few and far apart. At Lake Te Anau, 41 miles long and the largest in South Island, we stopped to call on Dr. Orbell, the rediscoverer of the takahe. His home was easy to find for it is ringed by a line of wapiti antlers set in concrete. There are 34 of these heads and the biggest has 16 points. Whether or not the famous doctor shot this army of stags I do not know, for he was not in Te Anau and had not been for some months. The lodge is his summer cottage; he lives and practices medicine in Invercargill down on the South coast.

Just before one arrives at Milford Sound, the deep water fiord on the coast, one drives through a three-quarter mile tunnel which is about the size of a rabbit warren and almost as gloomy. A week before we arrived an avalanche blocked the entrance so that the only way out of Milford was by plane or crayfish boat.

There are two ways to see the Milford Sound—by air or by sea—and since the air was too rough for flying, we were given, courtesy of the management, a special trip in the hotel's launch, Captain Jack Robinson commanding. Milford Sound is so deep—almost a mile—that no ships can anchor there and when a brace of French war ships steamed in recently they had to make fast to the cliffs. There used to be both whales and seals in the Sound but man has managed to eradicate most of them. Today the Sound is part of the national park and a few seals are starting to come back.

On the drive back to Te Anau where we took the plane for Christchurch, we stopped at Lake Manapouri, a strikingly lovely body of water which was threatened by a hydro-electric scheme which would raise the water level about eighty feet, and mean the flooding of a great area of forest. Peter MacIntyre, our artist friend in Wellington, is fighting this project as are many other conservationists in New Zealand, but the chances are that the politicians will have their dam. The urge to dam rivers seems to be one of the least attractive by-products of civilization. In most democracies cheap power, even where there is really no need for it, wins elections.

At the last minute Irene decided to take the four-day hike on the Milford Track, a spectacular foot track through the high mountains with good rest houses at the end of each 10 mile day. I would like to have joined her but could not postpone my Australian appointments, so she met me in Canberra a week later.

EIGHTEEN

Australia

FROM CHRISTCHURCH ON the Pacific shore of South Island, New Zealand, to Melbourne, Australia, on the Tasman Sea is only a matter of five hours by air, but the cities might well be in different planets and travellers must adjust accordingly. The pace of the little sheep-raising center corresponds to that of the meandering flocks in the high pastures while Melbourne rockets along like the mechanical rabbit in a greyhound race. This may be because there is more incentive to hurry in a less regulated state and it may be because Melbourne is the business center of the country. Australia is the smallest, driest, and flattest of the continents but it also is the only one occupied by a single nation and that, in these days of envious and aggressive neighbors, has very great advantages. Furthermore, with only eleven million people and three million square miles of territory (even though a good deal of it makes only kangaroos happy), Australia is absorbing 100,000 immigrants a year and can continue to do so for many decades to come.

Thanks to my old State Department colleague, Lincoln White, who was our consul general in Melbourne, I was introduced on the afternoon of my arrival to the leading conservationists of Victoria, Australia's fifth state in terms of size, but first in terms of progressive conservation. A. D. Butcher, Director of the Fisheries and Wildlife Department of Victoria, gave me a comprehensive briefing on the problems of his state and his views on conservation in Australia generally. He felt that the newly organized Australian Conservation Foundation was a highly commendable effort to correlate conservation from a national standpoint. A great deal of the credit for this organization must go to the Duke of Edinburgh who takes a vigorous interest in Australian wildlife. It was the Duke's eloquent appeal that may have saved the noisy scrub bird. Due to his efforts, a plan to build a town in the center of its last remaining habitat near Mount Gardner in western Australia was temporarily shelved.

All of the ten conservationists present stressed the necessity of a broad survey of Australian wildlife. Today the six states, two internal territories and nine external territories, all have their own conservation problems and, lacking a master plan, do not always correlate their efforts. They felt that while the federal government might help toward the cost of such a survey, much of the money would have to be privately raised. Unfortunately, however, gifts to aid wildlife are no more tax deductible in Australia than they are in New Zealand. In the press interviews which I gave *The Age* and *The Sun,* the two leading daily newspapers of Melbourne, I urged the importance of tax deductibility for this pressing cause.

A long list of Australian birds and animals are in grave danger of extinction, and unless something is done about them, they will soon follow the white-footed rabbit rat, the rufous-rat kangaroo, the western native cat, the eastern barred bandicoot, the magpie goose, the osprey and the turquoise parrot into oblivion. In Victoria alone, the threatened list includes the red kangaroo, the bustard, the eastern native cat, Leadbeater's possum, the pootaroo (rat kangaroo), the smokey mouse and the broad-toothed rat.

A study made by the British branch of the World Wildlife Fund shows that of 56 animals, birds, and reptiles in danger of extinction, eight or 14.3 per cent, are in Australia. Yet Australia has only 1/285th of the world's population and more space to protect fauna than dozens of smaller nations. Some recent reports were shocking; only a few weeks before we arrived, the Fisheries and Wildlife inspectors of Victoria had caught hunters with 3,000 ducks shot out of season; Cape Barren geese, the handsome grey goose whose numbers have been drastically reduced, were still shot and their eggs taken; kangaroos while far from rare, were being slaughtered at a rate which many experts felt would eventually exterminate them. By a strange irony, their flesh was being used as pet food for dog and cat lovers.

As a guest of Geoffrey Downs, Director of Soil Conservation for

Victoria, and Miss I. Watson, Information Officer for the Fisheries and Wildlife Department, I spent a pleasant and interesting day at the Sir Colin MacKenzie Sanctuary, some thirty-five miles northeast of Melbourne in the foothills of the Dona-Buang Mountains. Originally tribal lands of the Yarra Indians who called it "Coranderrk" from the delicately flowered Victorian Christmas bush, the area includes Badger Creek and some fine old trees. MacKenzie, an orthopedic specialist who was knighted for his work with people suffering from the after effects of poliomyelitis, persuaded the Victorian government to declare the area a sanctuary for Australian fauna. The park, which runs to some 450 acres and is partly financed by the state government and partly by private donations, is considered the best of its kind in Australia.

V. C. Mullett, the Director, laid aside a rare caterpillar he was studying and took us for a personally conducted tour of his domain. He showed us the biggest outdoor aviary I have ever seen and possibly the largest in the world. 200 feet long, 100 feet wide and 42 feet high, the wiring is so fine that one almost has the feeling of being in the open. The purpose of this bird palace is primarily to house lyrebirds, the shy magnificent bird whose mating displays are the wonder of ornithologists and the public as well. A big bird with a tail like a peacock, the lyrebird is not endangered but is so wary that it is seldom seen even in the wild reaches of the Australian Alps, the Victoria Mountains and the Blue Mountains of New South Wales. Furthermore, it mimics the cry of other birds so that it is hard to track it by its call.

But perhaps the lyrebird's most enviable trait is its ability to summon all the females within earshot of its mating call and when they are all lined up, take his choice and ignore the unlucky ones. Lady lyrebirds are all full of hope but all but one are doomed to disappointment.

From the subject of lyrebirds, Miss Thompson switched to birds which appeal to man internally instead of spiritually and told me about the "mutton birds," shearwaters whose young are still eaten by the coastal folk of Australia. Tasting somewhat like mutton, the young birds are caught before they are able to fly and canned. A better fate should be given them for few birds brave so much to breed. Flying across thousands of miles of ocean from as far away as Alaska, these shearwaters arrive in November and after breeding and laying their eggs start the long journey back to the north in April.

The sanctuary contains examples of the only two mammals in the world which are bred from an egg—the platypus and the echidna or spiny anteater. Three platypi swam happily around a glass tank and conducted a spirited hunt for some fresh-water shrimps which the director put in for our benefit. Evidently their sense of sight and smell was poor, for the shrimp managed to survive for quite a while before being cornered. In a country where almost all animals are marsupial with pouches for their young, the female platypus is an exception and incubates her eggs by folding her body around them. When the young are born they are right up against her mammary glands (she has no nipples) from which milk oozes.

The echidna, which looks like a porcupine with a golf peg for a nose, is a land animal which lives on grubs. The female develops a pouch each season and lays her single egg directly into it. Her milk supply is also laid on in the pouch. Neither the platypus nor the echidna is rare but both are rigidly protected.

To me, one of the most fascinating of the many exhibits is the brolga or native companion, a great grey crane with a red snood on its head. Armed with a foot-long pin-sharp beak, the brolga male will not hesitate to attack if bothered and a double-spaced wire is kept around his area. The cry of the birds is raucous and often gives away the location of the nests which are built on the ground.

A good deal of study has been given to the problems of wildlife education and I was impressed by the opinions of both Downs and Miss Watson. Downs, who attends most of the World Wildlife meetings and is a friend of Dr. Fairfield Osborn of the New York Zoological Society, whose views he much admires, believes that this enlightenment should extend beyond the birds and beasts to the general ecology of the land. What good is a habitat if the forest is burned down, or a swamp area if it is drained, or a plain if it is flooded by dams?

Indiscriminate slaughter of kangaroos was causing a great deal of discussion. Leading propagandist against it was Professor Jock Marshall of Monash University at Clayton, Victoria. According to the professor, 200,000 kangaroos a week were being shot in New South Wales alone. Operating under a permit from the state government, more than a hundred "hunters" were working a 90,000 square mile area in between the Murray River and Cobar. The good shots earned as much as $250 for a six-night week. Spotlights were used and as the light was often uncertain, great numbers of kangaroos were wounded and flopped away in the night to die days later in agony. The dead animals were butchered on the spot, carried to the nearest freezer and sold for 5 cents a pound. Some of the frozen meat was exported for human consumption to Hong Kong, Singapore and Japan, but most of it was processed into pet food for local use.

Professor Marshall, in an eloquent newspaper article, cited the near extinction of the American bison which was reduced by just this kind of professional hunting from nearly 5 million in 1870 to a few hundred in 1890. It was only through the personal efforts of President Theodore Roosevelt and a handful of other conservationists that the few survivors were protected.

Downs is vice president of the Australian Conservation Foundation and we had a lengthy discussion about its objectives and relationship to the possible formation of an Australian Wildlife Appeal, similar to those set up in England and America. Downs told me frankly that initial efforts to interest people in an appeal had failed, partly because it had been inexpertly explained—he did not refer to the Duke of Edinburgh, but to a less articulate duke who came out from England to sell the idea—and partly because Australians felt that whatever money they raised should be spent in their own country and not abroad. It was his opinion that no new effort should be made then to revive the appeal idea but that all efforts should be made to concentrate on improving and financing the Australian Conservation Foundation. Aside from a nominal donation by the central government, the Foundation was virtually without funds and urgently needed the means of setting up an office. The idea of fund-raising operations to finance the Foundation had evidently not so far been explored by the men I talked with.

Like New Zealand, Australia's ties with Britain came under severe strain during the last war. First the fall of Singapore and then Churchill's insistence that Australia keep her army in the Middle East even though her homeland was in danger, made many Australians take another look at their alliances. The result was the ANZUS Pact which throws the full weight of the American war potential on Australia's side in the event of attack. Britain's effort to join the Common Market also shook Australia to her economic heart, and there is still a feeling among some of the businessmen I talked with in Melbourne that Australia will only find a market for her agricultural products in England while de Gaulle lives. They fear that a less European-minded French

Premier may allow England to join the Continent. In the meantime, exports to Japan are increasing steadily and the hotels are full of earnest little groups of Japanese armed with Nikon cameras and order books.

Against this background of economic uncertainty and worry—to say nothing of Red China's long-term need for more land—the objective of my visit, conservation of Australian wildlife, would seem a hard subject to get people excited about. In fact, this is not so. By and large, Australians love the outdoors, spend a lot of time there, and have more interest than most peoples in the animals and birds which share their continent. The minute I brought up the matter of wildlife, everyone, from taxi drivers to ministers, brightened up and expressed their views. "I've lived here forty years and I ain't yet seen a kangaroo," said a Melbourne waiter; "and I don't want them sheep farmers to shoot them all before I do."

To keep the kangaroo around as well as the other examples of Australia's unique wildlife, a dedicated band of men was working hard in the Division of Wildlife Research of the Commonwealth Scientific and Industrial Research Organization. Among the most eminent of these was Dr. Robert Carrick, a lean Scotsman who came to Australia from Aberdeen, and was considered the best scientist in his line in the Dominion. The story of just what Dr. Carrick did came out in dribblets. During a long and very pleasant lunch with him and his wife in the sunlit dining room of the Rex Hotel, I learned that he was among other things a "population ecologist" and was working to help solve one of humanity's most pressing problems—exploding populations—by the study of birds and animals. He promised to take us to his research station and explain in detail.

Discussing the Australian Conservation Foundation, of which he is a member of the governing board, Dr. Carrick said that although a national drive would begin soon to raise money for it, he did not see how sufficient funds could be collected without important help from the government, and the one and only person in the government who could immediately assure these funds was the Prime Minister, Sir Robert Menzies. He urged me to leave no stone unturned in my effort to see him and present this pressing case.

My friend, Ambassador Owen Davis, with whom I served in South Africa, gave a dinner for me and invited among others, Dr. H. J. Frith, Chief of the Division of Wildlife Research, and M. L. Tyrrell, Private

Secretary to Viscount de L'Isle, the Governor General. Tyrrell, a big, outgoing man, who has served a succession of governor generals, told me that he had arranged a luncheon for me with the Duke of Edinburgh and Viscount de L'Isle but that our decision to stay longer in New Zealand forced him to cancel it. The Duke had left for Singapore and de L'Isle for Perth, far away in Western Australia. In any case, de L'Isle had finished his tour in Australia and would be leaving in a few months.

Frith, a thin, rather truculent gentleman with decided views on everything from kangaroos to politics, told me that his division, like the others in CSIRO, was purely a research organization and had no power whatever to inaugurate or enforce conservation programs in the various states or the federal areas. In this it differs from our Fish and Wildlife Service which does control game laws for the whole country when it comes to migratory waterfowl.

Dr. G. Sawer, Professor of Law at the Australian National University, who wrote the constitution for the Australian Conservation Foundation, told me that various changes had been made in this charter and that soon it would be incorporated. The next move in his opinion—and Tyrrell and Frith both agreed—was to put all possible pressure on the Prime Minister to make a respectable grant to the Foundation and change the tax laws so that gifts to it would be deductible. They all felt that anything I could do to get the PM interested would be most helpful.

Seventy years old, Sir Robert Menzies had led his country for sixteen years, a record for an Australian prime minister, and he ruled with a sharp tongue and firm hand. Except for a brief period when he reduced credit to head off inflation, Sir Robert presided over a flourishing economy for all of his terms in office. The economy continued to expand at six per cent a year, there was full employment and a shortage of skilled workers that even the 100,000 new immigrants a year did not fill. And it was this generally prosperous state of the Australian economy that made the members of the Conservation Foundation believe that Sir Robert would not object to easing the tax laws for gifts to wildlife. The amount of money lost to the treasury would not be great, and the cultural rewards would be important.

The Federal district runs to about 180 square miles and it takes about an hour to drive out of it and into the rolling hills of New South Wales. In the lovely Molonglo Valley we spent the day at the 5,000 acre cattle and sheep ranch of Alexander Scott. Known as graziers, the ranchers of Australia, whose domains take up most of the great flat country are, in many respects, the most typical Australians. They live close to the land and the windows of their comfortable old houses look out on vast vistas of pastures lined by stately eucalyptus and dominated by huge steel blue skies. One of the worst droughts in recent history had turned the grass brown and the river had shrunk to a brook. But Scott's garden still bloomed with masses of flowers, and white cockatoos sailed through his shade trees.

The question as to whether men like Scott would be interested in supporting a new kind of zoo was raised the following evening when we went with Dr. M. F. Day, an entomologist of CSIRO, and his wife to call on Dr. and Mrs. Stephen Boyden of the Australian National University. Boyden, a young man with a large black beard, has conceived of a "biological center" which would dramatize the importance of biological science in relation to human affairs. Instead of cages of exotic animals, the exhibits would consist mainly of Australian fauna and include reptiles as well as mammals and birds. An important part of the center would be research.

"The master plan for the center," said Boyden as he caressed a stumpy-tailed lizard, "will be presented to the National Capital Development Committee within the next few weeks." This committee allocates the land and Boyden hopes to get at least 100 acres for his center. Whether the center would be part of the Australian National University, or be set up under one of the Ministries of the government, had not been decided. In any case, Boyden wanted to have it run by a board consisting of scientists, government, and civilians.

Discussing the rare animals which might find a home in the center, Boyden laid aside the lizard, by this time rather sleepy from handling, and picked up a corroboree frog, a shilling-sized little fellow which was discovered by an American. It seems that ten years ago Dr. John Moore, chief of the Department of Zoology of Columbia University, saw this brightly colored frog and named it corroboree after the painted designs with which the aborigines deck themselves for festive occasions.

The matter of funds for Boyden's center led back to that font of all power—Sir Robert—and both Day and I advised him to present the plan in as dramatic a way as possible so that the Prime Minister would be able to visualize the theme and be assured that the voters would like it. I liked Boyden and liked his plan.

Gymnorhina tibisen, otherwise known as the Australian magpie, has solved a problem which has many intelligent humans scared stiff. This nine-inch black and white bird limits its breeding in accordance with the food supply of the territories which it inhabits. We may, in fact, learn a great deal from the studies which Dr. Robert Carrick has been making of the magpie population around the headquarters of the Wildlife Division of the Commonwealth Scientific and Industrial Research Organization a few miles out of Canberra.

Dr. Carrick, an enthusiastic and kindly scientist who responds quickly to interest in his researches, devoted the better part of a day to showing us how he studies the magpies. He chose them because they are the most sedentary of the Australian birds; each may spend its entire life in an area of 10 acres or so and can thus be banded and watched from the nest to the grave. Magpies, like many human societies, are sharply divided by their living arrangements. Of the 1,000 birds resident in the area under study, about a quarter live in "Territories" where they have food all year round, trees for nesting and all the appurtenances of an ornithological Park Avenue apartment house.

From two to ten birds occupy each territory which varies in size from five to twenty acres. The average number of adults in each group is three and males seldom outnumber females although there are male Moslem magpies who acquire several wives and some strong-willed females who manage two husbands. There is no relation between the size and quality of the territory and the number of birds which occupy it but the inhabitants must be able to defend their holding, and this is a full-time business. Four-fifths of the magpies do not have territories, and turning bandit, spend a great deal of their time trying to eject the magpie aristocrats from their choice habitats. They seldom succeed for virtually all the successful breeding is done by the territory dwellers and the job of defending the territory is shared, but defense of the nest is carried out vigorously by the female alone.

Because of this intense desire to protect their habitats and nests, the magpies are easily caught. A member of the unwashed flock is introduced in a cage into a territory and immediately the permanent residents swoop down to attack it and get caught themselves. Elaborate banking enables Dr. Carrick and his staff to tell the age, territory and other pertinent facts about any given bird.

From his studies which have gone on for ten years, Dr. Carrick has drawn some extremely interesting conclusions. These are: territorialism and associated socio-sexual interactions limit breeding to about one quarter of the adult population of magpies; the inhabitants of the territories are buffered against important mortality from disease—they do not have to seek their food in areas frequented by other birds—and lastly they have a balanced diet within their territory and are generally in good shape.

As common as the magpies and as interesting to study are the Australian kangaroos which occupy a number of runs behind the administration building. J. H. Calaby, one of the senior scientists of the Wildlife Division, took time out from a busy schedule to show us some of his long-legged pets. Kangaroos vary from the tiny muskrat kangaroo, which weighs in at 1½ pounds, to 180 pound monsters that can tear a man to bits with their powerful hind legs. We were introduced to several of these vindictive males who promptly reared on their hind feet and challenged us to come inside the wire. In addition to ripping with their long claws they can bite. Baby kangaroos spend eight months riding around in their mother's pouch and we watched a six-month-old infant being extracted from the pouch to be weighed and measured. About the size of a large hare, the little fellow was frightened and kept trying to disappear into orifices in our pants which were not made for kangaroo hideouts. His mother was too shy to stand still while he jumped into her so she had to be held and then the baby jumped in.

Asked about the current furor over the slaughter of kangaroos by professional hunters for dog food, Calaby said that in his opinion the common species are in no danger but he favored more reserves for them. He also pointed out that Captain Sturt, the explorer who crossed what is now New South Wales in 1840, mentioned seeing only a few kangaroos. This is one of the areas where they are now found in thousands and Calaby believes that the increase was a direct result of the pasture provided for the sheep and cattle. The old forested areas simply did not produce enough grass to sustain large populations.

An authority on mammals, Calaby is the Australian correspondent for the Survival Service Commission of the International Union for the Conservation of Nature and is the man who corrects the "Red Book," whose data is of so much use to me on these conservation missions. He told me that since Harper's *Extinct and Vanishing Mammals of the World* was published in 1945 by the American Committee for International Wildlife Protection there has been some good news for certain species. The brush-tailed phascogale, the pouched mouse, the tiger cat, the Tasmanian devil, the banded anteater, Gunn's bandicoot, the honey mouse, the red-necked pademelon, the Tasmanian wallaby and the Dama wallaby can all be taken off the danger list.

So can the koala which now thrives under strict protection. Thirty-five years ago it was widely believed that this little marsupial was doomed to extinction. Once widespread in Victoria, it was almost wiped out by disease in the 1890's and later its numbers were drastically curtailed by "hunters." So successful has the conservation program been that Victoria alone has liberated more than 7,000 koalas to stock some fifty areas.

The other side of the coin makes gloomier reading. Of the 229 species of native mammals, marsupials comprise 119 and Calaby lists 42 of these as being in danger of extinction. Of the 67 rodents he lists 11 in danger. Many of the threatened species, however, occur in remote and unsettled country and the range of others is inadequately known. Calaby believes that there are only twelve species whose habitats are known which might benefit from the establishment of reserves where they now hold out. These are the red-tailed phascogale, eastern jerboa-marsupial, southern planigale, eastern native cat, Tasmanian tiger, western ringtail, Leadbeater's possum, hairy-nosed wombat, island wombat, brush-tailed rat-kangaroo, potoro, and our friend the broad-tooth rat.

With the exception of the two wombats and the Tasmanian tiger, all of these animals are nocturnal, and so small that they are seldom seen and consequently excite very little interest in the public. They are safe from direct human interference but destruction of their habitats may well send them into the Valhalla of the dodo.

Some species have always been rare. There is the famous case of the Eyrean grass-wren. First collected by F. W. Andrews who made a pastoral survey of the Cooper's Creek area in 1875 (he was accompanied by three Afghan camel drivers and three aborigines), this little bird occupied a country "so frightful" that its numbers were necessarily very limited. Andrews made no notes and the two skins which reached the British Museum were named by John Gould. Time passed and it was not until 1914 that another reference to the little wren turned up.

A. White, while collecting in the Musgrave and Everard Ranges of South Australia, reported seeing one. In 1923, F. Lawson also reported seeing one in the upper Finke River area in the Northern Territory. In 1960 an effort made to relocate the wren was unsuccessful.

In 1961, a well-equipped expedition set out for the Macumba river with the do-or-die purpose of finding the grass-wren. They travelled more than a hundred miles over trackless country before they reached a water hole on the Macumba. The temperature was 105° when they camped and set out to explore the area which consisted mainly of flood flats, studded with salt-bush and cane-grass. On the day they had to leave, due to exhaustion of their supplies, they found a single bird and later two more were located and it was decided to drive them into a mist net made of nylon. Imagine the disappointment of the collectors when the wrens flew right through the net even though it was the finest they had.

Our travels in search of rare animals are sometimes affected by politics and war. In 1963 we were unable to penetrate the northern sections of the Yemen to search for the oryx because of Nasser's invasion of that unhappy little country, and while in Australia I learned from the Portuguese chargé d'affaires in Canberra that diplomatic relations had been suspended between his country and Indonesia. He added, however, that consular relations, a kind of second-grade contact, were still being maintained between Dr. Salazar and Sukarno so that our visit to Timor did not have to be cancelled. Portugal was not the only country worried over Sukarno. Bung, as he was known to his weary people, had also made some wild claims about the Australian half of New Guinea which adjoins "West Irian," the Indonesian segment of the big island.

When Captain Bligh was governor of New South Wales, he paused at Tasmania to perform a good deed. He planted an apple tree and today Tasmanian apples are among her leading exports. But the big island south of Australia—it is actually 1,000 square miles larger than Ceylon—is chiefly known in the wildlife world at least, for two more exciting reasons. Chief of these is the Tasmanian "tiger" which is not a member of the cat family at all but a big brownish-grey wolf-like marsupial with dark brown stripes on its back. Whether or not the thylacine still roams the back lands of the island is open to conjecture but there is no doubt that at least one did three years ago because a fisherman killed it.

The strange tale was told to me by Dr. Eric Guiler, Senior lecturer in Zoology at the University of Tasmania and without doubt the leading authority on the thylacine. The fisherman, who lived at Sandy Cape, a tiny settlement far up the almost deserted west coast of the island, heard a noise late at night in the tin-roofed shed where he kept his bait, and grabbing a flashlight went to investigate. In the weak beam he saw two eyes, and seizing a heavy piece of wood, hit the animal on the head and killed it. In the morning he found a half-grown male tiger lying dead in the hut, and covering it with a piece of tin, went to tell his friends the great news. After celebrating his triumph with numerous drinks, he returned to the hut to find the tiger gone. Weeks later, the police were able to establish but not prove that one of the fishermen had stolen it and tried to sell it to a wealthy animal collector on the mainland, but the story had gotten so much play in the papers that the collector did not dare buy it and the fisherman grew scared and probably dumped it in the ocean. A week or so following the killing of the animal, however, the Animals and Birds Protection Board of which Dr. Guiler is chairman, sent a man to the site of the killing who was able to get samples of hair and some dried blood. Laboratory tests subsequently showed that the animal was indeed a tiger.

Encouraged by this evidence that the tiger might still survive, Dr. Guiler, in 1963, persuaded the Premier of Tasmania, the Honorable Eric Reece, to give him 2,000 pounds Australian to conduct a search. The investigation, which went on for seven months, involved the setting of some 700 snares per night and baited traps. Footprints and droppings of the tiger were seen near several of the traps but none of the wary animals were caught. Since then, reports of sightings have been increasing and careful sifting of the evidence has led Dr. Guiler to believe that a few of the reporters have actually seen tigers.

To see a tiger myself, I went to the Tasmanian Museum, a fine new building, whose prime exhibit is a mounted family of three tigers. Among the strangest animals I have ever seen, the thylacine male has a huge head and a mouth so large that it seems quite capable of swallowing a pumpkin. About the size of a medium-sized dog, this male probably weighed about fifty pounds. The female was considerably smaller and her head was much more in proportion to her body. Data about the breeding of the thylacine is shrouded in some mystery but Dr. Guiler believes that the average litter consists of three or four pups which are carried in the pouch for some months before being placed on the ground and fed with meat by their parents. The breeding season is believed to be from November to December with the young being born in January.

The thylacine was not always rare. In the early days of the colony, they were fairly common on both the mainland of Australia, where they are now extinct, and on Tasmania. Known as a sheep killer as early as 1836, the tiger was proscribed and the Van Diemen's Land Company retained a trapper to hunt them down. In 1840, the company offered a bounty of six shillings per scalp. The first government bounty of one pound per animal was paid on April 28, 1888, and the last on June 5, 1909. According to the records, bounties were paid on 2,268 animals.

Dr. Guiler, who has done a great deal of research on the old records, believes that the sheep killings laid to the thylacines were greatly exaggerated. He found that one of the landowners who voted for the bounty in the parliament of 1886 claimed to have lost 30,000 sheep to these killers and the fact was that his entire holding of sheep was only slightly above 30,000. That many of the sheep owners did not regard the thylacine as a serious menace was indicated by the fact that 11 out of the 24 members of Parliament voted against the bounty. Wild hogs undoubtedly accounted for more sheep than the rather slow-witted marsupials.

By studying the records of bounties paid out by the Lands Department for the years 1888 to 1909, Dr. Guiler was able to place on the map where the killings took place. The study indicated that most of the animals were killed on the east coast and in the central highlands. Few bounties were paid on the west coast, and Dr. Guiler doubts if the thylacines were ever numerous in this area of high rainfall, rain forest and button grass plain. Yet today it is the wild and virtually uninhabited west coast where the last thylacine to be positively identified—the one killed by the fisherman—was seen.

There is plenty of room all over Tasmania for the thylacine to hide. Only 300,000 persons inhabit an island of 26,000 square miles and a third of these live in the capital of Hobart. Not many miles out of the city, the sheep farms begin and the landscape alternates between forests of eucalyptus with dense underbrush beneath the trees and more or less open park lands. The holdings are large with a ratio of one sheep to ten acres and, except for the yearly muster, few people ever ride over the wild ranges. The soil, moreover, is so poor that it cannot be tilled for agriculture and many of the original settlements have been abandoned.

Dr. Guiler would like to make another attempt to find the thylacine but the question arises as to what to do with it or them if they are caught. Study and release is the obvious answer but even more satisfactory would be the creation of a reserve, preferably on an island, where the species could be propagated without risk of losing them to unnatural causes. A sanctuary for the thylacine fits in well with a pet project of Dr. Guiler's on which he has been working for some years. Off the east coast of Tasmania lies Maria, a 23,000 acre island which would be just about perfect as a reserve for Tasmanian fauna. Most of the island is Crown land and could easily be proclaimed a sanctuary by the Governor but the rest is privately owned and would have to be acquired under the "resumption of land" laws. This means that the land would be bought by the state on the death of the present owners.

But full title to Maria might take another twenty years to acquire and, in the meantime, the thylacine might vanish from the earth. Therefore, it seems to me that every effort should be made at this time to find the tiger and, if necessary, keep it or them in a zoo or similar park until the island is ready. The cost of another expedition is not great and in view of the rarity of the objective, well worth the effort. Tigers have been kept for periods in zoos and one was kept in the Bronx Zoo for a few years.

First cousin of the tiger is the devil, a fox terrier-sized marsupial with the head of a pig, wire-like whiskers, and a wet nose. Emitting whining snarls, it attacks and devours the deadly blacksnake and is not above nipping off a finger if given half a chance. To cap all these charms, the devil has an unpleasant odor and is far from rare in Tasmania even though it has ceased to exist on the mainland. The pair I saw in the wildlife park outside Melbourne were among the least attractive animals I have ever seen. Modern agriculture seems to favor the devils and they are now so numerous in parts of Tasmania that as many as 100 have been taken from 100 acres of land. Some sheep owners claim that young lambs are eaten by the devils but the presence of lambs' wool in the devils' stomachs may simply mean that they ate lambs already dead. Examinations of a number of specimens indicated that the devils eat a wide variety of food and are especially fond of scrub wallaby, possums, birds and, sad to say, other devils. The farmer's loss of pasture to wallabies may, in fact, be controlled by the devils and he should not grudge the few hens which they admittedly sometimes snatch.

The primary reason why the tiger and the devil survive in Tasmania is due to the fact that the dingo, the hunting dog of Australia, and the fox have never been introduced into the island. The absence of these enemies has also permitted many of the smaller marsupials, such as the bandicoots and rat-kangaroos, to survive. The potoroo, a rabbit-sized kangaroo which looks like a bandicoot, is fairly common in Tasmania but was believed extinct on the mainland until recently when two small colonies of them were found in western Victoria.

Shooting is popular on the island and the bag limits generous. The wildfowler can take 15 ducks and some black swan, while the upland hunter can collect 3 pheasants, 15 quail and some snipe. Big game available consists of deer, kangaroo and wallaby. Those interested in more exotic sounding bags can hunt mutton birds and wattle birds.

Alan Moorehead, in *Cooper's Creek*, describes the blacks which the explorers Burke and Willis met as "naked aborigines, caught in the timeless apathy in which nothing ever changes or progresses; they built no villages and planted no crops; except for a few flea-bitten dogs they possessed no domestic animals of any kind. They hunted, they slept, just occasionally they decked themselves out for a tribal ceremony but all the rest was a listless dreaming." We know more about the aborigines now and the anthropologists take a very different view of them. Dr. A. P. Elkin of the University of Sydney puts it this way: "We have been repeatedly told that the Aborigine is lazy but actually he is conserving or rather recovering his energy. We are apt to forget the powers of endurance the hunter needs in the long relentless chase after the kangaroo, the wallaby or the emu." We shooters of modern shotguns should remember the Aborigine stalks his ducks with a spear and will take an hour to approach close enough to kill the bird.

Who are the Aborigines? In the first place, they do not belong to the European, Mongoloid or Negroid divisions of human beings. They have their own division, the Australoid, which also includes the aboriginal hill tribes of India and the Veddahs of Ceylon. I made several trips into the Veddah country and do see a striking resemblance between the shy little people of the Ceylon jungle and the plains dwellers of Australia. Both have wavy, wildly tangled hair, both have chocolate brown skin, and the males of both races are very hairy while their hands and feet are slender. Migrating from the North, the Australoid infiltrated the East Indies as well as India and Ceylon and small groups of them can still be found in Malaya, Indonesia and New Guinea. From these islands they worked their way to Australia bringing with them the dingo, the dog.

By 1788 when the white man began to take an interest in Australia there were about 300,000 Aborigines, divided into 500 tribes. This did not mean that the Aborigines were in Australia only long enough to increase to that figure. Like the magpies, the Aborigines maintain a balance between population and food resources. They practiced and still practice both infanticide and abortion when in times of severe drought the lives of the adult members of the tribe are threatened. But other factors have led to their decline and today there are only 80,000 in Australia and none in Tasmania.

Giving the Aborigine full marks for adapting his life to the land, Dr. Elkins makes the point that the white man after 175 years is able to live on only the fringes of the continent while the Aborigine has lived for thousands of years all over it. Not only in what is called "good blackfellow country" but in the waterless deserts he has survived because "in the course of centuries, through experience and experiment he has evolved a three-fold adaptation: intellectual, technological and psychological."

We dined in Sydney with Tillman and Peggy Durdin, old friends from China days. Till, now with the *New York Times,* is their correspondent for Australia, New Zealand and the Pacific and had recently been to New Guinea. I told him of our interest in the bird of paradise. For centuries the long white tail feathers of this lovely bird have been a symbol of royalty. The maharajahs and kings of Nepal used to wear them in their helmets and even today the king of Nepal wears them on festive occasions. The official present of the United States to Nepal on the coronation of the present king was a set of bird of paradise feathers furnished by the Smithsonian Institute. They were more appreciated than the cars and assorted doodads of other countries. The feathers have always been used as currency by the inland tribes of New Guinea but the most urgent reason for killing the birds was the export market for the feathers which Australia banned in her half of the island.

Sir Warren Macdonald, the chairman of the Commonwealth Banking Corporation who is senior vice president of the Australian Conservation Foundation, was away during my visit to Sydney, but he called me and arranged for me to see Donald Malcolmson, the energetic and able young man who is chairman of the working committee of Foundation. Malcolmson, who was in on the founding of the Foundation following Prince Philip's visit to Australia two years before, told me that his committee has ironed out the wording and is prepared to present a finished draft to the 70 councillors who make up the governing body of the Foundation. He hoped that this body would be able to meet in Canberra in the near future and after ratifying the constitution get down to raising money. He agreed with me that it was necessary to press the matter of making gifts to the Foundation tax deductible and said that Sir Garfield Barwick, the president of the Foundation, was studying the matter. Gifts to the National Trust are now deductible and it seems only logical to include living things as well as houses.

Malcolmson also believes that a survey of all Australian fauna should be made so that there is less duplication in the state efforts, and that a broad plan of educating the public should be undertaken. All this, of course, takes money as the treasury consisted of only 2,000 pounds Australian donated by the government as an earnest symbol of its interest in the project. He was sure, however, that sufficient sums could be raised from the big corporations to meet the costs of an office and a paid secretary. We discussed possibilities for this important job and he asked me for recommendations based on my talks with conservationists in his country. We agreed that diplomacy may be just as important as knowledge of wildlife in the running of such an organization, and that certain men who qualify in one field do not in the other.

Far below us the baked yellow plain which is the vast heartland of Australia lay shimmering in the sun. It is 2,000 miles from Sydney on the Tasman Sea to Darwin on the Timor Sea and most of the time one flies over desert. We passed Cooper's Creek, where only a century ago the explorers Burke and Willis established a base for their epic journey into the unknown interior.

Imperceptibly the rust browns and vivid yellows of the central desert of Australia merged with the greens of the coast and finally we slid down through a cloud burst with appropriate rainbow to the landing field at Darwin, capital of a moist tropical world which has nothing in common with the temperate climate and hustle and bustle of Sydney.

At the gate to meet us was His Honor, Roger Dean, Administrator of the Northern Territory, a realm five times the size of England, Scotland and Northern Ireland, which runs from the trackless sands of the interior to the palm-fringed shores of the Timor and Arafura Seas and encompasses 500,000 square miles but holds only about 50,000 people —less than a small town in America.

Darwin has 18,000 inhabitants and most of them, like those in Washington, work for the government. Basically their job is to administer, keep healthy, educate and police the people of the Territory. Twenty thousand of these are aborigines and the rest pretty much of a mixture of whites and yellows. The houses are all built on stilts in deference to the white ants and without air conditioning the nights must be a bit sultry. There is an ancient jail with a wooden wall whose inmates used to go home of nights; and a good many churches, two of which are modern and, Irene says, spectacularly so.

My purpose in going to Darwin was primarily to visit Melville Island where the Tiwi, one of the few remaining aboriginal tribes which retain some of their pristine culture, have their ancestral abode. Primitive peoples, living entirely on the land, gather a vast store of knowledge about wildlife. Legends of the Veddahs, the jungle people of Ceylon, told of strange birds and animals which may or may not exist there today, while the Bushmen of the Kalahari Desert in southern Africa have a wealth of myths, some of which are based on fact. Many years ago the quagga, half zebra, half wild ass, was located by bushmen. From the pygmies of the Ituri Forest in the Congo came the first hint of the existence of the okapi, the half giraffe, half zebra.

The Tiwi live on Melville Island, a million and a half acre reserve 2½ times bigger than Belgium—some 30 miles from Darwin. To get there I chartered a Beechcraft and with Harry Giese, Director of Social Services for the Nothern Territory, flew across the aquamarine expanse of the Timor Sea. Heavy white clouds with ominous grey bottoms dotted the horizon and our pilot made us promise to start back not later than 2 P.M. when the monsoon would blanket the coast.

Responsible for all of the 20,000 aborigines in the Northern Territory, Giese, a tall good-looking man in his late 40's, likes his job and likes trekking in the outback. His staff consists of 538 Europeans and 5 aborigines and his charges speak 70 different languages and are scattered over about one-sixth of all Australia, where the country is so vast and the population so sparse that cattle stations run to 10,000 square miles and much of the land has never been surveyed.

As we flew to Snake Bay, the landing strip on the far coast of Melville, he told me something of the history of the island. First settled on the 26th of September, 1824, by Captain Gordon Bremer R.N. of the H.M.S. Tamar, the influence of the white man was progressively hard on the natives. Later came the Japanese pearling fleets and later still the European buffalo hunters. It was not, in fact, until 1911 when the Sacred Heart Mission was established on Bathhurst, an island separated from Melville only by a narrow channel, that the Tiwi began to get along with the white man.

Mission stations in the aboriginal reserves are subsidized by the Australian government and in the Northern Territory by the Catholics. Methodists, Church of England, Lutherans and the Aboriginal Church of Inland Missions all work in the same vineyard. No two missions are allowed to work in the same area, however, so there is none of the godly but fierce competition that used to amuse and confuse the Chinese in my days in the Middle Kingdom. I was interested to hear the Summer Institute had begun to work on the languages of the aborigines. The objective is to develop an alphabet and eventually teach the natives to read in their own tongue.

Giese told me that leprosy was introduced by the Chinese but is now under control. Venereal disease has also run its course but there is still a good deal of trachoma and dysentery. Plural marriage was greatly discouraged by an early Belgian bishop who bought up the entire class of 12-year old virgins from the Tiwi families of Bathhurst and then sold them, one to a man, for marriage purposes only. Today polygamy is rare, even among the pagans. I particularly wanted to go to see the Tiwi of Snake Bay because most of them are still pagans while the Tiwi of Bathhurst are Christians.

Missionaries still work just as hard on Melville and run the school which we duly inspected. Because they had heard that I was interested in the fish and animals of the sea the Tiwi sang me a song about the dugong, that strange sea cow whose plight has taken up so many pages of this book. Unlike the manatee, the dugong's cousin which inhabits the Amazon, and whose future is uncertain due to unrestricted killing, the dugong of the Timor Sea still seems to be fairly numerous. The Tiwi hunt them with harpoons and the week before our visit two were killed and eaten.

Giese had arranged in advance for many of the old men who knew the legends of hunting and animals to gather at the house of the director of the settlement and there shuffled onto the porch four of the oldest men I have ever seen. Blue-black with shaggy hair and faces like gnarled oak, the elders of the Tiwi were glad to talk about the old days of hunting. Today the missionaries are training the young Tiwis that hunting is a sport for weekends only and should not be confused with the week's work. The Tiwi of Melville have built their own houses, cultivate the forests and grow some of their vegetables. Fishing still gives them most of the proteins and we were served giant mangrove crabs and baramundi, a delicious fish.

Black Joe, whose Tiwi name is Wamhawichmay, told me of hunting the wallaby with throwing sticks and Big Jack, Nownu in Tiwi, spoke of spearing fish with the beautifully made spears which the Tiwi still produce. In dances and songs which the Tiwi sing at ceremonials they make up poems about the animals and the words are never the same.

Some of the old boys had hunted on Cape Dawn Peninsula which is near to Melville and I was surprised to learn that buffalo, deer, banting cattle and ponies abound there. All, of course, are exotics, brought in by the whites in the early days. The ponies came from Timor and are sometimes caught, tamed and ridden by the aboriginal children.

Hunting exploits are recited at one's funeral and Giese took us to the groups of carved logs where the dead, after being sent on their way with proper ceremonies, are at last buried and then surrounded by a picket fence of these curiously carved and painted poles. The ceremony known as Pukamani lasts for days.

The poetry of the Tiwi has been rhymed in English and I will quote a poem called The Rain Comes:

> The frogs are moving, whispering in the trees,
> Djapara on his sea-girt island home
> Sits in the night. The humid western breeze
> Communes with him. The white sea foam
> Lies on the beach. The little ant

Carries its eggs. The signal's plain.
The women stoke their fires and chant.
The earth is dry and thirsty for the rain.

At the bar of the Fannie Bay Hotel and later in his pleasant home, I talked with Douglas Lockwood, the correspondent for the *Sun* of Melbourne, who has written some first-class books about the aborigines (*The Lizard Eaters* and *I, The Aboriginal*) and knows a great deal about them. Several years ago he was part of an expedition to Western Australia which made contact with aborigines who had never before seen white men. He said they were fascinated with the tinned foods but not at all interested in pictures of themselves peeled off the polaroid cameras.

Conservation in the Northern Territory has for some reason become confused with the aboriginal reserves. The Wildlife Ordinance of 1963 which set aside 50,000 square miles as animal and bird refuges still permits the aborigines to hunt, trap and otherwise capture any living thing they imagine they can eat and as this gamut runs down to lizards and snakes little is safe in the areas in which they hunt. In the old days this would not have mattered much as the aborigines were so few that they could not possibly make much of a dent in the game—but today there are nearly 20,000 in the Northern Territory alone and their numbers are growing rapidly. Their rate of increase is a good deal higher than the white Australians and even higher than the emigrants from Southern Europe.

Listed as pests which can be destroyed at any time in the Northern Territory are wild donkeys—20,000 were said to have been shot in one station—wild camels, wild cats, wild pigs, wild goats, and all dogs and dingoes found in the bush. Also all foxes, black and navy rats, mice, little red fruit bats, Gould's fruit bats and all snakes. Virtually all Australian snakes are poisonous except the pythons. In certain areas red kangaroos and even wedge-tailed eagles are also listed as pests and can be shot on sight. All rifles and shotguns have to be licensed and the police are charged with enforcing the game laws.

With Bruce Paine, the District Veterinary Officer, whose duties run to wildlife as well as cattle, we drove to Fogg Dam, a bird sanctuary some 44 miles southeast of Darwin. Built for the Humpty-Doo rice-growing project which failed, the huge catchment is now a boon to the birds which during the 8-month dry period, when hardly a drop of water falls, congregate there in thousands. Even during the rains a trip there is highly productive. Brilliant azure kingfishers darted among the bushes, a flock of magpie geese allowed us close enough to photograph them before they took off like lumbering bombers. Four huge Jabiru storks, black and white with blue necks walked sedately among the lily pads, while snow-white spoonbills and egrets stood around them like so many stately courtiers. On a lone dead tree a wedge-tailed eagle brooded.

We had driven out to the dam part of the way on the Stuart Road and nothing makes one realize the isolation of Darwin more than this single hard-surfaced highway that leads for nearly a thousand miles to Alice Springs. There the road stops and one must take the railway to Adelaide.

NINETEEN

Timor: Last Outpost

RISING FROM THE blue expanse of the Timor Sea we saw an island whose peaks were hidden in the clouds and whose mountains and valleys were jade green in the afternoon sun. Nothing could differ more from the flat sun-baked lands of the Northern Territory of Australia, 350 miles to the South. We had left Oceania and were in Asia, for Timor is the largest island of the Lesser Sundas. The people that inhabit it are Asians; the animals which roam its jungles, and the birds which throng its trees are Asian fauna.

Last outpost of an empire that once extended from Goa in India to the richest of the spice islands, Timor has been Portuguese since before Columbus discovered America. It was in 1460 that the first explorers landed on the eastern end of the island. Later the Dutch conquered part of Timor and today Portugal and Indonesia share the 300 by 60 mile island and, like Canada and America, have a long unguarded border; but unlike the neighbors in North America, relations between Dr. Salazar and Sukarno were not serene. Diplomatic relations were broken a few weeks before we flew to Timor and the Indonesian president announced that the days of colonialism in the East Indies were over.

But Dili, the sleepy little capitol of the Portuguese Overseas Province of Timor, could not have been quieter. True, every other man in the street was a soldier but this was only natural as the main garrison was stationed there and all males of the half million population had to serve their time in the army. Few of the troops were white and I heard that Portugal's European contingent did not number more than a few thousand.

Timor has some strategic significance. When the Japanese took it in 1942, they interdicted the passage of allied ships through the Torres Strait and forced all supplies from Europe to go South of Australia adding 1,200 miles to the voyage. Command of Timor and her airfields would have given Sukarno, and perhaps even more significant—his Red Chinese backers—another leg toward expansion southward.

There were, however, definite advantages for Sukarno to allow Portugal to remain in Timor as there were for Red China to tolerate Macao, the tiny Portuguese colony near Hong Kong. Both provinces— all Portuguese territories over the world are now called Overseas Provinces—are places for trans-shipment of goods, and since Sukarno denied his people access to Singapore and its western products, Timor was one of the few places where he could still get some of these necessities.

Whether or not this mundane consideration tipped the balance, the Portuguese would certainly do their best to defend themselves; and in order to underline this point, the governor was Lieutenant Colonel Jose Alberty Correia, former chief of staff of the garrison at Macao.

The guard of native Timorese with drawn krisses snapped to attention when I went to pay my formal call on His Excellency. At the door I was met by Captain Jose Maria de Mendonca, the Governor's military secretary, and escorted to a small and efficient-looking office where H.E. rose to meet me. A young man in his mid-forties with a precise and direct way of expressing himself, the Governor said he had had numerous signals about us and wanted me to know that it would be his pleasure to see that we went anywhere and saw anything we wanted on Timor. He then outlined a schedule which included all the places we wanted to go and detailed Captain de Mendonca and his wife to accompany us. A more generous and agreeable Governor I have yet to meet.

First on the itinerary was a trip to Ermera, a coffee-growing district high in the mountains. It was the rainy season and roads, which under the best of conditions are bad, were terrible. Furthermore, many of the bridges were washed out so that we had to ford rivers which almost washed the Land Rover away. We passed small bands of natives, all of whom stopped, removed their hats, and raised their hands in salute.

As we chugged up the winding mountain road, the scenery increased in grandeur and would have been grander still if we did not have to see across a yawning chasm a few inches from our wheels. Timor has some magnificent forests and we passed trees ten feet in circumference which overhung the road like the roof of a cathedral nave. I saw few birds aside from the jungle cocks and crows. A wild pig occasionally broke across the road and once I saw the head of a small deer. In more than fifty miles we passed only a few small settlements.

The objective of our drive was reached where the Administrator, F. Meneses, a cousin of Captain de Mendonca, ruled some 60,000 people with 14 police. Meneses was expecting us and had asked the head men of the neighboring villages to stage a dance. Unlike the steaming coast, Ermera is 5,000 feet up and we almost shivered as we watched the dancers. All male with a female orchestra of bronze gongs and drums which accompanied them, the dancers imitated the fighting cocks whose prowess they so greatly admire.

Life in the capital is not easy. Dili has endemic malaria despite the fact that this disease has been wiped out in hundreds of less savory places. Housing is scarce and the postmaster general, doctor and other members of the administration shared the Miramar with us. Only a few of the streets are paved and a cloud of dust follows the roaring jeeps and Land Rovers. The water must be boiled and gastronomic adventures with green vegetables, except at the hotel, are extremely unwise. But hardest on the Europeans is the sense of isolation. Except for the weekly plane to Darwin and the infrequent ship to Portugal, there is literally no contact with the outside world but the radio.

But Dili is a great metropolitan center next to Oe Cussi, a Portuguese enclave more than a hundred miles down the coast in Indonesian territory. Thanks to the governor, we were allowed to visit it and, accompanied by the de Mendoncas, boarded one of the two government-owned Doves, and staying well outside the 12 mile limit demanded by the Indonesians, flew across a pale green sea until we came in and landed gently on a pasture recently forsaken by a herd of water buffalo.

Antonio Pite, Administrator of Oe Cussi, was on hand with a jeep to show us his domain. Consisting of 803 square kilometers, inhabited by some 20,000 people, the enclave is a perfect background for a Somerset Maugham novel. The main street, on the sea, consists of the big house of the Administrator, the school where a few white nuns teach and look after a flock of dark children, and the garrison where one white officer, five sergeants and a platoon of native soldiers represent authority. Scattered beneath the great fig and palm trees are the thatch-roofed houses of the population. Little, rather sad-looking people, the Timorese are a mixture of Malayans, Papuans and Polynesians, and while quite pretty in their early youth become extraordinarily ugly in later life.

It was in Oe Cussi at the house of the administrator that I first had more or less definite news of *Felis Megalotis*, the rare cat which was the reason we came to Timor. The pilot of our plane had heard an officer commanding one of the inland districts say that he was trying to trap and mount a species of wild cat that was rare on the island, but according to the natives, definitely existed.

That the cat does exist there is no doubt, but unless I was prepared to spend some weeks in the jungle, my chances of seeing it were remote and the nature of the terrain, to say nothing of the risk from fever, effectually ruled out this kind of verification. I did, however, talk to people who had seen the cat and described it. The wife of the Administrator at Ermera saw it one evening cross a road in front of her jeep in the north end of her district. She said it was stubby-tailed like one of our bob-cats and had a tawny coat. It was quite unlike and larger than any of the domestic cats which have gone wild and are often found in the bush. The place she saw it was wild and remote from the nearest village. This information tied in with what little I have been able to learn about *megalotis*. A nocturnal hunter and extremely shy of man, it is said to haunt the densest jungles of both Timor and the neighboring island of Rotti.

Timor is as innocent of conservation as Eve was of clothes. There are no game laws and anyone can shoot anything, any time. The local sport is highjacking deer with the lights of a jeep at night. However, the nature of the terrain is such that probably very little is killed. Outside of the European officers and the Chinese merchants, almost no one owns a jeep and even these rugged vehicles are often defeated by the nature of the roads.

The Portuguese, however, enforce game laws in Angola, where they have saved the giant sable, in Mozambique and in their other African provinces; and I see no reason why Timor should not join this progressive movement. At dinner with the Governor I suggested that he have a survey made of the island's fauna and then consider some laws to protect the rare species like *megalotis*. I also talked conservation with Barbosa, the Director of Tourism, and pointed out to him the advantages of interesting visitors in Timor's fauna. There are a great many tropical birds and enough grey monkeys, deer, wild pig, wild buffalo to make interesting viewing, if a preserve were formed and roads built.

A rumor that a rare cat had been seen recently at Maubara, 50 kilometers up the coast toward Oe Cussi, prompted us to drive there and even though the cat turned out to be of the common civet variety, we had a fascinating day. Captain Mendonca had phoned the local King and His Majesty had ordered out his cavalry escort. Mounted on tough little Timor horses (they are not ponies), the guard of fifty lancers wearing their traditional turbans and gay colored tunics was as fine a show as I have seen since I saw a dress parade of the 17/21 Lancers in India in 1935. The King himself, mounted on a bay stallion, was a sight to behold. On his turban he wore a gold crescent; around his neck ropes of red beads, every four inches of which signified ownership of a bullock. He carried a silver-mounted sword and his stirrups were old gold coins on loops into which the big toe fit.

The flag of Portugal headed the squadron and after giving me the official salute, the King passed his men in review. Later, over tea in the palace, His Majesty told me something of the history of Maubara. He personally remembered the record to his sixth great grandfather who ruled over many more than the 15,000 persons over whom the present King, Gaspar Nuseas, now reigns.

The local kings of Timor still have considerable prestige and their authority is backed by the Portuguese. Gaspar, and the King of Oe Cussi, whom we also met, are two of the most powerful on the island. During the last war Gaspar's father remained loyal to Portugal despite all the efforts of the Japanese to sway him. There is a Portuguese memorial over his grave, donated by a grateful government.

The small European population of Dili have few chances to get away and enjoy themselves, and all of the invited guests were pleased when Barbosa took us in his launch for a day's outing to Atauro, the purple island which looms like Bali-Hai across the water from Dili. Atauro is one of the string of islands which stretch along the southern boundary of the Flores Sea, but all the rest, including Wetar, Alor and

Flores, are Indonesian. It is partly ringed by a coral reef and we had a wonderful time swimming with goggles and watching the multi-colored fish dart through their subterranean jungles. I saw a purple star fish and a giant clam, quite capable of trapping the unwary swimmer.

Among the guests was Guia Perreira, the Chief Administrative Officer of the Government of Timor, whose duties include everything not on the military side. Approached about the importance of conservation, he immediately agreed to look around the island for a suitable area which might be proclaimed a sanctuary. As I suspected, he said that Timor now has no game laws and nothing is protected, but the state of the roads and the lack of guns among the natives effectively limits hunting. Perreira is also the press officer and I urged him to invite my friend Tillman Durdin of the *New York Times* to visit Timor. The island has touristic possibilities but even in Australia, next door, few people have heard of it.

Today, no one on Timor seems to know where Captain Bligh landed after his epic journey by open boat from Tahiti in 1788, but since he passed through the Torres Strait and crossed the Arafura Sea, it is logical to suppose that he stepped ashore at one of the little forts which guard the south coast of the island. The forts are still used and except for the silent cannon, are pretty much the same as when Bligh saw them. Such a bastion of Portuguese rule is the Fort of Tranqueira, some forty kilometers down the coast from Baucau, the sleepy town where once a week the big plane from Darwin arrives.

We stopped at the fort on our way from Baucau, to which we had flown in a government plane from Dili to Lospalmos, the capitol of the District of Lautem, where we were to spend the night with the Administrator. (Timor is divided into 11 administrative districts, each under an administrator and subdivided into 40 subdivisions each under a Chef de Poste.) Near Lospalmos a rare cat had been sighted and it was to check on this, as well as to see the south side of the island, that we were prompted to accept the kind invitation of Eduardo Barbosa, the Director of Tourism, to make a three-day trip with him by Land Rover from Baucau.

Unlike the rugged north coast, where the capitol of Dili is situated, the southern shore of Timor is one of gently rolling country where much of the island's rice is grown. We noted that although buffalo are used to prepare the paddy fields for planting, they perform this operation by simply stamping about. No plow is used. One crop of rice is grown per year, perhaps because in many places there is not sufficient water or fertilizer for a second crop. The villages of Lautem are unique in the great peaked roofs of the houses, which give the huts the look of squat tea urns with huge knitted caps over them. Purpose of the thatched roofs is to store grain where the rats, pigs, ants, and other predators can't reach it. All of the houses in Timor are built on stilts, but those of Lautem are by far the highest we saw.

We passed numerous sluggish, crocodile-haunted rivers and saw grey monkeys chattering in the trees. The Timor jungles are not as dense as those of Central Africa, but they are rich in the size of their trees. We passed massive wild fig trees whose branches formed domed rooms of perpetual twilight, tall teaks and many varieties of eucalyptus. Creepers twined the trees together and once I saw a brilliant yellow snake glide along a branch. Timor has many poisonous snakes and among them is the yellow cobra, but since cobras are ground snakes the one I saw must have been a different species.

Lospalmos lies on an upland plateau, more than 1,000 feet above the sea and we passed droves of Timor ponies, water buffalo, and goats pasturing on the rolling prairie. Just outside the town the Land Rover refused to function and we had to be pulled into the Administrator's house behind a truck loaded with firewood.

From Lospalmos we drove on little used country trails to Tutuala, the most remote of the subdivisions of Lautem, where Ignacio de Rosario Perreira, the 26-year-old Timorese Chef de Poste (the great majority of the Chefs de Poste are Timorese) showed us the sights. At the end of the island, Tutuala lies 1,500 feet above the ocean and one can see both the Timor sea on the south, which is known as the Tassi or male sea because of its turbulence, and the Savu Sea or female sea on the north.

We almost failed to reach Barican that night. One of the four rivers which we had to ford on our journey to Lautem had risen and Barbosa, who had once been detained at this river for seven hours, was all ready to call for horses. Ten miles on the tiny Timor horses would have been quite a canter. Fortunately, the Land Rover got through.

After a good dinner at our pension, the Posado de Santiago, the colonel of the garrison of Baucau and some of his young officers came to call. One of these, a hunter and amateur zoologist, told me that he had seen *megalotis* several times near Baucau and that a friend of his, a lieutenant of the cavalry stationed at Maubisse, high in the mountains (about the 6,000 foot level) had also reported seeing one. Both descriptions checked with that of the wife of the Administrator at Ermera and with the data given me by numerous Timorese natives.

Singapore is a great and exciting city of almost two million people, three quarters of whom are Chinese. The standard of living is one of the highest in Asia and one can buy anything from a Cadillac to a clothespin without leaving a city block.

The British presence is still an important factor in Singapore. By treaty with Malaysia, Her Majesty's Government still controls the air fields and naval installations of the island and, at present, Admiral Beg, Commander in Chief of British Forces in the Far East, has a force of some 70,000 men in the area.

We had a delightful luncheon with Philip Moore, the Deputy British High Commissioner, who in addition to being an able diplomat is a sportsman and takes a keen interest in wildlife. He and his wife gave us a run-down of the national parks and a good deal of information about local citizens interested in conservation. Originally, I had planned to spend at least a week in Malaysia, go up to Kuala Lumpur, pay my respects to the Prime Minister, and see some of the game parks, but a change in our reservations for Russia and Mongolia necessitated a general speed-up and it was necessary to cut down on this leg of the trip.

Despite the limited time, I did manage a very good session with Dr. J. L. Harrison, Professor of Zoology at the University of Singapore, and thoroughly knowledgeable on Malaysia's fauna conservation problems. He said that the slandang are probably down to 500 head and are constantly being poached. The herd in the King George V Game Park, Malaya's only sizable reserve, amounts to only about 20 head. He estimates there are probably a dozen Asiatic rhino left and most of these are in Selengor. The Chinese demand for rhino horn for aphrodisiac purposes is so great that the horn from the stuffed rhino in the Sarawak Museum was stolen and a plastic one which replaced it was also stolen. What a surprise some rich old Chinaman will have when he tries to dissolve the plastic in his tea.

Banting, the handsome wild cattle, are still found in pathetically few numbers in Trengganu. Harrison felt, however, that all three of these big animals were getting some protection, while three other less attractive species may well be in worse shape. He cited the crocodile, which is now raised commercially in ponds, but since the supply of small crocs has virtually dried up with the stoppage of trade with Indonesia, the few remaining large crocs in Malaysia are under greater pressure. Leathery turtles, which lay their eggs on only one beach in the Peninsula, are growing so scarce that this beach has become a tourist resort with the onlookers encouraging the turtles to produce, a state of affairs hardly guaranteed to please the shy lady turtles.

The dugong, that mermaid-like sea cow that I have reported on from Ceylon and the Amazon, is becoming rare in Malaysian waters. Harrison says there are no reliable statistics about it and that a survey of the dugongs, as well as the crocodiles and leathery turtles, is urgently needed.

The orang-utan occurs in both North Borneo and Sarawak, now states of Malaysia, but there is a great deal of smuggling. I learned that young orangs can be bought in Singapore despite the strict prohibition against their importation and sale. Estimates of the number of these big apes vary but there are probably not more than 3,000 in Malaysia and 2,000 in Indonesia. Dr. Tom Harrison and his wife of the Sarawak Museum are the experts on the orangs.

Singapore Island consists of only about 224 square miles, but contains 8,000 acres of parks and reserves within its boundaries. As a guest of Dr. Chew Wee-Lek, a Cambridge-trained botanist, I was driven to the Catchment Area and shown a rain forest of great trees. Many small animals live there, including wild pigs, mouse deer, porcupines, two species of squirrels, and two species of wild monkeys. There is also the Singapore rat, a rodent found no place else in the world. Dr. Chew told me that during the war a tiger swam over to Singapore from the Sultan's game park and maintained itself for some days in this primeval reserve in the middle of the city.

With more than 4 million people crowded into a bit less than 400 square miles, it is hard to imagine that Hong Kong has any space left for ants, much less a respectable list of animals and birds. One forgets that, due to the rugged terrain, humans can only live on 62 square miles of the islands, and the remaining 336 square miles are the haunts of deer, pigs, pangolins, porcupines, civet cats, and assorted rats. Although some of these and almost all of the birds are protected by laws, enforcement of these laws is no easier in the Crown Colony than it is in the vast plains of Africa, and poaching is rife. Most of it is not for food but for "sport." Cut off from more fertile fields of hunting by the communists, the weekend shooter takes his shotgun and light rifle into the hills and stalks almost anything that moves and is not wearing clothes.

None of these animals is in any danger of extinction as they occur all along the Chinese coast, but there is a rare bird, the Chinese egret, which is said to nest in Hong Kong. Hard to distinguish from the common egret, it was decimated by plume hunters in the late 19th century and has since shown little ability to recover. According to the Red Book, the last two birds collected of which we have a record is a pair from the Yellow Sea coast of Korea. Specimens collected in South Shantung Province in 1937 were available for study in Peking in 1937. Originally, however, it was found in Fukien, Kwangtung, Kiangsu, Shantung and Taiwan, and was even said to have wintered in the Celebes, the Philippines and Thailand, although most ornithologists refuse to believe they nested so far south.

Concern over Hong Kong's fauna has been mounting for many years, but it was not until recently that an effort was made to do anything about it from the standpoint of establishing reserves and tightening up the game laws. Encouraged by such well-known members of the World Wildlife Fund as Peter Scott and Ian MacPhail, the Hong Kong government obtained the services of Dr. Lee Talbot and his attractive wife Marty, who is also a scientist, to make a study of the colony's wildlife ecology, and recommend measures to conserve it. The Talbots were in the Far East on a mission for the World Wildlife Fund to study wildlife resources of parks in a number of countries and were able to wedge in the Hong Kong study after having completed their jobs in Indonesia and the Philippines, and before they began work in Thailand and Malaysia. They had just completed their report on the day of our arrival in the Colony.

Prepared for the Agricultural and Fisheries Department of the Hong Kong Government, the draft report which the Talbots kindly showed me strongly recommended that National Parks be established and that a Nature Conservancy Council be organized. The report, in fact, endorsed the proposals made by the Forestry Officer of the Department of Agriculture and Fisheries which Peter Scott thought highly of during his visit to the Colony the previous year.

While today the Hong Kong Hills are clothed in green, the vegetation is mainly scrub and bears little resemblance to the tropical rain forests which covered the island up to 1,000 years ago. According to the zoologists, elephants, tigers, and leopards roamed the countryside while dugongs and crocodiles infested the estuaries. Deforestation has since severely affected the vegetation and soil and probably the climate of the island. Constant burning and cutting of protective covering has laid the land open to torrential rains resulting in erosion and increasingly severe floods.

Despite this drastic change in habitat, some of the finest big game of China have held on and only recently become extinct in Hong Kong. The last known leopard was shot eight miles from Sha Tau Kok in December, 1957, while the South China tiger disappeared from the Colony seventeen years ago. Even the Asiatic wild dog, a wily and hardy scavenger that has survived in many parts of China's barren provinces, is now only a memory in Hong Kong. No recent reports have been made of the Eastern Chinese otter and the crab-eating mongoose and the chances are that both no longer live there.

The beaches of many islands which make up the Hong Kong Colony were used by the green turtles to lay their eggs. Although the turtles are greatly respected and even worshipped by the fishermen as symbols of longevity, their eggs are not, and for countless generations the eggs have been taken from the nests, pickled and fed to babies to prevent diarrhea. Such a policy of living on capital could not continue forever and in 1963 only one green turtle was known to have returned to Hong Kong. An attempt by Professor J. G. Phillips of the University of Hong Kong in cooperation with the Department of Agriculture and Fisheries to save the eggs of this last survivor met with failure. The villagers of Lamma island promised to protect the eggs and were offered a reward for each hatched egg received by the University. Instead of this, they dug up all the eggs, reburied six, and demanded a reward for finding the nest.

The giant salamander, which grows to five feet, used to be found in the streams of Hong Kong and is still imported into the Colony. According to Dr. Phillips, one can buy them alive in the market for 4 shillings a catty or 1⅓ pounds.

The Emperors who ruled the Middle Kingdom from the Dragon Throne in Peking did so by the Mandate of Heaven and when this mandate was withdrawn they and their dynasties crumbled into the good earth of China. Hong Kong's mandate is less spiritual. In fact, a good chunk of it ends in 1998, when the lease by which the Crown

Colony holds most of the New Territories on the mainland expires. Without this land and water from the Chinese rivers, the existence of the Colony would be precarious, so say the least. But until then, barring a sudden decision by Mao or his successors to take it over, the future of Hong Kong is reasonably stable and in order to give its 4 million inhabitants some place to escape from their incredibly crowded cities to enjoy the peace and fresh air of nature, a series of national parks and nature reserves is now under consideration.

In order to see some of these projects, I spent several long and interesting days with E. H. Nichols, Assistant Director of the Department of Agriculture and Fisheries, and P. H. Daley, the Forestry Officer. Crossing on the ferry to Kowloon on the mainland, we drove to the Tai Lam Chung Catchment area where a range of newly forested mountains drain their brooks into a series of small blue lakes. One such stream, the Shing Mun, might be stocked with trout, for it rises at the 2,500 foot level and flows clear and cold for several miles down a shaded valley. Old tea terraces ridge the hills and the only sound is the twittering of the birds and the drone of the crickets. Except for a few tiny farms far down the stream, the vistas are all pastoral scenes of rural China even including an ancient grave where the spirits of long-forgotten ancestors still enjoy the blessings of "wind and water."

The Sai Kung Penninsula is another site which the Department would like to turn into a national park. Attached to the mainland by a narrow neck, the area would be an excellent one for fauna as it would require a minimum of guards to patrol the entrance. The plan envisions a first zone comprising facilities for parking, restaurants, and possibly a nature museum; and a second zone where the aged and the very young could stroll on prepared pathways with picnic areas. The remaining, and by far the greater part of the peninsula, would be left wild and stocked with all types of indigenous fauna. I personally see no reason why the Asiatic leopard could not be reintroduced, providing there are sufficient wild pig and deer to satisfy its appetite. To the best of my knowledge there has never been a case in Krueger Park in South Africa of one of the big spotted cats eating a tourist. In fact, they are rarely seen during the day.

A third area is the Mai Po Marshes which are now the habitat of a good number of birds and could be the home of many more if adequate protection were available. It was in these marshes that Frederick Hechtel, President of the Hong Kong Bird Watching Society, saw a

Chinese egret, the rare bird about which my friend, Col. Jack Vincent, editor of the Red Book, wants more data. Hechtel said he saw only one specimen and that was in 1963. A census made by the Society in 1960 showed that there were eight egreteries then, of which two contained a total of nine occupied nests. Those two were near the hamlet of Yuen Long. In 1963 a member of the Society reported that the Chinese egrets were apparently breeding at Shau Tau Kok on the border between the New Territories and Red China. Today it is thought that the birds are breeding only in the Shau Tau Kok area.

Extremely hard to distinguish from the common egret, the rare Chinese species has blue face markings, but these appear only during the breeding season. The one other difference is that the Chinese variety has a different number of plumes and carries them at a slightly different angle. Lord Medway, a British ornithologist, believes they occur in Malaya; and Mr. Metson, of the American Consulate here, reports that they are also found on Taiwan.

In addition to my journeys around the Colony, I spent some profitable hours with Professor J. G. Phillips, head of the Department of Zoology at Hong Kong University. A slight young man in his early thirties, Phillips has already made a name in his field and has been an important instigator of wildlife projects in the Colony. Dr. Patricia Marshall, an attractive assistant professor in his department, has also been a keen promoter of the cause. She showed me an exhibit of almost all the species of animals and birds that occur in the Colony. Hundreds of students were viewing them with fascinated interest, especially the live exhibits. There was a small wild boar, several mongooses, a fox, and some well-fed rats. Birds included a pied harrier, herring gull, eagle owl, brown shrike, francolin and violet whistling thrush. Pat Marshall and Dr. Charles Grant, a forestry expert at the University, drove me high into the wilds of Hong Kong Island and showed me the hut where a good deal of zoology field work is done.

Just before I left, a round table meeting was held to discuss the whole subject of conservation, and to it were invited all interested parties in the government, the university, and private life. I outlined the objectives of the World Wildlife Fund, sketched some of our missions, and told of my trips and talks in the Colony. It was generally agreed that the Talbot recommendations for parks and reserves should be implemented, and that a board of prominent citizens should be chosen to advise the government department selected to run the conservation program.

The next move was to discuss with the Governor the importance of these recommendations. As is the case in virtually every one of the twenty-three countries which we have so far visited in Africa, the Middle and Far East, and South America, the decisions can only be made at the Summit. We dined with Sir David Trench and later we had a long private talk in which I outlined in detail the proposals made by the Talbots and stressed the point that they were basically the suggestions made by the Department of Agriculture and Fisheries and the interested men at the University of Hong Kong such as Professor Phillips. A colonial officer who has served all over the lot, the Governor is sympathetic to conservation generally and I believe will do his best to see that Hong Kong gets some parks and reserves. On my last day I held a press conference and saw to it that our recommendations were duly reported.

TWENTY

Taiwan: Viable Fortress

HIGH ON A green mountain top, the flag of free China snapped in the breeze as we dropped through the clouds and landed at Taipei. I was glad to see it and glad to be back. It was ten years since I had been to Taiwan and seventeen since I first flew there on a visit from Nanking during the last days of the Republic on the mainland. Admiral Jerauld Wright, our Ambassador, met us at the airport along with representatives of the Chinese government, the Asia Foundation, and the Chinese Association for the Conservation of Natural Resources.

The Generalissimo's ruling that Taiwan is simply a province of China where his government is temporarily detained, is reflected in the laws. Originally framed in Nanking for all of China, they are still in force on the island. The basic game laws, for instance, apply to tigers among other animals which flourish in South China, but have never roamed the Taiwanese mountains. In fact, local game laws for the island have never been issued and their absence is a source of worry to the members of the Chinese Association for the Conservation of Nature and Natural Resources, the recently formed body dedicated to doing something about Taiwan's vanishing natural resources.

Secretary of the Association is Hunter Han-ting Eu, a bright young Taiwanese who cares greatly about wildlife and with little help is doing all he can to save it. Harold Coolidge, my colleague on the World Wildlife Board, helped him organize the Association, which now has a twenty-one-man Board of Directors and some 500 members.

234

Working with interested government agencies, the Association framed a National Park Law to establish nature reserves, which was then sent to the Executive Yuan for consideration. If passed by that body, it will go to the Legislative Yuan where it can become law and where an agency to run it will be designated.

As in Hong Kong, the decision to establish national parks depends greatly on the key men and the good will of C. K. Yen, the Premier, and Chieh Huang, the Governor of Taiwan, is vital to the project.

The Japanese during the fifty years they ran the island proclaimed a number of national parks but had not gotten around to doing much about them by 1945 when Taiwan was lost to the Allies. In fact, it was not until recently that anyone of importance began to worry about conservation and even this initial stirring might not have gone far if the Asia Foundation, a privately financed American cultural organization, had not given Hunter Eu and his friends a grant to pay for the formation of the Chinese Association for the Conservation of Nature and Natural Resources. The grant was made by Edgar Pike, who then headed the Taiwan office of the Foundation and is now in Hong Kong where he responded to my plea for conservation books for the schools by giving another grant. The present representative of the Foundation in Taiwan is Walter Mallory-Browne who is interested in conservation and, I believe, will also be of help to the cause.

According to the Red Book, two pheasants and a deer are in danger of extinction on Taiwan. The Mikado pheasant is restricted to the mountain areas of the island, usually above the 5,000 foot level. Nothing is being done now about protecting these beautiful birds from the Aborigines who hunt them for food, and unless a special reserve with guards is set up, the chances of their survival is not good. Luckily the Ornamental Pheasant Trust, a British organization devoted to saving rare species of pheasants, has been able to purchase Mikados from Taiwan and has bred up a sizable stock of them. When and if the Chinese government is willing to provide a secure reserve, the Trust has said they would be glad to provide birds to help stock it.

Swinhoe's pheasant, although reputedly more abundant than the Mikado, is thought to be growing very rare. There are about 220 in the world zoos and perhaps an equal number in private collections. The Pheasant Trust has indicated that it would return to Taiwan some of these pheasants for breeding if the authorities set up an adequate park for them.

One of the rarest birds in the world, the Japanese ibis used to be seen in many of the provinces of mainland China and occasionally on Taiwan. There are only 12 of these birds in Japan. The Chinese egret, about which I reported in Hong Kong, is also said to be an occasional visitor to Taiwan.

To find out all I could about these rare birds, I visited the Taipei Municipal Zoological Garden where I was taken around by Superintendent Ching Chih Chai, and Professor Dien Zuh-Ming, Curator of Birds at the Taiwan Museum. I saw and photographed a pair of Mikado and a pair of Swinhoe's pheasants. Both are handsome members of the pheasant tribe and said to be fine eating, hence their decline. Superintendent Ching, who gets most of his birds and animals from the aboriginal trappers, believes that the Swinhoe's pheasants are not in as critical shape as the Mikado because more are offered him by the mountain people. Although discovered and described by the English collector, Walter Goodfellow, in 1906, the bird was named after the Emperor of Japan who then ruled Taiwan. In addition to trapping by the aborigines, who eat it as well as take its feathers for ornaments, the Mikado suffers greatly from its natural enemy, the Formosan yellow-throated marten.

Neither Dien or Ching had ever heard of the Japanese crested ibis or the Chinese egret visiting Taiwan. Asked about the possibility of their still being found on the mainland, they said they doubted it because any birds as rare as these would certainly be mentioned in the mainland ornithological magazines which are on sale in Hong Kong.

I was pleased to find a thriving herd of 49 Chinese Sika deer in the Garden's zoo. The Formosan Sika is a sub-species, known as *taiouanus,* and herds of it are now in captivity in various parks and zoos in England and in the Bronx Zoo in America. The Taipei herd should be added to the Red Book list.

According to Ching the Sika is now very rare on Taiwan. The Aborigines hunt it vigorously for its antlers which, when in velvet, are highly valued as a potent aphrodisiac. The current price is $5,000 Taiwan dollars or about $125.00 a pair. Only the male has horns, but both sexes have medicinal uses in the opinion of Chinese doctors.

Although not in the Red Book, the Formosan cloudy leopard most certainly should be. It is so rare now that only one has been shot in the past few years. This was a young female killed by an Aborigine on January 13, 1964 in the northeast section of the island at the 2,000 foot level. There are three poorly mounted specimens in the Taiwan Museum from which I deduce that the Formosan species is one of the smallest of the leopard family, probably weighing no more than 70 pounds. It is even smaller than the snow leopard which is really not a leopard at all but an ounce. The rosettes on the skin are large, irregular, and cloudy.

The Formosan bear is almost near the point where its questionable survival entitles it to be listed among the rare animals of the Red Book. There is a single specimen in the Taiwan zoo and few skins have been offered for sale by the Aborigines in recent years. Similar to the sloth bears of many countries in Asia, the Formosan species has a white "V" on its chest.

The Formosan serow is still said to be maintaining itself on the more inaccessible of the mountains. An expedition mounted by the U.S. Naval Medical Research Unit No. 2 in 1960 procured three specimens from the Aborigines who trapped them. Few of these wild goats are shot as they have become extremely wary of man in long centuries of bitter experience.

Natural enemies account for only a fraction of the wildlife destruction on Taiwan. Canniest and most implacable destroyer is man, whose bows, spears, and guns are always ready, and whose traps, snares, and pitfalls stud the ancient game trails. These hunters are not "sportsmen" from the cities, but Aborigines whose meagre diet demands meat— and how else can they get it except by hunting?

On Taiwan, the 10 million Taiwanese-Chinese and the 2 million mainland Chinese don't get along very well, but both tend to look down together on the 300,000 Aborigines and occasionally still call them barbarians. Only a few decades ago, the tamer Aborigines who had adopted Chinese ways were called Pe-po-hoan, or People of the Plain, while the mountaineers were called Chi-hoan or Raw Barbarians. A few really integrated Aborigines were called Sek-hoan or Ripe Barbarians. Like the American Indians, the Aborigines of Taiwan made the mistake of arriving first. Probably of Malayan stock, they migrated north with the ocean currents and arrived long before the envoy of the Suy Emperor claimed it for his master in 620 A.D..

The first Europeans were the Portuguese who founded a settlement in 1590. Later came the Dutch and Spanish, who were both evicted by the famous Chinese pirate, Koxinga. An early conservationist of sorts, Koxinga imported a pair of tigers whose progeny were reported for some decades before the line died out. In 1686 the Chinese Emperors restored their rule over the island and held it until 1894 when it was ceded to Japan at the close of the Sino-Japanese war.

The Aborigines today are the only inhabitants of Taiwan who are issued free shooting permits. Furthermore, free bullets are given them by the police and no tax is levied on income derived from hunting. No wonder the Sika deer is near extinction. A pair of its antlers in velvet will bring an Aboriginal family sufficient income to supply their few wants of manufactured goods for the next year.

To see something of the Aborigines and their remote mountain haunts, we spent three days flying and driving around the island. Taking off from Taipei airport in the early morning, we flew due south to Hua Lien, a little fishing port on the Pacific coast of the island. Hunter Eu of the Forestry Department accompanied us, and at the Hua Lien Airport we were met by a jeep station wagon driven by the best and most careful chauffeur in the employ of the Joint Commission on Rural Reconstruction, who furnished our transport through the mountains.

The Toroko Gorge Road, completed a few years ago, is an exciting and spectacular ride. Cut from the living rock, the narrow, one-lane passage twists and turns through a series of tunnels and frequently leaps the rushing Takiri River on fragile-looking bridges. There are often no guard barriers, and the drop is seldom less than 500 feet.

Tourists go to Toroko, but seldom beyond it. The reason why is easy to find. The road ceases to be asphalt and becomes a gravel track; the guard stones virtually vanish and every mile or so there are gangs of ex-soldiers repairing the most recent landslide. Taiwan has frequent earthquakes and the shale which makes up most of the mountains is prone to slide. The bridges are metal but the floors are wooden and the boards are spaced widely enough to afford excellent views of the river far below.

Beyond Toroko the road starts to climb and does so steadily until the 6,000 foot level when we suddenly entered a world of mist. The great spruces—we saw one with a circumference of 35 feet whose age is said to be 2,000 years—are festooned with hanging moss. Hemlocks cling to the steep cliffs; and only one bird was seen, a solitary raven perched on a dead branch glaring at us. As we approached the Ho Huan Pass at 7,800 feet, we climbed out of the mist and into a bright

36. Notornis, South Island, New Zealand

37. Paradise duck, New Zealand

38. Kiwi, New Zealand

39. Tasmanian tiger

40. Frilled dragon

41. Melville Island aborigines constructing a canoe

42. Thatched house in Lautem, Portuguese Timor

43. Tribal chief, Portuguese Timor

44. Rice paddies, interior of Taiwan

45. Aerial view of Tasmania

46. Przewalski's horse

47. Milking a Bactrian camel, Mongolia

48. Partridge, Mongolia

49. Red-tailed shrike, Mongolia

50. Lake Baikal, Siberia

51. Baikal seal

52. Siberian tiger

blue world where the birds sang again, and spread below us was a white lake of mist.

Just as the sun was setting, we arrived at Li Shan and were ushered into the new hotel in the style of a Chinese palace which rambles beneath Mount Sylvia, 13,000 feet high. After a very good dinner made in the Fukien manner, we interviewed a group of young Aborigines especially summoned from the nearby villages. They confirmed the rumor that the cloudy leopard survived until recently. One lad's father had killed one ten years ago and another said that there are still tales of its appearance in the remote mountains of the central range. Anyone who has ever seen the wild and rugged peaks of this massif will concede that anything might be living there. Using ten-power glasses, I searched many of the high slopes where the timber is a primary stand and the matted undergrowth would make exploration all but impossible.

Few of the villagers possess guns and those that do rely mostly on ancient muzzle-loaders. There are a few old Japanese rifles around, but it is hard to get bullets for them. Most of the game is caught by traps of which three types are used. A sapling is bent over and attached to a loop on the ground. When the animal enters the loop and trips it, the sapling is released and hangs the unfortunate beast in the air. Conventional iron traps are also used and there is a variety of cage traps for smaller game. Large game such as serow and sambar are hunted with a pack of local dogs which drive the quarry toward the passes where the Aborigines wait to shoot or spear it.

Sambar, serow, and pig seem to be in good supply, but I was able to get no definite word about the Sika. All had heard of this small spotted deer, but none had seen one. The mountains of Taiwan are laced with streams, and as there are 51 peaks over 10,000 feet in altitude, the torrents in which they breed are always cold and clear. The Japanese introduced rainbow trout with considerable success, but since they left no one has made any effort to control the fishing and there are virtually no trout left.

The impossibility of conserving game or fish on Taiwan until adequate laws are passed and enforced was brought home to us when we picked up two forest wardens on the road. One was armed with an old Japanese rifle and hand-loaded shells, while the other had a sack full of nets for birds. They said frankly that they always hunt and trap on their inspection trips. Since their pay is about 50 U.S. cents per day, one can hardly blame them for wanting to supplement it with additional income, to say nothing of an occasional meal of meat. Both boys were Aborigines of the Tyal tribe and were Protestants.

Instead of staying on the East-West Cross Island Highway which leads to Ku Kuan, Tungshih and Fengyuan, we took the seldom traveled feeder road to Wushe and climbed over a 10,000 foot pass in four wheel drive. Trees live at various altitudes and highest of all is the Taiwan fir. On the summit, we left even these hardy evergreens and emerged on a series of sky meadows of bright yellow grass.

Between Wushe and Puli we left the Aboriginal area—a permit was necessary to enter it—and drove along the fertile rice-growing valley from which one climbs to the Sun and Moon Lake, perhaps the most famous of the Taiwanese tourist attractions. While sitting on the porch of my hotel and looking over the misty lake, I jotted down my impressions of conservation in Taiwan.

The only hope for much of the remaining game (such as the sambar and the serow, to say nothing of the rare species like the Sika and the cloudy leopard) is to proclaim a series of sanctuaries where no one can hunt and no one can lumber. Possible areas for such parks would be Toroko Gorge, the Li Shan, Sun and Moon Lake, and Yu Shan south of the lake. Parks should be at least twenty-five square miles in area and should be patrolled on all roads which have access to them. The local Aborigines in these areas should be given rations of meat and then punished if they persisted in hunting. A survey should be made of the parks and a census of the game now in them. Sika could be introduced from the herd now in the Taiwan Zoo, and a breeding stock of both Swinhoe's and the Mikado pheasant could be procured from abroad, probably without cost aside from that of transportation. The cloudy leopard survives on the mainland and it might be possible to buy a pair through Hong Kong. Stocking the rivers with trout would be no problem.

The cost of setting up these parks and patrolling them would not be great. I understand that some 10,000 soldiers are retired from the army every year. Why not use a few thousand of them as game and forest guards in these Parks? They would probably like the job.

But quite aside from the possible profit and certain cost of the parks, the Republic of China is one of the great nations of the world and should have national parks. America, England, and every nation in

Europe has them. Even the Russians and the Poles have important national parks. The Government of China owes such parks to its people.

From Sun and Moon Lake we drove to Taichung where at Tung Hai University we called on Professor Johnson Chen, the venerable author of the only book on wildlife so far written in Taiwan. Although primarily a marine biologist, Dr. Chen is keenly interested in all of Taiwan's animals and birds and told me he is distressed over the present senseless slaughter. He said he would be glad to prepare for me an up-to-date list of all forms of wildlife which are now in danger of extinction. The list includes several species of fresh water fish which Dr. Chen said have now been exterminated in all but a few of the remoter rivers. The chapel of Taichung is of beautiful modern design and was presented by my old boss, Harry Luce of Time Inc., who spent most of his youth in China.

TWENTY-ONE

Of Whales and Men

IN THE ANCIENT Chinese calendar of the Twelve Beasts, which in the remote past was adopted by the Empire of the Rising Sun, 1965 was the Year of the Snake, a form of wildlife greatly respected in the Orient for its ability to survive. Unfortunately, there is no Year of the Whale to call attention to the sad fact that certain species of this world's greatest mammal are in peril of extinction. Their survival now depends entirely on the willingness of the Japanese, Russian, and Norwegian whaling fleets to reduce their killings to a point where the blue whale, as well as the fin and humpback whales, have a chance to build up their dangerously reduced numbers.

Governing body for the whale-catching nations is the International Whaling Commission, which in 1960 appointed a committee of three eminent scientists to make a broad survey of the condition of the Antarctic whale stocks. The savants reported that drastic action must be taken immediately if the industry is to be maintained on a continuing basis. Their studies indicate that the blue and humpback whales are "in serious danger of extermination," and that the fin whales have been seriously depleted and are far below the levels of "maximum sustainable yields."

Faced with this grim forecast, it was assumed that the whaling nations would instruct their delegates to approve wide conservation measures when the Commission met in July of 1965, but four of the seventeen nations represented refused to go along and the meeting

242

ended in complete failure. Japan was primarily responsible. It was her objection to the reduced quotas urged by the scientists that wrecked the effort to save the whales. Subsequently, Russia, Norway, and the Netherlands also refused to approve the conservation program. Since then, the Netherlands has sold her last pelagic fleet, and Norway has made it plain she would be glad to go along with the reforms, but can not afford to unless Russia and Japan also agree.

Largest of the five whales which are commercially fished is the blue. It is now estimated that less than 2,000 of these 100-foot monsters still survive. The Committee had recommended complete protection for them for a number of years, failing which they predicted a "distinct risk of extinction." Next largest is the 90-foot fin whale whose numbers have been so depleted that the average catch per catcher ship has declined from 3.3 fin whales in the 1955–56 season to 1.0 in the 1964–65 season. As of the present, the world population of these whales can only support an annual catch of about 4,000 fin whales, but in 1964–65 the industry killed 14,000—about 10,000 more than the stock can stand. Of the three smaller whales, the humpback is also in very short supply and the sei and sperm are beginning to show a marked decline.

The industry is now based primarily on the fin whale, since the blue is too rare to count on and the smaller whales are less economic to hunt. If the industry is to survive, therefore, the fin whale must be allowed to recover. Given this opportunity, the scientists say that there is no reason why it would not be possible to breed back the fins to a point where yearly catches of 20,000 whales could be safely taken.

One of my primary reasons for going to Japan was to see what could be done to persuade the Japanese Government to put pressure on the whaling fleet owners to restrict their kills of all whales and, in any case, to refrain from taking Blues. I began the campaign by enlisting the support of our then Ambassador, Edwin Reischauer. I was able to brief him on the whale crisis, as well as profit from his opinions on the passing scene in Japan. Deputy Chief of our Embassy was our Minister, John Emmerson, an old and good friend of mine, who not only put us up in his pleasant house, but arranged for me to meet many of the persons in Tokyo I wanted to see.

John takes a broad interest in wildlife and gave attention to the plight of the whales.

From Arranie Suomela, the Fisheries expert of our Tokyo Embassy, I learned that even though the four rebel whaling nations refused to agree to the Commissions' recommendation that the 1964–65 quota be reduced to 4,000 blue whale units, Japan, USSR, Norway, and the Netherlands, subsequently agreed (unofficially) to restrict their total kill to 8,000 BWU. (A blue whale unit is the standard measure in the industry: 1 BWU equals 1 blue whale, or 2 fin whales, or 2½ humpback whales and 6 sei whales. Sperm whales are not classified in BWU's.) The figure was, of course, ridiculous because the industry could not find enough whales to fill such a quota, and all the fleets fell below their individual allotments.

Three Japanese companies own seven pelagic fleets. Only one of these, the Polar Whaling Company, gets the bulk of its income from whaling.

The Russians have four fleets.

Suomela, who was formerly a Commissioner of the United States Fish and Wildlife Service and knows a good deal about survival statistics, told me that unless the whaling nations agree to rest the whales now, the industry will be destroyed in three years. He showed me figures clearly indicating the steady decline of the past ten years in the blue, fin, and humpback kills. As the killer boats find fewer and fewer of the big whales, they try to make up their quota with the smaller ones and greatly increased kills of the little sei whales are beginning to be reflected in decreasing numbers.

I also discussed the sad case of the whales with Japanese friends and came to the conclusion that my campaign to put pressure on the Japanese Whaling Companies should be a three-pronged attack. I would see the Minister of Agriculture, whose word is law to the whaling fleets. I would bring up the subject with all members of the Imperial Family with whom I talked. And, lastly, I would say exactly what I thought about the Japanese whalers in my press conference.

Japan never ceases to amaze me. In 1935 I had never seen a nation more war-like, and in 1945 more completely defeated; and now, twenty years later, more prosperous. Leading Asia in the field of industrial expansion, the Japanese should also take the lead on conservation. Unfortunately, however, this is far from the case. There is no over-all authority to look after wildlife, and I can find no reason to believe that such a department will be organized. Ministries, such as Education, Agriculture, and Fisheries, have some interest in conserving natural resources, but only where the livelihood of a substantial number of the population (as in the fishing industry) is concerned.

I noted a general interest in conservation among the people I talked with, but even though they were in an economic bracket which could afford charity, they complained that since such donations would not be tax-deductible they could give only small sums. Like those of Australia and New Zealand, the Japanese tax laws are antagonistic to charitable donations from individuals or corporations. Family deductions are limited to $60.00 per year and corporate deductible contributions can be made only to a special list of charities designated by the government. Wildlife is not on this list.

Diplomats have many opportunities to sell the conservation idea to prominent Japanese. In addition to briefing my own Ambassador, Minister, and the various counsellors I had a pleasant lunch as a guest of Dudley Cheke, the British Minister. Fluent in Japanese and a long-time resident of Japan, Cheke has a wide circle of friends whose good opinion is important to us. He told me that so far, at least, he had noticed no results from our initial effort. Van Gulik, the Dutch Ambassador, and De Frees, the Dutch Minister, with whom I served in China, were most helpful in making arrangements for me to see people of importance to our cause. De Frees arranged my meeting with Prince Hitachi, the younger son of the Emperor, and with Yoshinori Maeda, the President of the Japan Broadcasting Company.

A call on the president of a big Japanese company is almost as stylized as calling on royalty. I was met at the entrance of the building by the President's personal secretary, escorted to an elevator, whose operator bowed to me and to the secretary. On the executive floor I was handed over to a pretty girl secretary who bowed and took me in immediately to the President. An energetic stocky Japanese in his mid-fifties, Maeda has one of the most important jobs in the country. His company's radio and television programs reach almost all of the nation's 100 million people.

After the ritual tea, Maeda told me that he was a former news-paper man and had spent considerable time in Viet Nam. We talked of political developments in South East Asia and of the role Japan is now playing in them. Finally getting down to conservation, he said he had read with interest the blue print for starting a national appeal which was sent him from London. Asked what he thought the next step should be, he said that a prominent Japanese should be named to head the appeal and suggested former Prince Yamashina. I then raised the question as to how much money he thought could be raised, and he told me frankly that in view of Japan's stringent tax laws he did not think very large sums would be realized.

On the subject of the blue whale, Maeda was not as enthusiastic as I had hoped. He seemed to think that the Japanese whaling concerns are much too smart to live on capital, and the extinction of the animals from which they derive their profits is not good business practice. I cited some figures and told him that the newspapers would have the story from our standpoint.

One of the most interesting men I talked with about the possibilities of a Japanese Appeal was Dr. H. E. McClure, Chief of the Migratory Animal Pathological Survey, being carried on for U.S. Armed Forces Institute of Pathology. A red-headed scientist with and abiding affection for his work, McClure makes bird-banding (which is his chief interest) a fascinating subject. In the foreword to a pamphlet called *An Asian Bird-bander's Manual*, he says:

> Bird-banding or ringing is one of the most exciting and most satisfying of hobbies or research activities. The use of a gun has an important part in ornithological research, but the trap and net can lead into completely new avenues of thought and discovery. With a gun, a specimen is taken to the laboratory, with a camera, an instant is recorded, but in ringing, the bird is the primary objective. It is to be captured, studied alive, fully recorded, ringed, and released uninjured, both physically and emotionally. Only the patient, the soft-handed, and the considerate person may band. All others become useless in the field. Bird-banding is a condition of thought, an attitude, without which the would-be ringer had best desist from his efforts.

The results of the banding program answer many questions, not the least of which is the ability of birds to carry infectious diseases. Research has proved that a bird which lives part of the year in the Northeast of the United States has carried disease to an island in the Caribbean.

McClure said that the Russians are banding birds in the Lake Baikal area, and egrets have been found in Thailand and Malaya with Soviet identification rings.

Another American who is well versed in the conservation situation in Japan is Thomas L. Blakemore, a lawyer who has practiced in Tokyo for many years and is, in fact, the only American who has been admitted as a full member of the Japanese Bar. A gunner who also takes a wide interest in conservation, Blakemore has tramped over most of the Japanese Islands and is now interested in an expedition to find a rare wild cat which has been reported on Iriomoto-Jimo in the southernmost part of the Ryukyu Island chain. The cat, which is reported to have a short tail like our bobcat, a spotted dark coat, and stripes on the head, is trapped and eaten by the natives who usually throw away the skeleton and skin. The hide and part of the skeleton of one was discovered by the Japanese novelist and amateur mammalogist, Yuju Togawa, who immediately suspected that the cat was a new species, or subspecies, he had never seen before in Japan. This proved to be true, and the forthcoming expedition to trap a specimen is the result.

Blakemore told me that the Japanese otter is now so rare that he doubts if more than a few dozen still exist. My concern over the Japanese bear he labeled as premature. He has shot a number of these big bears—the males can weigh 1,000 pounds—and said they are still fairly plentiful in the northern island of Hokkaido. He added that hunters are just starting to use hounds to hunt them, and if restrictions are not introduced, this method might well result in greatly increased pressure on them. The Hokkaido wolf, the largest in the world, was exterminated by hunters in 1916. Hunting with hounds is also becoming popular as a means of bringing boar to bay. The hound used is called a "Plot" which Blakemore says "calls as it sniffs," a colorful way of saying it gives tongue when on the line.

According to Blakemore, Japanese hunters, unlike most of ours, pay strict attention to closed areas and are careful not to hunt in the territory which has been set aside by the government as "lying fallow," in other words, where the game is being allowed to replenish itself. The Japanese serow, the wild pig, and the deer all seem to be in good supply. He did not know if the Japanese deer is the Sika which has almost been exterminated in Taiwan and Northern China, but from his description, I rather think it is the same.

Responsibility for wildlife is divided between the Ministers of Agriculture and Education. I had appointments set up with both, but an extra session of the Diet prevented the Minister of Agriculture from keeping our engagement and my dates with the Royal Family came during the only spare time available to the Minister of Education.

His Imperial Majesty Hirohito is the 124th Emperor of Japan and even though his nation is no longer an empire in the colonial sense of having possessions, the ruler of 100 million of Asia's most progressive people is still regarded with awe and veneration by the vast majority of his subjects. In private life a kind and gentle man, he is said to be happiest when cataloguing his collection of marine biological specimens. I was not able to obtain an audience with the Emperor during my short stay in Tokyo, but I was able to see several members of the Royal Family; and I have every reason to believe that the objectives of my visit—to publicize the plight of the blue whale and to inquire into the possibility of setting up a Japanese Appeal for the World Wildlife Fund—were relayed to His Majesty.

Prince Chichibu, the Emperor's brother, whom I knew before the war, died some years ago, but his charming wife, the Princess, invited me to call and bring my wife and daughter. It was a warm spring day and the doors to the garden were open when the lady-in-waiting ushered us in. The Princess, looking much the same as she did when I first met her ten years ago, seemed genuinely pleased to see me and immediately asked what she could do to help my wildlife mission. I told her in some detail about the blue whale and she said she would repeat the gist of my plea to the Emperor. She added that since His Majesty is an expert on marine wildlife he would be sure to take an interest in the blue whales.

Although the moated grounds where the Royal Family lives are in the middle of Tokyo, they are so extensive and the walls are so thick that the roar of the city can be heard only faintly. Two varieties of pheasant, Reeves and Lady Amber, live in the grounds, and Her Highness called them by clapping her hands.

My second call was on Prince Hitachi, the second son of the Emperor, whom Prince Bernhard had originally interested in the World Wildlife Fund when he was in Tokyo for the Olympic Games. A shy young man of twenty-two, the Prince studied zoology and knows a good deal about the wildlife situation in Japan. He told me he was worried about the Japanese crane and the crested ibis. He had not, however, heard of the sad state of the blue whale and asked me to go into detail about it. I also asked him to mention the matter to his father, the Emperor, and he said he would be glad to.

Asked whom he thought would be a good man to head up a Japanese Appeal, the Prince said that he rather favored Mr. Maeda, but was not in a position to know how much time he or anyone else could give to the cause. Except for his shyness, which he will certainly get over as time goes on, it seems to me that the Prince himself would be an excellent president of the Appeal. The Royal Family has great prestige and anyone asked by a member of it to help would never hesitate to comply.

Although not a member of the Royal Family, Prince Yoshimaro Yamashina is closely related to it and looks a good deal like the Emperor, but is taller. Known today as plain Dr. Yamashina—he stopped using his title during the MacArthur days when the nobility was abolished—the ex-prince runs the Yamashina Institute for Ornithology and Zoology, the only one of its kind in Japan. Housed in a crowded heatless old building with mildewed ceilings, the Institute receives a small yearly stipend from the government but depends on private donations for field work. I gathered that Dr. Yamashina himself has to foot many of the bills.

Seated in his dusty office with files stacked to the ceiling, the Doctor, with a kindly smile, told me about the status of Japan's rare birds and said that if I only had the time he would be happy to accompany me to see them. There are exactly one dozen Japanese crested ibis left and the only reason why this corporal's guard of these stately birds survives is because in 1959, when the total was down to four, the Government purchased a 1,000 acre reserve for them on the Noto Peninsula. Common in the middle years of the Nineteenth Century, the crested ibis was almost exterminated by man between 1870 and 1890 when a sudden fashion craze produced a market for their feathers. The Japanese breeding grounds were rediscovered in 1930, but the felling of the trees in their habitat, both during and after the war, almost caused their extinction. Today's tiny flock is always in danger from pesticides when it ventures into the surrounding countryside.

To feed her teeming millions Japan must produce every scrap of food she possibly can and this means the intensive use of fertilizers and chemicals to kill parasites. Despite this driving incentive to produce, many Japanese told me that they had read Rachel Carson's *Silent Spring* and were worried about their birds.

Almost as rare is the Japanese white stork which also suffers from the increasing use of pesticides in the paddy fields. There are today just 13 of these storks, but two of this number have been trapped and are now breeding in the safety of a large pesticide-proof enclosure. The hen who is sitting contentedly on five eggs may not be aware of it, but the whole ornithological world is keenly interested in her family.

The short-tailed albatross now has a total population of 54 and is confined to Torishima Island in the Bonin group. Man's desire to "sit soft" is responsible for the near extermination of these handsome birds. A hundred years ago more than a million of them inhabited the coastal islands and attracted the devastating attention of the fishermen who eked out their livelihood by killing the albatross and stuffing their fine white feathers into cushions.

Dr. Yamashina and his staff have banded 7,000 birds and are keenly interested in making contact with ornithologists in Mongolia where many of the ringed species migrate to breed. He cited in particular the hawks and herons and asked me for any information on the Baikal teal, one of my objectives in the Lake Baikal region.

What is the attitude toward animals of the average subject of the Emperor in this the 40th Year of Show or enlightened peace, the name given his reign? This is a hard question to answer for the Japanese have two sharply contrasting sides to their natures. Recently one of the swans in the moat before the Imperial Palace grounds was found killed by vandals and every newspaper in Tokyo called for punishment for the villains who perpetrated this heinous crime. Yet the average Japanese is highly insensitive to cruelty to animals. Conditions in the dog pounds in Japan are said to be so appalling that they would not be allowed to exist in any nation in Europe or America.

Nor do these harsh conditions interest most Japanese, even though they are good Buddhists and nominally at least have been taught to revere life in all forms. The only organization dedicated to preventing cruelty to animals is the Japan Animal Welfare Society and half of its membership of only about 1,000 consists of foreigners. I heard that the Society is able to carry on only because of massive donations from abroad, particularly from Lady Cascoigne in England.

There is no effective anti-cruelty law in Japan and a cook who baked a cat alive in a well-known restaurant in Tokyo was fined a mere $5. Furthermore, it was only because the Japan Animal Welfare Society succeeded in giving the crime wide publicity in the papers that the culprit was fined at all. In order to express "sorrow," the manager of the restaurant gave the Society a donation of another $5.

While the really rare birds are today getting a good deal of protection, little is done to insure the protection of the many migratory wildfowl which breed in Siberia and Mongolia and come to Japan occasionally. The before mentioned Baikal teal, which breeds in Eastern Siberia, west of the Yenisee River, and on the north shore of Lake Baikal, sometimes comes to Japan and has been seen there by Prince Yamashina. There is, however, an Imperial preserve at Saitama where these teal often winter. The falcated duck, which ranks in beauty with the mandarin duck and the Carolina wood duck, is a rare visitor to Japan although some have been reported breeding in the northern island of Hokkaido.

During my years in China I often admired, and sometimes shot, the wild geese which came honking down from the north. These included swan geese, greylags, bean geese, bar-headed geese and the much rarer lesser white-fronted. Most of these geese and the myriads of ducks and teal that come with them, bred in the vast swamps of Siberia and Mongolia. Many of these wildfowl still winter in Japan and do not have adequate protection. Curiously, the bean geese were rigidly protected during the feudal days in Japan. Englebert Kaampher, a Dutchman, wrote in 1692 that these geese were common and so tame that they would not flush at the approach of man. At the end of Tokugawa Shogunate, the geese declined rapidly and are now rare. According to Jean Delacour's excellent book *Waterfowl of the World*, some of these geese wintered in the moat of the Imperial Palace in Tokyo until 1923 when the last of them were reported there.

TWENTY-TWO

In the Workers' Paradise

As the soviet Motor Ship, *Baikal*, cut her way through the choppy straits between the Japanese islands of Honshu and Hokkaido, an unlikely group of scientific capitalists gathered in the bar and manufactured with considerable success a flock of martinis out of vodka and vermouth. It was the first of a generation of odd drinks which the first World Wildlife Fund Mission to Russia and Mongolia would consume on their long journey from the wastes of Siberia to Moscow, 4,500 miles away.

There is much to be said for group traveling in Russia, especially if the group is small, intimate, and composed entirely of old and good friends. I could not have been blessed with a better team. John and Lucy Hanes, Mary and Oz Lord, and my daughter, Phillippa, made up a party of congenial experts in many fields. John is an ornithologist of note; Lucy well versed in the Russian language; Mary, through her years in the United Nations adept at getting along and charming all types, even the Commies; Oz Lord is a master maker of martinis; and Phillippa, a first-class rider of horses and designer of textiles, two accomplishments that may well be our best passport to popularity among the Mongols.

Life in the Workers' Paradise has improved appreciably since I last visited Russia in 1957. At that time, I spent several weeks on a ship in the Black Sea and the difference between the accommodations on that ancient barge and the *Baikal* are great. Built several years ago in East Germany, the 4,500 ton passenger and cargo ship is modern, clean, and fast. The food, while strong on fried items and piles of rather heavy bread, is edible; and the service, consisting of husky gold-toothed waitresses, is good. Choice of drinks has increased greatly in eight years and there are several fairly palatable table wines.

Our fellow passengers were a fascinating spectrum of colors. They ran from deep dyed reds to the fellow-traveling scarlets, and sympathetic pinks. There were also Japanese businessmen who are as near to being colorless as even Nehru could have wished. The largest group consisted of delegates from the General Council of Trade-Unions of Japan who were wending their way to Moscow as guests of the Soviet government to take part in the May Day celebrations. According to several Japanese businessmen with whom I talked, the trade-union men are Socialists with more than a modicum of sympathy for the Soviet system. This delegation got an elaborate send-off from the Yokohama Dock consisting of cheering masses, red flags, and general signs of solidarity. The crew of the *Baikal* smiled approvingly.

Although the *Baikal* does not dock at Vladivostock, Russia's principal port on the Sea of Japan, it docks at Nakhodka a short distance down the Bay. Our only contact with Vladivostock was through some of the ship's maids and interpreters who turned out to be students at the University of Vladivostock earning extra pay by taking occasional trips. One of the most interesting of these was a bright young man who, when asked where he came from, said he was a Jew from Armenia. I could not help thinking that a similar remark to an American of the same race would be answered by the laconic "I'm a guy from Brooklyn."

John Hanes' collection of telephoto lenses drew immediate response from a group of Japanese free-lance photographers, and between us we piled a table full of enough expensive cameras and binoculars to start a store, or record a war. John did not neglect his ornithological duties and reported a rather unusual number of gulls sitting on the sea, even though we were a good 25 miles from land. Most of these sea birds were common gulls, but he also sighted a kittiwake gull, a black-tailed gull, a glaucous gull, a sooty shearwater, a puffin and a cormorant. Just as the sun went down and the lighthouse on the tip of Honshu started to twinkle, I saw a flight of 8 great geese probably greylags.

It was cold in the North Pacific in April and I blessed the Air Attaché in Tokyo who gave me a flight jacket, complete with fur hood and a Japanese Olympic Games badge carefully sewn over the U.S. designation.

Grey barren cliffs, topped by frequent radar stations, ring the little harbor of Nakhodka on the Siberian side of the Sea of Japan. Inland, the hills rise to snow-capped mountains and nowhere in the sweeping vista is there a tree. A cold wind blew down from the steppes and a few hungry gulls wheeled in our wake. The *Baikal* dropped anchor and a group of hard-faced officials came aboard.

Appearances, however, are often deceiving. The customs men proved polite and asked me to open one of my six cases. Our battery of cameras was passed without a question being raised (even the telephoto lenses, in a case like that of a large pistol), and the parting remark of the chief immigration officer was that he hoped we would like our journey.

At Nakhodka, we boarded the train for Khabarovsk and what a good train it was. Instead of the dirty and cramped four-bed sleeper that I had taken eight years ago from Moscow to Odessa, we found ourselves in a modern, air-conditioned wagon lit carriage with two beds to a cabin, wash basins, bedding, etc. An English-speaking head-waiter (who had spent many years in Shanghai), supplied us with red caviar and bottles of vodka and wine. The dinner was not fancy, but substantial.

The Trans-Siberian Railway from Nakhodka to Khabarovsk runs due north through flat, treeless plains. For hours there is nothing but dead brown grass, and then the train slips through a lonely hamlet of battered wooden houses and a few thin cattle. No wonder Mao looks with envy on the vast open spaces of Oriental Russia. Nor are the enviers far away. For most of the 100-mile journey, tracks run from within two to about twelve miles of the Red Chinese border.

Contact with Russians, which was extremely difficult in 1957, is much easier today. On the train we had a number of frank conversations with Russians of various backgrounds. The net of their opinions was that they were finding life a good deal more pleasant under the present rulers of the Kremlin. Not only were there many more creature comforts, but the old uneasy evasiveness with which they spoke to all foreigners seemed to have vanished.

We arrived at Khabarovsk after two days and one night on the train. A city of some 400,000 persons—the Intourist girls each told us different population figures—it is certainly one of the leading, if not the leading, city of Siberia. The streets are broad, the Park of Culture and Rest spacious, and the statues plentiful. There were, of course, none of Stalin or Khrushchev, but there were also none of Aleksei N. Kosygin or Leonid Brezhnev.

But our reason for going to Siberia was primarily to spot wildlife, not the political game, and we were lucky in interviewing Petrovitch Sysoev, the Director of the Khabarovsk Museum, about Siberian tigers and other rare game of the area. A spade-bearded gentleman of about sixty, the Director had spent many years in the Siberian bush and had personally caught three tigers, two of which were stuffed and on exhibition in his museum. According to him, the Siberian tiger is only found south of the 48th parallel and has grown rare primarily because man is invading his habitat and the wild pig on which he lives is growing scarce. He estimated that there are not more than 100 Siberian tigers left. They are fully protected and permits to catch them alive— not shoot them—are carefully supervised. On the wall of the Museum was an oil painting of Russians catching a tiger. Dogs were used to run the tiger to bay and then, as the dogs closed in on its flank, the men flung nets at it and entangled it until they could secure its paws.

Leopards are also found in the Pacific Maritime Provinces of Russia, but like the tigers, they are rare and now have full protection. The mounted specimen in the museum looked white with large dark rosettes and I thought it must be an ounce, the so-called snow leopard of Tibet and Sinkiang, but the Director said it was a true leopard.

John Hanes inquired about the birds and was shown some badly stuffed specimens of white storks, bustards, blue herons, and other large birds that the Director said are now protected. The museum, in fact, is rather a sad little place, but the towns of Siberia are all relatively new—Khabarovsk was founded in 1858—and culture has not so far been very high on the priority list.

Intourist had us scheduled to stay in Khabarovsk through May Day, but the minute we mentioned a desire to see something of the countryside they quickly arranged for us to leave for Irkutsk on a plane which they had denied existed up till then. The reason was, of course, that the area is considered a sensitive one for two reasons. North of it are the Soviet atomic testing areas and near it are the armies which watch Red China.

Some of our fellow passengers on the *Baikal* were allowed to continue to Irkutsk on the Trans-Siberian Railway, but it was carefully explained to us that flying was a better way to travel. The fact that John was a former Assistant Secretary of State in charge of Security; that Mary was one of our delegates to the United Nations; and that I was a former Ambassador who served during the war as Chief of Intelligence for OSS in the Far East, was evidently not overlooked.

There was also a noticeable improvement in Soviet air transportation. The TU 104 jet, which we boarded at Khabarovsk for Irkutsk, was a much more comfortable plane than the one I took eight years ago from Moscow to Tashkent. These planes were faster, covering the 3,000 kilometer trip in just about three hours. Seating capacity was about 100 and most of the passengers were Army, Navy, and Air Force men. In place of the old four classes, there seemed to be no distinction in the seating.

Glistening white in the afternoon sun, Lake Baikal lay ice-bound below us. I had hoped that the ice would have broken up so that we could see the rare inland seals and the nesting grounds of the Baikal teal, but learned later that the lake is never navigable until late May, a fact that had not permeated to the New York office of Intourist. Losing altitude, we coasted along the shore and then followed the Angara River to Irkutsk, the capital of Siberia.

The weather was almost balmy when we landed, but the temperature inside the airport was somewhat chillier. We had all been told by our Intourist guides in Khabarovsk that we could take pictures any place, and John Hanes quite logically assumed that this applied to photographing lakes from the air as well as from the ground. Scarcely had we entered the building and settled down to wait for our baggage, when John was summoned to the office of the manager of the airport. Scenting trouble I went along in my capacity as "leader of the delegation." It seemed that an Air Force Lieutenant had noticed John's photographic effort over Lake Baikal and promptly reported him as a potential spy. John agreed to expose his last five pictures (and thus save the film). The Russians allowed that this might make matters right and we all ended up shaking hands. The incident passed off easily, but it served to make us remember that even though there is a thaw it has not warmed the ground very deeply.

The Hotel Siberia, Irkutsk's only one, was crowded. How a city of 400,000 can get along with only one hotel is a mystery that only the men who run Russia's economy can understand. Nevertheless, we were given "deluxe" suites and a peg-legged porter trudged up three flights to them with our mountain of baggage. Even though we were way over the allowance for air travel, we were not charged extra on the Khabarovsk-Irkutsk run.

Life for the middle class had improved since my last trip. Leonid Ivanovitch Mazhevitch, our Intourist guide for Irkutsk, told us that he paid only 10 roubles a month for a one-room, bath and kitchenette apartment plus heat, light and water. He did not tell us his exact salary, but I would guess it to be between 150 and 200 roubles a month. 90 roubles a month of this goes for food, and probably about 10% for clothing. A good suit costs R 150 and a poor one R 50. This is a great deal less than suits cost eight years ago in Moscow. The quality seemed much better. Shoes cost R 25 a pair but they are shoddy looking. A small crowd admired mine when I had them shined.

May Day in the Communist world is a great event. Every town of any pretense is decorated with flags, huge posters of the current rulers of the Kremlin, and a reviewing stand where the party big-wigs can review the happy masses. This year, however, it was decided to omit the army units which used to add a certain grim note to the festivities and concentrate on "demonstrations." Getting from our hotel to the reserved to see the parade—there was no grandstand with seats—was no easy job.

The demonstration consisted of busty girls, clad in various athletic costumes and waving streamers of various colors; groups of ordinary people carrying flags and representing factories, schools, etc.; and a few companies of soldiers without side arms. We wearied in about an hour and some of us started back to the hotel only to find that the only way to get there was to join the parade which went past it. Accordingly, Lucy, Phillippa, Oz and I became an integral part of the Lenin Tractor Factory group (sans tractors, however), and marched steadfastly under red banners for five or six blocks. The picture, if anyone bothered to take it, would look fine in the *New York Times*.

In addition to the trickle of tourists or other foreign groups—we were the only Americans that year—there was a small group of French hunters who signed up, at $1,500 per person, to shoot Russian bear. Just as unsporting as the polar bear hunts of Alaska and Norway which take place in airplanes, the intrepid slayers of the Siberian bear leave nothing to chance. The system works this way. As everyone knows, all bears hibernate during the winter at which time they are half asleep and about as ferocious as koalas. The Russian forest guards find a cave where a bear has dug in, bring the hunter to the entrance, and then prod the bemused bear out into the open with sticks, whereupon a brave Frenchman opens up with his high-powered rifle.

Responsible for this legal murder is Transtours, a Soviet travel agency specializing in trips to the USSR and other nations of the Red bloc. I understand that drives of Polish deer can also be laid on for a price. For the flat fee, the Parisian hunter gets eight days in the Soviet Union and a guaranteed shot at a bear which can weigh up to 1,000 pounds. The Siberian bear is similar to our brown bear and is one of the world's largest carnivori, but if left alone is not considered dangerous unless cornered or with young.

To be sure that the French hunters do not waste their time, they are not summoned by Intourist at Irkutsk until the bears' hibernating lair has been definitely established. Then a cable is sent to Moscow, which notifies Paris, and the hunter leaps aboard a plane, jets 4,250 miles from Paris to Irkutsk, and is rushed out for the moment of truth, with all conceivable odds against the bear.

Viktor Boichenko, the director of Intourist at Irkutsk, had been unable to keep up with the demand. Earthquakes, which are common in this part of Siberia and Mongolia, disturbed the bears and many of them had left their hibernating lairs ahead of time.

John and I wished to see what wildlife we could and organized a picnic in the country. Except for a few collections of drab little huts, where office workers grow their vegetables, there are no suburbs in the Workers' Paradise. One leaves the city and plunges into the sombre rolling countryside of Siberia. Collective farms till huge acreages of potatoes and wheat and when the fields stop there is the forest stretching for hundreds of thousands of square miles to the North. Most of the Siberian forest is Taiga, the heavily timbered swampland that is really only negotiable in winter. Patches of old snow dotted the ground and on rising ground we could see the white peaks of the Primorsky Range.

By any standard Lake Baikal in the wilds of Siberia is a mighty body of water. Not only for its size, which is 12,160 square miles, about the area of Belgium; nor for its depth, which averages 2,400 feet, the deepest in the world; nor even for the sheer volume of its water which makes it the biggest depository of fresh water on the globe; but for the emerald clarity of these waters and for the rare and fascinating life which inhabits them.

In its transparent depths, which contain almost as much water as all five of our Great Lakes in America, swim omul, sig, sturgeon and *Comephorus baikalensis*, a fish capable of withstanding great pressures like its distant cousin, the coelacanth of the Madagascar Channel. Inland fresh water seals disport themselves along its banks and in small Lake Frolikha, which connects with Baikal by a river, lives a species of trout unknown elsewhere in the world. Surrounding the lake is the Taiga, the almost impenetrable swamp forest of Siberia from which comes the sable and a king's ransom of other famous furs.

Baikal is wracked by earthquakes and lashed by violent storms. Despite this, the vast expanse of clear water absorbs heat up to a depth of 600 feet and influences the coastal temperatures to a point where they are 5 to 7 degrees warmer in winter and cooler in summer than the adjacent areas. There are in fact more sunny days over Baikal than there are in many health resort regions of the Black Sea.

The day we drove to Baikal was not that bright but a wan sun did try to warm the barren countryside and on the Argana River the ice was almost gone. We learned that the Argana flows so swiftly out of Baikal that a large area around the mouth is never frozen and is the favorite resting place of thousands of migrating wildfowl. John saw golden-eye, red-breasted mergansers, goosander, old squaw, and red-necked grebes. Most of the lake itself was still frozen and stretched away in a sheet of ice to the snow-capped mountains on the further shore.

In addition to seeing the lake, our objective was to talk with scientists of the Limnological Institute, a recently formed scientific organization set up to study the lake and its varied fauna. Miss Valentina Ivanovna Golkina, a substantial lady who runs the Institute Museum, met us and took us for a conducted tour of her small but extremely interesting set of exhibits.

Our primary interest was the status of the inland seal, one of the only three races of fresh water seal in the world. (The other two are in the Aral and Caspian Seas.) My friend Harold Coolidge saw these seals on his honeymoon before the War and reported at that time that they were scarce. Strict conservation has since paid off for these little seals and today there are 60,000 of them, so many that hunters are allowed to shoot 3,000 a year.

The Russians had some experience of the exhaustibility of the ocean fur seals. Between 1786, when the Russian explorer Gerasim Pribilof discovered the islands in the Bering Sea where the seal congregated to breed and drop their sleek pups, and 1866, when the Czar sold Alaska to the United States for $7,200,000, the seal population of the islands, originally estimated at upwards of 5,000,000, has been depleted by 50%. But we ignored this dangerous statistic and by 1911, when a Fur Seal Treaty to restrict the kill was signed with Canada, Japan and Russia, the seals were down to 3% of their original numbers. Kipling's haunting tale, The White Seal, tells of a few who escaped the slaughter.

The sable, whose fur coat brings the highest prices in the fur world, is receiving protection in the Baikal region. A large area has been set aside where no trapping is allowed at any time.

The caviar-producing sturgeon is also protected and can only be caught in one small bay of the great lake. They are not killed, but only "milked" for the caviar and then returned to the water. Sturgeon do not produce eggs until their nineteenth year and continue to ovulate every other year from that time until they die at a great age. Miss Golkina told us that the ichthyologists do not know how long a sturgeon can live but believe that it is possible for them to survive for 200 years. The best egg-producing years, however, are from 20 to 50.

Our efforts to get some information about bird banding led nowhere. Miss Golkina said that there is a group of men doing this at the upper end of the lake—there is no road around Baikal so one must wait till the boats can get there—but she did not know anything about their work.

Baikal is the source of some excellent food fish and we lunched on pickled omul and fried grayling, both worthy members of the piscine family. Omul eat only plankton and must be caught with nets. Pike and perch also abound in the shallower bays. A unique species of dogfish also lives in the lake.

John Hanes made some enquiries about the upland game around the lake and found that there are two species of capercailie, the huge grouse. The white-billed capercailie is a forest dweller and the black-billed variety is indigenous to the high mountains. The hazel grouse, which looks like the European red grouse except that it is lighter in color, is abundant.

The only bird which John saw in the museum that he did not recognize was a small duck called *Nyroca Fuligula* which may well be some sort of teal that does not migrate outside of Russia. It is not listed in the Japanese or European bird books.

We could get no data on the Baikal teal or the falcated duck, both of which are said to breed on the lake. However, the migrations had not started and there were very few waterfowl or even upland birds about. John saw some Siberian buntings, marsh tits, and white wagtails.

Rumors of creatures far more exotic than the inland seal and the rare teal keep recurring in the far north of Siberia and even though we could learn nothing at Irkutsk about the possibility of such unknown animals, I think the gossip is worth reporting.

The legend of a great creature is current among all the tribes of Siberia and Mongolia. The Yukaghir, whose lands reach from the Lena Delta to Kolyma, call the mammal the olhut, which they say lived not long ago and was contemporary with their ancestors. The Yakuts and Ostiaka, true Mongols, call the mammoth "mamantu" and describe it as a giant rat which lives underground. Further south in Manchuria and Mongolia the legendary mammal is known as a "tai-shu."

It is a hairy monster with tiny eyes and a short tail and it digs enormous tunnels in the snow with two teeth shaped like picks. The *World of Animals*, a book written by K'ang-Hsi, the first Manchu Emperor, in 1662, says: "There is in the North a kind of big rat as big as an elephant which lives underground and dies as soon as it comes into the air or is reached by sunlight. These fen-saii weigh 10,000 pounds, have teeth like elephants and the natives of the north make bowls and combs from them." The fact is that Siberian natives have found mammoth tusks 16 feet long and weighing 450 pounds. In the early 1900's the province of Yakutsk exported an average of 152 pair of tusks per annum. Total tusks so far exported in the past 200 years come to more than 25,000 pairs out of this one province alone.

The trade is very ancient, and is mentioned in Chinese chronicles. In the 9th century Arab traders bought these tusks on the Volga. In more recent times, as late as 1935, mammoths have been found preserved in glaciers. In 1901 an almost perfect specimen was taken from the banks of the Berezovka River in eastern Yakutsk. It was covered all over with reddish-yellow woolly fleece and long black hair like horsehair between one foot and 1½ feet in length. A flap of skin under the tail protected the anus. The skin was lined with fat 3½ inches thick.

It had a concave head and small ears like the Indian elephant, to which it is related. Ten feet high at the withers, it was smaller than most elephants. The contents of its stomach showed it lived on plants which grow today in this area.

The point is that there is no satisfactory answer as to why these mammoths, adequately adjusted by diet and warm fur to arctic conditions, are no longer extant. The assumption was that the mammoth was a creature of the tundras but most of the remains are found in the forested Taiga. This vast wooded area covers 3 million square miles, ¾ the size of the USA, and is very inadequately explored. It is quite possible, according to Heuvelmans, that mammoths *do* exist today in this fastness. In 1918 a Russian hunter who had been in the Taiga told the French consul at Vladivostock that he found the tracks of a huge animal. It was two feet long and 18 inches wide. There were tracks of four feet. Later he found huge heaps of dung and broken branches. After weeks of tracking he came up with the beast which proved to be a big elephant with curved tusks and long chestnut-colored hair. The hunter was afraid and ran. Since then there have been other reports of huge elephants in the Taiga forest around the Gulf of Ob.

TWENTY-THREE

Mongolia: Land of the Wild Horse

IN 1963 A STOCKY little man with a moon face and slanting eyes introduced a completely non-controversial resolution in the General Assembly of the United Nations. The measure urged all the nations of the world to preserve their rare animals and birds and the man proposing this wise and timely action was the Ambassador of the Peoples Republic of Mongolia. Relegated to a few inches in the back pages of the papers, the resolution, which passed by unanimous vote, still made news in conservation circles and I decided that when the time came for me to make a swing around the Far East in behalf of the World Wildlife Fund I would certainly try and include this forward thinking but little known country of central Asia.

The time came and while the lengthy negotiations over visas were in progress—we do not recognize Mongolia and have no diplomatic relations with her—I did considerable research on the country of Ghenghis Khan and the rare species of animals and birds which inhabit its mountains, its far-flung pasture lands and its great deserts. Bigger than Alaska, Mongolia covers 626,000 square miles and is bounded on the north by the Siberian Province of the Soviet Union; on the east by the Red Chinese Province of Manchuria; on the south by Chinese Sinkiang and the Great Wall; and on the west by the Turkestan Province of the USSR. Most of the northwest is the steppe well-watered by lakes and rivers but the south includes the Gobi and Ordos Deserts. The average altitude is 4,200 feet and the temperature swings from 110 degrees in summer to 50 below in winter.

Such a vast land could support many millions of people but today only one million Mongols live in it and undoubtedly for this reason a wide variety of rare game still survives, or at any rate is reported still to survive. Most interesting of these to me is the Mongolian wild horse, the only true wild horse left in the world. Distinguished from other horses by its erect mane, lack of forelock and a head relatively larger than that of the wild ass, the Przewalski, named for the Russian explorer and scientist who reported it, is now among the rarest animals in the world.

There is some doubt as to whether they still exist in Mongolia. The last wild ones were captured there between 1942 and 1945. Of these animals only one mare was used for breeding and she is now at the Askaniya Nova Zoo in Russia. For the past twenty years there has been little information coming out of Mongolia about the Przewalski horse and none of this could be authenticated. Both natives and even experienced hunters mistake the wild ass or Kulan for the Przewalski. Occasionally, however, a report reaches the outside world which evokes interest in scientific circles and in a recent paper by V. D. Treus, published in a Ukranian newspaper and translated and sent to me by Dr. Malcolm McKenna of the American Museum of Natural History, it was stated that in 1963 some wild horses, said to be Przewalski, were caught near "Jargalantu" (Khobdo) situated at 91 degrees 45 minutes East, and 48 degrees, 0 minutes North. This area is just west of Lake Usu Nur in the Altai Mountains. It is possible for some people to fly to Dzirgalantu, the largest town of the area, but evidently not for foreigners. The border with Red Chinese Dzungaria, a division of Sinkiang, is nearby and Mongolia's relations with Mao's government being what they are a tight watch is kept on all the border areas.

I did hope, however, to find some recent news and particularly to check up on the claim of O. Cevegmed, the Mongolian zoologist who claims that in the winter of 1959-60 two herds of Przewalski were seen in the mountains of Bajtag-Bogdo and Tachin Shara Nuru. Following this revelation Professor Dementiev of Moscow organized an expedition to these areas and also to the Gobi Desert where there have also been scattered reports of wild horses. No traces of wild horses were found although local shepherds in both areas said they remembered seeing them twenty years ago.

Luckily for the world a number of this rare species survive in zoos. According to the Przewalski stud book there are now 114.

The Mongolian wild ass is still said to be fairly common in central Mongolia. Known also as the Chigetai, Dziggetai, Kulon or Kulan, this attractive little grayish-colored ass with a median black stripe from mane to tail makes good eating and few Mongols can resist taking a shot at it.

The saiga has suffered for centuries due to the demands of the Chinese pharmaceutical trade. Like other Asian ungulates its horns hold the promise of sexual vigor (even though this has been medically disproved) but since the cooling of Mongolian relations with Red China and the subsequent ouster of some 10,000 Chinese laborers the market for saiga horns has sagged. The saiga looks like a combination of animals. The pronounced nose resembles a hare; the thick neck that of an ox; and the horns are very similar to those of an Indian black buck. According to reports the saiga is in no danger, but like everything else in Mongolia is shot on sight.

The third animal about which I hoped to find some recent data is the Gobi argali, the great wild sheep whose horns resemble battering rams. Roy Chapman Andrews shot some in the Central Gobi in 1926, but Sowerby, in 1937, wrote that the extinction of these fabulous sheep in Inner or Chinese Mongolia was almost complete. Whether or not they still exist in Mongolia proper I hoped to find out by journeying to the border of the Gobi in the area where they are said to survive.

There are only two ways to get to Mongolia and, as Americans, we could not go through Peking, the city where, before the war, I used to see the golden dust come swirling down from the Gobi. The alternative is via Irkutsk and from the city we set out in a grey drizzle for the flight south over the somber forests. By the time we arrived the sun was beating down from a cloudless blue sky and the little city of Ulan Bator, the capital of Mongolia, lay shimmering in a broad plain surrounded on all sides by white-capped mountains. Customs, which can be a trial in many newly emerged nations, were perfunctory and soon we were aboard a bus under the charge of Guichintsoo, a doughy-faced Mongol youth who had just spent six months in England trying to learn English and should have spent several years longer.

Ulan Bator is a curious mixture of the old and the new. Most of the people still live in gers or yurts, the round felt tents that sheltered their ancestors in the days of Ghenghis Khan, but these are now towered over by blocks of flats and public buildings of recent design. A few factories with tall chimneys spouting smoke are also mixed in with the yurts and apartment houses. A little river, the Tola, runs through town and from it comes all of the drinking water, apparently unfiltered. Our hotel, the only one in operation, was the Ulan Bator, a Chinese construction job with Czech furniture. The food was whimsical. Breakfast consisted of caviar, brown bread, cold peas, and sweet coffee. Lunch of caviar, heavy soup and mutton cooked in grease. Dinner about dittoed lunch. Only by liberal doses of Scotch whiskey and vodka could we get the meals down. A sampling of the food stores indicated that most people got only the mutton, cheese, and butter. There were no cans of fruits or vegetables and, of course, no fresh available.

The diplomatic corps was heavy on the socialist side and light on the free world. The USSR, North Korea, North Viet Nam, Czechoslovakia, Hungary, Poland, Cuba, and Peoples China are all represented by ambassadors while the only resident non-communist diplomat was the British chargé d'affaires, R. A. Hibbert. An intelligent and pleasant gentleman of about forty, Hibbert, his wife and an assistant, have living quarters and an office in the Ulan Bator Hotel. Mongolia is recognized by a few of the western nations, but, except for Britain, no diplomatic establishments are maintained there and the western ambassadors to Moscow or Peking simply appear to present their credentials.

About half the people on the streets dress in Mongolian national costume of a padded silk or wool del and boots and the rest in uniform or in shoddy-looking European clothes. There were quite a few motors about with most of the trucks of Chinese construction and most of the cars of Russian. The Russian imitation of a British Land Rover is quite comfortable. The shops had few goods and of questionable quality, and clothes are very high even from our standpoint. However, everyone looked well fed and warmly dressed.

Sightseeing in Ulan Bator was not always rewarding but the museum and the old palace of the Living Bhudda were well worth the effort. Dr. Roy Chapman Andrews, who led four expeditions into Mongolia, told me about meeting the Hutukhtu, when that gay old spiritual and temporal monarch was in his dotage and delighted in shocking his ministers by asking them to hold two wires through which he immediately sent a current of electricity. Although the third highest dignitary of the Buddhist Church, only the Dalai Lama and the Tashi Lama of Tibet being superior, Hutukhtu made no secret of his wife and various incidental female friends. It was, however, this Living Buddha, Bogdo-Gegen, who became the first ruler of an independent Mongolia after the break-up of the Manchu Empire in 1911. From the fall of the Khans in the 14th century to that time Mongolia was merely an ill-governed and unimportant province of China.

In 1922 when Dr. Andrews first visited Urga, as Ulan Bator was then called, it was picturesque but none too savory. Death was something to be avoided. He saw a man carry his young wife out of their yurt and leave her on the open plain. She was very ill and the man did not wish her to die in the yurt and thereby bring a curse on him. Bodies were not buried in those days. They were simply left for the dogs and carnivorous birds. The Chinese called ravens "Mongol coffins." Dr. Andrews saw a great many skulls lying around but was told that it was a serious offense to touch one. No one bathed and the stench, especially inside the yurts was awful. Sexual morality was unknown and a large proportion of the people had venereal disease. The prison consisted of a nest of wooden boxes, 4 feet by 2½, so that prisoners could neither sit nor lie. Some were also chained and had their hands manacled. The only opening was six-inch hole through which food was given them. In winter, the prisoners were given a single sheep skin.

The year before Dr. Andrews' visit communism got its start in Mongolia when Sukhe Bator, a young revolutionary, called in the Bolsheviks to help him defeat Baron Ungern-Sternberg, one of the White Russian generals operating under Admiral Kolchak, who was then making a gallant stand against the Reds in the Far East. Ungern-Sternberg with a force of 11,000 men had taken Urga and set up an anti-communist government with Bogdo-Gegen, the Hutukhtu, at its head. But Ungern-Sternberg's severe methods—he believed firmly that the only good communist was a dead one—scared the easy-going Mongols and after losing the support of the Hutukhtu and the Mongolian nobility, he was defeated and executed.

Bogdo-Gegen lingered on as a constitutional monarch until 1923 when he died. In 1924 the country was declared a republic and the communists, who had formed a coalition with the nobility and large landowners in order to oust the White Russians, started to turn on the rich "enemies of the people." The big land and herd owners were in due time liquidated but the collectivization of the nomads, who make up ninety per cent of the million persons who inhabit Mongolia, was a much harder job. Love of freedom and independence are basic characteristics of the nomad everywhere and by 1956 fewer than one-fourth of them had been forced into collectives. Since then the heat has been applied more persistently and today virtually everyone in the nation is enrolled in some variety of socialist collective state farm or industrial project.

Yet despite all the drab trappings of communism the Mongols seem to me to rise above them more than any of the subject peoples. The national costume, which the Russians have discouraged among their own satrapies like Kazakstan and Uzbeckistan, is still the favorite dress of the Mongols and the gaiety of the silken dels seem to shame the humdrum dress of socialism. The Russians may well have been occasionally sullen under the Czar but under the communists the expression has become set. Not so the Mongols who laugh a great deal and try to enjoy life. This is especially true on the steppe where there are no listening devices, no prying party members, who are not at least neighbors and friends, and where the simple sweep of the boundless vistas mocks regimentation.

Flying is still a relatively new experience to the Mongols and they never take it lightly. If the government planes operated on time the pilots might lose face. On the two occasions we took to the air in Mongolia the aircraft were respectively five and four hours late. There were a number of excuses but the one we chose to believe was the simple one that the pilots needed a longer time for breakfast. We did not really mind waiting but it was somewhat unsettling to see one of the mechanics start to sew up a hole in the side of one of the tires while another Mongol gremlin oiled the wings with a long can. Finally, along with a horde of uneasy peasants, we were allowed to board and luckily were able to sit together. Two large buckets in the aisle were not there to put out fires; virtually every Mongol was sick and very sick.

Our objective was Ur Kangi, a yurt and brick village some 300 miles south of Ulan Bator and within jeeping distance of the Gobi Desert. On the pasture where we landed (no pictures please) were lined up four Russian jeeps. There were four grinning drivers and a representative of the local government who would do the catering. We took with us, as we did all the time in Mongolia, our two official guides, Tsedendorg, the vice chairman of the Mongolian Tourist Agency and Guichintsoo, the interpreter. The former was an alert powerfully built Mongol with an intelligent and rather cunning face. The interpreter we named Dumpy and never was a name more aptly bestowed. Not only was Dumpy abysmally ignorant of his country's history and statistics but his command of English was so limited that he virtually never succeeded in really understanding what we wanted to convey. Both he and his boss were, of course, good communists and party members. Out of the population of a million there are only 40,000 of these hard core boys and they have most of the good jobs. Dumpy was one of seven Mongols who had been sent to the University of Leeds, probably through the good offices of Professor Owen Lattimore, the Mongolian expert, who is currently lecturing there. As I remember Leeds it is not a city where one would be apt to defect.

Driving in Mongolia has a good deal in common with a race on the Indianapolis Speedway. The steppe is usually smooth, there are no fences, and one takes one's own line with only one basic objective—to beat the other guy. Phillippa and I picked a good driver and an engaging fellow as well who always smiled, even when his motor went dead twice in the middle of a river and we had to be hauled out ignominiously by another jeep. In five days of continuous driving over all kinds of country we only blew one tire and never turned over once.

At the little nomad settlement of Guchin Us, meaning 30 wells, we stopped for lunch. The Mongols eat about five times a day and we were always being faced with large assortments of rather poor food. The inn at Guchin Us was an exception or perhaps it was the extremely pretty Mongol girl that waited on us. She had braided black hair at least four feet long; white pearl-like teeth; and a complexion not yet weathered by the rigorous Mongolian climate. She gave us big bowls of fermented camel's milk, hard-boiled eggs, caviar (the Russians must supply the Mongols with tons of caviar, probably to keep them pliable), and brown bread.

That evening we spent our first night in a yurt or ger. Capable of withstanding the fierce winds of the steppe and yet of being taken down and loaded on camels the ger is about as perfect a home for a nomad as one could find. Furthermore the gers are warm in winter and cool in summer. They can be fitted with a stove and a pipe which sticks out of the roof. There are no windows and only one low door. We had beds made up with a single quilt and a blanket. The toilet was a tiny house far out across the steppe and washing was done in a basin filled with cold water. Outside a round moon hung low in the sky and as we went to sleep we heard the moaning sound of the camels tethered outside. Phillippa and I were happy to be there.

From this settlement we drove south through passes in the mountains to the edge of the Gobi. Baga Bogda, an 11,759 foot peak, one of the easternmost of the Altai range, towered over us and we passed patches of sand, a sure sign of the approaching desert. At a little brook a herd of camels had been gathered and after lunch we rode them. The two-humped Bactrian camels are much more comfortable than the one-humped dromedaries of Africa and the Arabias and seem considerably less vicious than their cousins of the Sahara and the Rub El Khal. Perhaps the stick inserted through the soft part of the nose to which is attached the rope by which the camel is guided plays some part in this docility. A sharp twitch of the rope can give the camel considerable pain. There is no girth on a Bactrian camel saddle and one balances by the stirrups.

The local herdsmen told us that there were snow leopard and wild goat in the mountains and at one of the yurts we saw two skins of very large leopards. Not a true leopard, the snow version has black rosettes on a white background and is actually an ounce. Enquiries about wild horses or camels met with no encouragement. Even the old men had not seen or heard of them. Yet this is the area where in 1877 Przewalski, the Russian explorer and scientist, reported wild camels for the first time. Sven Hedin, the Swedish explorer, also saw them there.

By 1900 the wild camels were hard to find and harder still to shoot. Hedin mentioned Abd-ur-Rahim, a hunter who esteemed the flesh of wild camel and made his living shooting game but was only able to account for 13 camels in seven years. Requiring water only every eighth day in summer and every fourteenth in winter the wild camel inhabit only the driest and wildest part of the Gobi. They can scent a man at 12 miles. In the rutting season the bulls fight fierce battles and carry ugly scars.

By the time Roy Chapman Andrews began his central Asiatic expeditions in 1918, the game had been thinned out a great deal and Andrews expressed the fear that many species would soon be extinct. But Andrews' main interest was not the animals of today but the animals of millions of years ago. Central Asia, the oldest continuously dry country in the world, was never covered by ice and in the sands of the Gobi the various Andrews expeditions found a treasure house of rare fossils. There was the Entelodon, a giant pig-like animal; the Baluchitherium, the largest mammal ever to inhabit the earth; the Shovel-toothed mastodon, an elephant with a dredge in its mouth; the Chalicothere, a claw-hoofed mammal with the head of a horse but hoofs replaced by giant claws; and the Andrewarchus, the largest of all flesh-eating mammals.

On the way back from the Gobi we sighted three bustards, but before John could photograph them one of our guides unlimbered his rifle and was making the sand leap around the feet of these great and slow-moving birds. He missed, but proved a point which I have all along suspected. Every Mongol who wants to shoot does so and aims at any animal or bird that he believes belongs to no one. We remonstrated with the "hunter," but it did no good and later in the journey he took a pop shot at a duck and later still at a hawk.

We were told by Dumpy that there are game laws and he promised to get us a copy of them. Of course, he never did, but in any case it did not matter because no one seemed to have heard of them. Conservation in Mongolia is simply another western word whose significance they have not yet grasped.

Only camels can survive in the Gobi and all of the collectives in the area we visited are camel collectives. To see how these functioned, we called on one of the herders whose prowess in camel breeding had been recognized by a medal which he proudly wore on his del. The breeder, a good-looking Mongol with a broad smile, said that he had 245 camels under his care of which 20 belonged to him personally. In the old days he might have owned the entire herd or, on the other hand, might have been simply a hired hand.

While the herdsman's wife served us fermented camel's milk and curds, I looked around the ger. There was a large radio, a suitcase, a box for clothes, a bed, a mirror stuck full of family photographs, and a stove. We asked the polite questions: Is your family well; are the camels fat; is the grass good—in this case, camel-thorn good.

I asked about the Almas, the Abominable Snowman of the Gobi, but the herdsman only smiled and shook his head. To a "progressive" modern camel farmer tales of these strange fur-covered myths smack of the old days and traditional superstitions. But perhaps it was simply Dumpy's usual inability to get our point across.

We were in Mongolia in early May when it can still be very cold, especially at night. If I had not had the U.S. Air Force flight jacket which I borrowed from our air attaché in Tokyo, I would have been damn near frozen. Actually we had only one snowstorm and that lasted only a few hours, but there were other grey days. Gloves and a warm cap were also useful.

All of us ate everything that was put before us including cucumbers and various green vegetables and none of us, to my knowledge, had any stomach trouble. The water was supposed to be boiled, but I believe never really was. If it looked too murky we added vodka or whiskey.

In a shallow depression of the grassy mound lay a pile of rubble and, glancing idly over it, I saw the glint of color beside the rotting bones of a long dead camel. The shard was glazed with emerald green and may well have once graced the palace of the sons of Ghenghis Khan for the fragments and two stone turtles are all that is left of Karakorum, the great capital of the Mongol Empire. Utterly destroyed by the Ming Emperor Yung Lo in 1380 the site, aside from elementary digging by Mongolian archaeologists in 1960, is today simply part of a state farm where the herdsmen, mostly ignorant of their history, pasture their flocks.

Even before the great Khans made Karakorum their capital it was the principal town of Wang Khan, pronounced by the Nestorians Ung Khan or John, the fabulous Prester John, the Christian King, whose fame spread over Europe. Ghenghis Khan defeated Prester John but kept some of his wise men at his court. Most of the facts are still shadowy because the Mongols have no literature to speak of. The written language is different from the colloquial and the religious books, the only record of any reliability, are written in Tibetan.

But from the records of the conquered peoples we know that Ghenghis Khan was born about 1165, the son of a minor chieftain whose rule extended to only 40,000 tents. The chronicle says that Ghenghis arrived in the world with "clotted blood in his hand" and never were the auspices more correct. Before he died in 1227, the great Khan whose names ranged from Mighty Slayer, Scourge of God, Perfect Warrior and Master of Thrones, made himself ruler of the world from Armenia to Korea and from Tiber to the Volga. He died in the year of the Mouse in the Cycle of the Twelve Beasts.

Communism tried to destroy Mongolian Buddhism as it does all religions but there are still said to be believers and to administer to their spiritual needs, the present government allows about 100 monks to practice. Only two main temples are open and one of these, Erdeni-Tsu, which is situated at Karakorum, we inspected. Two old monks, the only ones in residence out of the complement of 10, received us and took us through the temples. Built in 1586 and containing many

Tibetan pictures and idols, the temples although clean had a neglected look. Only one butter lamp flickered before the great statues of the Buddha and the offerings of rice were obviously old and stale.

On the day we spent driving to the falls of the Orkhon River, it became suddenly cold and grey and for several hours it snowed hard. These sudden changes in temperature are hard on the animals and account for much of the livestock losses especially among the new born. Two fierce looking dogs, descendants undoubtedly of the war dogs which were trained to eat the enemy wounded in the days of Ghenghis Khan, left the cadaver of a horse on which they were feeding and dashed after us snapping at the tires.

The Mongolian loves his horses, sings about them, and never walks when he can ride. From the age of four the children go to school on horseback and outside every ger a horse is tied. Really very small, the average height cannot be more than 12 hands, the Mongol horses are incredibly tough. Dressed, I weigh nearly 200 pounds but the pony I mounted took off at a good canter. The saddles, wooden and very narrow, are uncomfortable for westerners. So are the stirrups which are very short so that the Mongol rides almost standing up on the withers. Phillippa, a really good rider, impressed the Mongols immensely.

So important is the horse that it was formerly used as a medium of exchange. One "bot" equalled one horse, or one cow, or seven sheep, or ten goats. One-and-a-half bots equalled one camel.

I particularly liked the Mongol songs about horses which are sung to the accompaniment of a two-stringed violin, called a Morin Khour. The instrument has a sound box of stretched python skin and a carved horse's head at the top. There are two kinds of Mongol songs, the long ones and the short ones.

Always we looked for wildlife but aside from birds saw little of it. On the Orkhon River a flight of three bar-headed geese landed on the bank and allowed John and me to get close enough to photograph them with John's long telescopic lens. Another time we saw a big hawk but before John could bring his camera to bear one of our guides whipped out his .22 rifle and started to shoot at it. This was too much and we gave all of the men with us a lecture on the stupidity of shooting harmless hawks and for that matter shooting anything just to see if they could hit it.

Roy Chapman Andrews covered about the same territory on one of his expeditions and I made notes of the game he saw. Where are the

Mongolian gazelle that used to teem on the plains? Where are the wolves that Andrews clocked at 40 miles an hour? And the antelope which reached 60 miles an hour over short distances? We did see bustard (the ones the men shot at); shoveler ducks, teal, demoiselle cranes, crested lapwings, and sand grouse. But the only wild animals we noted were the little blond gophers that make their holes on the plains. Carriers of bubonic plague, these gophers have bright yellow fur but are too small to process.

The ponderous progress of an aged tortoise is lightning-like compared with the ability of the bureaucratic machine of the Peoples Republic of Mongolia to get things done. On the day we arrived in Ulan Bator I explained at length to our official interpreter, the egregious Dumpy, that I wanted very much to get an immediate appointment with the Director of the Academy of Sciences, the senior savant of the nation. He promised to expedite this simple request. On the evening of the day before we left the capital for good, an appointment was confirmed with the Director.

This was probably not entirely Dumpy's fault. So suspicious are all Communist regimes of foreigners that no department which is not specifically set up to handle the outlanders likes to have a chance on seeing them. Undoubtedly Prime Minister Tsedenbal, Foreign Minister Dugersuran, and Tserentsoodol, Chief of the division of Ministry of Foreign Affairs, which handles non-Communist affairs, all had to be consulted before we could see Dr. Shirenden of the Academy.

The Academy occupies spacious quarters on the top floor of the state library before which stands an heroic statue of Joe Stalin, probably the only remaining one in Mongolia. Dr. Shirenden and four of his staff, including an assistant who spoke good English, received us cordially and after exchanging pleasantries answered questions. Asked about Przewalski's horse, the primary reason for our journey to Mongolia, he replied that scientists of his Academy had seen "four or five small herds the previous year in the Altai Mountains." He also indicated this area, which is on the border of Chinese Dzungaria, on a large wall map. Questioned as to steps being taken to preserve these last remaining herds he said that the Ministry of Agriculture has jurisdiction over conservation and that "watchmen" have been assigned to guarding the herds. Reminded that the Soviet expedition of 1962, which visited the same area, had not only been unable to find any

Przewalski but had even been unable to find any locals who had ever heard of them, he shrugged his shoulders.

Asked about the status of the wild camels, he said that small herds of these also survive and differ from the domesticated camels, which have gone wild, by their smaller size and extreme wariness. He said they are found in the Gobi area. He said that the kulon, or wild ass, is plentiful. According to the Director, game laws covering the protection of these three rare species as well as seasons for hunting other animals are in force. Asked for a copy of these laws he said he did not have them.

Despite these somewhat vague answers both John Hanes, who accompanied me, and I felt that the Director and his people were genuinely anxious to establish some scientific contacts with us. He requested us to send him directly any books we had dealing with the conservation of animals. He added that Dr. Shagdarsuran, head of the Department of Zoology of the Academy, would be delighted to correspond with our scientists in America about fauna. He also said that Dr. Namnandorg, head of the Department of Geography, would be glad to correspond with our people in regard to palaeontology or archaeology.

I then asked what the reaction of the Academy would be if American scientific circles supplied an expert to come to Mongolia with a view to gathering more information about the rare fauna. Here he grew a bit wary and said he felt his own scientists had the situation well in hand. What he really meant was that he did not have the authority to answer such a question without consulting the Ministry of Foreign Affairs. At this point he brought up the matter of American recognition of Mongolia and said it was hard for his country to deal with people whose government did not recognize her.

He then introduced the subject of mounted specimens of animals and archaeological objects and said that such exchanges or sales between his country and ours would have to be handled through the Ministry of Foreign Trade.

Asked by John Hanes if the Mongolian ornithologists band any birds, he said they did but was unable to supply any further information on the subject. He did say, however, that he was sure the Mongolian banders would be glad to exchange information with our own people in Japan. I asked if we could write about this in care of his office and he said we could.

On our departure he gave me a book written in Mongolian which he said gave details about the animals, birds and fish of his country. Incidentally, Shirenden himself is an historian and does not have much personal interest in conservation but is a highly intelligent man who sees fully the importance of the subject to Mongolia.

My own feeling is that if rare animals, such as Przewalski's horse and the wild camel, still survive in Mongolia it is due to luck and their natural wariness rather than any real effort to save them on the part of the government of the Peoples Republic. The game laws mean nothing to the average citizen who shoots what he wants whenever he wants. The fact that members of our own party fired at birds even though they knew the purpose of our mission was to protect wildlife was not the result of a desire to affront us: the men saw no reason why they should not shoot as they always have.

TWENTY-FOUR

Some Results to Date

IT IS ONE thing to go and find out how rare a species is becoming and another to do something about it. In some cases I was able to persuade the powers that be to meet the costs of saving their birds and animals and in others I had to ask the American Appeal of the World Wildlife Fund wholly or partly to finance necessary conservation projects. In the following I will touch on some of the reports that have come in since I completed my three missions.

Soon after our 1963 mission to Africa, an expedition paid for by the American Appeal, was mounted to save Hunter's antelope (hartebeest). Inhabiting the desolate border country between Kenya and Somalia, these rare antelope were under increasing pressure due to the tribal warfare which periodically flared between the Tana River of Kenya and the Juba of Somalia. We had to act quickly and Major Ian Grimwood, then Chief Game Warden of Kenya, immediately set out with trucks for the border area, where he rounded up thirty young antelope and transported them back to the Tsavo East National Park in Kenya where they would be safe from the hungry warriors.

In my long journey up the White Nile in the Sudan I talked with a number of game wardens, local chiefs and others interested in saving the rare birds and animals that live along the great river. Virtually none of them had any knowledge of the principles of conservation but they could all read English and were delighted when I promised to send them small individual libraries of the basic books on this and allied subjects. It took nearly a year for these books to make their way

by ship from New York to the Red Sea ports and then by caravan over-
land to the Nile but they finally arrived and I have had grateful letters
from all the recipients.

My talks with the Emperor of Ethiopia resulted in a tightening of
the laws protecting the Walia ibex and the mountain nyala; and a fact-
finding expedition by Leslie Brown later in 1963 established the habitats of these endangered species. Mr. Brown's investigations, which
were partly financed by the Swiss National Appeal of the World Wildlife Fund, were of great value to both the Fund and to the survival
service of the International Union for the Conservation of Nature.

Following a long and pleasant interview with Aden Abdullah Osman, the President of the Somali Republic, the old game laws, framed
by the Italians, were updated. An amusing exchange took place during
our talk. I was particularly interested in getting some protection for the
wild ass and the President, after listening gravely to my plea, said in
effect; my country is under attack by the Ethiopians, my people are
largely illiterate, my treasury is nearly empty and you ask me about the
wild ass.

My efforts to get the government of Egypt to pass some laws protecting waterfowl from Spring and Fall slaughtering (the Egyptians
shot them on both legs of their yearly migrations) were unsuccessful at
the time but since then I have heard that the Governor of Cairo has
restricted the bags. However, he has not yet eliminated the market
hunters who are simply put to the inconvenience of hiring more guns.

The second part of the 1963 expedition was spent in the Near
East. The previous year Major Grimwood captured four of the almost
extinct Arabian oryx in the Eastern Aden Protectorate and my mission
was a follow up to see if there were reports of more of these rare antelope in the Rub Al Khali, the sand desert where the oryx live. I obtained no reports of further sightings of oryx but the officers of the
Hadhrami Bedouin Legion, the British sponsored defense force of the
Protectorate (known now as the Federation of South Arabia), promised to keep their eyes peeled as they patrolled the hinterlands and report to me from time to time through the Resident Advisor at Mukalla.
So far there have been only negative reports and it looks as if the last
oryx has gone from this 80,000 square mile tract of Arabia. However, a
few small herds are still reported in the neighboring sultanate of Muscat and Oman.

My reason for visiting the Yemen was also to find out if oryx inhabited this little known country and I did hear reports of sightings on the border of Saudi Arabia. Ever since then the war between the followers of the Imam Badr and those of President Sallal, aided and abetted by some 50,000 Egyptian troops, have kept the border in such a state of turmoil that there have been no reports of the oryx. Our diplomatic mission in Taiz is on the look out for any firm evidence that these shy little antelope may have evaded the hostilities.

King Hussein of Jordan has proved himself a good friend of conservation and has established a wildlife reserve at the desert oasis of Azraq. Not only is this the resting place of migrating wildfowl but in its environs are found desert gazelle. Several of us—including Guy Mountfort, who led an expedition to Jordan for the Nature Conservancy of London—have talked with His Majesty about the need for wildlife refuges, and we are all pleased by the results of these efforts.

One of the tangible results of my trip to Iran was the sending of Khosrow Sariri, Assistant Chief Inspector of the Game Council of Iran, to America on a leadership grant. Thanks to the interest of Julius Holmes, then our able ambassador to Teheran, Sairi, who was in effect the leading conservationist in his country, was able to study basic conservation for several months in America, and return with a great deal of useful knowledge on methods of preserving the rare wildlife of Persia.

Among the results of the 1964 mission to South America was the proclamation by Fernando Beluande Terry, the President of Peru, of a sanctuary for vicuñas in the high Andes. The project was first discussed at a dinner he kindly gave for my wife and me at the Palace in Lima. The vicuña are lucky, for Major Grimwood, who saved the Hunter's antelopes of Kenya and the oryx of Arabia, has been given the job of chief game warden of Peru.

News from the Falkland Islands has been good. Ian Strange wrote me in mid-1966 that as a result of a grant given him by the American Appeal of the Fund he had been able to complete his survey of the wildlife of the islands. This included not only the birds but the mammals such as the sea-lion, elephant seal, and fur seal. He also said that the government has proclaimed several more islands as wildlife refuges.

Soon after we left Tahiti, the first stop on the 1965 expedition, the Governor, Jean Sicurani, issued a proclamation protecting *Pomerea nigra nigra,* the little black flycatcher which was believed extinct since

1931. This order, which included other rare birds of Polynesia, was the first recognition by the French government of the importance of conservation in their islands in the South Pacific.

The Governor of Fiji, Sir Derek Jakeway, was also most helpful and promised to up-date and enforce the conservation laws. A proposal for a small grant for the publication of a list of Fiji's rare birds has been submitted to the Fund.

Australia is rich in rare species and among the rarest of these is the "Tasmanian tiger," the wolf-like marsupial known as the thylacine. A grant from the American Appeal, donated as a result of my trip to Tasmania, has enabled Dr. Eric Guiler of the University of Tasmania to continue his search for this all but extinct mammal, and in July 1966 I received a long letter from him with the exciting news that a den has been found.

Near the Savage River on the virtually uninhabited west coast of the island of Tasmania, a bushman, rummaging amid the ruins of the long abandoned Whyte River gold fields in the Spring of 1966, found a rusty boiler which was evidently being used as a lair by animals. There were dog-like tracks around the entrance and hairs sticking to the sharp edges of the boiler's mouth. The bushman was a simple fellow who might have paid no attention to the den if he had not remembered meeting Dr. Eric Guiler of the University of Tasmania several years previously and having the doctor urge him to be on the look out for "tiger." Carefully collecting the hairs the bushman sent them by fishing boat to Hobart where Dr. Guiler ascertained in his laboratory that they were indeed from a thylacine.

There are no rare animals or birds on the rocky islands and sliver of mainland that make up the Crown Colony of Hong Kong but there is some wildlife and to save it and at the same time provide the Colony's teeming millions with parks for peace and recreation the Governor, Sir David Trench, proclaimed a series of nature reserves. Plans for these refuges were worked out by the local conservation authorities and by a World Wildlife Fund mission consisting of Dr. Lee Talbot and his wife Marty who is also a Ph.D and a very attractive one too.

Our efforts in Taiwan were directed mainly toward persuading the Premier of the Republic of China that unless immediate action was taken the very rare Mikado and Swinhoe's pheasants and the endangered Sika deer would soon become extinct. Some months after we left the island I was pleased to hear that a commission had been established to draw up plans for these refuges. Conservation in many of the smaller nations depends on the drive of one man and Taiwan is lucky in having the dedicated services of Hunter Eu. Part of the grant enabling Hunter to study conservation at an American university was paid for by the American Appeal.

In every country I went to I did my best to persuade the governments legally to entrench their wildlife refuges so that succeeding regimes could not open the parks to exploitation. Unfortunately many of the parks in South America are wildlife reserves in name only. Lumbering and mining are both carried on in them and the workers, of course, have guns. Pesticides are also a hazard but most of the countries where rare game still lingers are underdeveloped and often cannot afford chemical spraying

We in America are a rich nation yet conservation is having a hard time. As Stuart Udall, the Secretary of the Interior, bluntly puts it in his fine book, *The Quiet Crisis:* "America today stands at a pinnacle of wealth and power, yet we live in a land of vanishing beauty, of increasing ugliness, of shrinking open spaces, and of an over-all environment that is diminished daily by pollution, noise, and blight." Aside from Europe where wildlife problems are met as well, if not better, than they are in America, most of the world does not have the means to keep the birds and animals themselves. In most of South America and most of Africa there is little understanding or even sympathy with conservation among the masses of the people. Hinduism and Buddhism forbid killing so that game is not under pressure from hunters in India and some neighboring countries, but the terrible increase in populations destroys the habitats and has the same effect on wildlife.

Before it is too late, the rulers of these nations must be sold the importance of saving their rare fauna and where they cannot afford to do this funds must be sought to help them.

INDEX